Continuity and Change in Latin America

Continuity and Change in Latin America

Edited by John J. Johnson

Contributors

Richard N. Adams
Frank Bonilla
Gilbert Chase
R. P. Dore
Fred P. Ellison

John J. Johnson
Lyle N. McAlister
K. H. Silvert
W. Paul Strassmann
Charles Wagley

Stanford University Press, Stanford, California 1964

Preface

In 1959 the American Council of Learned Societies and the Social Science Research Council established a Joint Committee on Latin American Studies whose basic goals were to improve communications among those interested in research relating to Latin America, to consider ways in which the development of such research might be furthered, and to administer a program of grants for field research.

The Committee, aided financially by the Carnegie Corporation, the Ford Foundation, and the Council on Higher Education in the American Republics, has moved steadily toward the achievement of its purposes. Individual research grants have been provided for seventy-five scholars working in many different branches of the humanities and social sciences and associated with fifty-eight different institutions throughout the United States. The Committee has, further, acted in an advisory capacity in planning the 1961 conference on the Status of Latin American Studies in the United States, co-sponsored by the University of California at Los Angeles and the Council on Higher Education in the American Republics. The Joint Committee also provided funds to help meet the expenses of both the First Inter-American Conference on Musicology (Library of Congress, 1963) and a meeting on Portuguese language development in relation to Brazilian area studies (University of Texas, 1964). Together with the Hispanic Foundation of the Library of Congress, the Joint Committee sponsored a conference of historians, which laid the basis for a "Guide to Historical Literature on Latin America" now being prepared with the financial assistance of the Ford Foundation.

The Joint Committee on Latin American Studies has also taken the major initiative in calling together four other conferences of wide scope. Two such meetings were primarily concerned with improvement of communications among social scientists in the Latin American countries and the United States. One, the Inter-American Conference on Research and Training in Sociology (Palo Alto, 1961), was held with the cooperation of the American Sociological Association and resulted in the organization by its Latin American participants of an active "Latin American Group for the Development of Sociology." The second, co-sponsored with the Instituto de Economía of the University of Chile, was the Inter-American Conference on Research and Training in Economics (Santiago, 1962), whose proceedings were distributed to economists throughout Latin America and the United States. The financial support of the Council on Higher Education in the American Republics made both these conferences possible.

Different in both nature and organization was the Joint Committee's seminar held at the Center for Advanced Study in the Behavioral Sciences at Stanford University from July 8 through August 23, 1963. During that seven-week period a continuing panel of the seminar discussed the condition of Latin American studies in the United States with visiting representatives of various disciplines. A report on that seminar, which was financed by a special Ford Foundation grant, has been prepared by Charles Wagley and will be published by Columbia University Press.

The present volume is the fruit of a fourth major gathering sponsored by the Joint Committee. Following two years of preparatory work under the direction of Professor John J. Johnson a meeting on Continuity and Change in Latin America was convened in Scottsdale, Arizona, January 30–February 2, 1963. Preliminary papers had already been distributed to all conference participants, together with detailed written analyses of those papers prepared by experts including Henry F. Dobyns, Cornell University; John E. Englekirk, University of California at Los Angeles; Orlando Fals Borda, Universidad Nacional, Colombia; Peter Gregory, University of Minnesota; Joseph Grunwald, Yale University; Albert O. Hirschman, Columbia University; Manfred Max-Neef, Organization of American States; Robert G. Mead, University of Connecticut; Manning Nash, University of Chicago; Juan Orrego-

Salas, Indiana University; and Robert A. Potash, University of Massachusetts. Their analyses were in themselves scholarly contributions, but neither written comments nor verbal suggestions made during the sessions have been included in this volume, since they have, in great part, been incorporated into the papers published herein.

Also participating in the Scottsdale conference were H. Field Haviland, Jr., Brookings Institution; Pendleton Herring, Social Science Research Council; John B. Howard, Ford Foundation; Harry William Hutchinson, University of Florida; John S. Nagle, Ford Foundation; Robert E. Scott, University of Illinois; Carl B. Spaeth, Stanford University; James F. Tierney, Ford Foundation; Schuyler C. Wallace, Foreign Area Fellowship Program; and Bryce Wood, Social Science Research Council. John Wirth of Stanford University served as rapporteur. Joseph A. Kahl, Washington University; Irving Leonard, University of Michigan; Stanley J. Stein, Princeton University; and Robert Wauchope, Tulane University, as members of the Joint Committee, helped in the preparation of the conference although they were unable to attend in person.

It is the hope of the Joint Committee that the papers contained in the present volume will both constitute a substantive contribution to knowledge about Latin America and act as a stimulus to further exploration. With full knowledge of the hazards of generalization, the authors have sought to make their observations apply to a substantial part of Latin America, although no claim is made that coverage has been complete.

ROBERT N. BURR
Chairman, SSRC-ACLS Joint Committee
on Latin American Studies

Contents

Contributors

RICHARD N. ADAMS is Chairman of the Department of Anthropology and Assistant Director of the Institute of Latin American Studies at the University of Texas. From 1949 to 1956 he resided in Peru and Central America, conducting research for the Institute of Social Anthropology of the Smithsonian Institution and for the World Health Organization. He is the author of *Cultural Surveys of Panama-Nicaragua-Guatemala-El Salvador-Honduras* (1957), *A Community in the Andes* (1959), and *United States University Cooperation in Latin America* (1960).

FRANK BONILLA is Associate Professor in the Department of Economics and Social Sciences of the Massachusetts Institute of Technology and a member of the Senior Staff of MIT's Center for International Studies. He has planned and directed large-scale opinion and attitude surveys in many Latin American countries and in India, Singapore-Malaya, and Japan. In 1960 he became an Associate of the American Universities Field Staff, and in that capacity wrote and lectured on Brazil and other Latin American countries. He has contributed chapters to recent volumes on nationalism, education and political development, and cross-national political research.

GILBERT CHASE is Professor of Music and of Latin American Studies and Director of the Inter-American Institute for Musical Research at Tulane University. He has served as Cultural Affairs Officer at the United States Embassies in Lima, Buenos Aires, and Brussels. From 1955 to 1957 he was Professor of Music and Director of the School of Music at the University of Oklahoma. He was

President of the Inter-American Music Council, 1960–63. His
books include *The Music of Spain* (1941), *A Guide to the Music of
Latin America* (revised edition, 1962), *America's Music* (1954), and
Introducción a la música americana contemporánea (Buenos Aires,
1958).

R. P. DORE is Reader in Sociology at the London School of Econom-
ics and Political Science. He has taught at the London University
School of Oriental and African Studies, and at the University of
British Columbia. He is the author of *City Life in Japan* (1958),
Land Reform in Japan (1959), and *Education in Tokugawa Japan*
(1964).

FRED P. ELLISON is Professor of Romance Languages and Director of the Language and Area Center for Latin American Studies
at the University of Texas. From 1952 to 1961 he taught the Spanish and Portuguese languages and Spanish American literature at
the University of Illinois. His primary interests are Portuguese
language development and Brazilian literature. His publications
include *Brazil's New Novel: Four Northeastern Masters* (1954), a
a translation of Rachel de Querioz's *The Three Marias* (1964), and
scholarly articles on Latin American literature and the teaching
of foreign languages.

JOHN J. JOHNSON is Professor of History at Stanford University. He was Chairman of the Conference on Latin American History in 1961. He is the author of *Political Change in Latin America: The Emergence of the Middle Sectors* (1958) and *The Military
and Society in Latin America* (1964), and the editor of *The Role
of the Military in Underdeveloped Countries* (1962).

LYLE N. MCALISTER is Director of the Center for Latin American
studies and Professor of History at the University of Florida. He
is the author of *The "Fuero Militar" in New Spain* (1957) and
articles in professional journals on civil-military relations in contemporary Latin America.

K. H. SILVERT is Professor of Government at Dartmouth College
and Director of Studies of the American Universities Field Staff.
He was on the faculty of Tulane University from 1948 to 1961.

He has written *A Study in Government: Guatemala* (1954) and *The Conflict Society: Reaction and Revolution in Latin America* (1961), and edited *Expectant Peoples: Nationalism and Development* (1963).

W. PAUL STRASSMANN is Professor of Economics at Michigan State University. He has worked as an international economist at the Central American Desk in the US Department of Commerce, and is now engaged in a study of technological change in underdeveloped countries, with the support of Social Science Research Council, Rockefeller Foundation, and Michigan State University–Ford Foundation International Programs grants. He is the author of *Risk and Technological Innovation* (1959) and numerous contributions to professional journals.

CHARLES WAGLEY is Professor of Anthropology and Director of the Institute of Latin American Studies at Columbia University. He is the author of *Economics of a Guatemalan Village* (1941), *The Social and Religious Life of a Guatemalan Village* (1949), *The Tenetehara Indians of Brazil* (with Eduardo Galvão, 1949), *Amazon Town: A Study of Man in the Tropics* (1953), *Minority Groups in the New World* (with Marvin Harris, 1957), and, most recently, *An Introduction to Brazil* (1963).

Continuity and Change in Latin America

Introduction

John J. Johnson

Since World War I an endless succession of scheduled and unscheduled changes has racked Latin America. There have been different changes, and different degrees of change, in the twenty profoundly different Latin American states, but change has been felt everywhere. Now, in response to the strides of modern science and technology, the pace and scope of the transformation are accelerating. The traditional structure is breaking down, and political and economic power are being transferred with increasing speed from the integrated haciendas to the as yet unorganized cities. A philosophy of constant change has supplanted one of stability. New frames of reference are being constructed; new outlets for discontent are appearing. It has become more and more fashionable to be revolutionary. Those who seek progress through reform contend directly with those who demand progress through violence. One way or the other, political and social reorganization is under way. Latin America has a new sense of purpose, and modernization has top priority on the list of attainable goals.

Social and Political Tensions

The transformation is taking place amid profound inter-class tensions. For one thing, traditional systems are being repudiated before viable substitutes for them have been found. Millions are abandoning established values for new ones that are transitory or rooted in the moment. The last remnants of mutual interest between the haves and the have-nots are threatened. The have-nots demand a new, more "democratic" type of relationship. Everywhere privileged groups are being held responsible for discrepancies between expectations and performance in the national economy, for inability to maintain law and order, and for the spectacular maldistribution of wealth. Aroused elements insist that the impoverished lower classes not only be protected adequately from want and tyranny, but be given political representation, education, and dignity.

The lower classes themselves are less interested in these abstractions. The average man is preoccupied with his own and his family's private problems, with the unemployment, the lack of buying power, and the other day-to-day frustrations that mirror the loss of stability at the national level. Juan Pueblo is deeply concerned with immediate goals. No longer accepting the gap between his "social rights" and his relative deprivation as natural or inevitable, he is self-willed and restless in his personal search for social justice, money, and status. He accepts impersonal representative democracy in principle, but he also places heavy reliance on such nondemocratic paths to glory as personal contacts and magic formulas.

The emergence of new groups and the concomitant progress of technology are revolutionizing Latin American politics and intensifying the political struggle. The new elements are increasingly aware that politics is a means of getting the things they want. They increasingly judge politicians by their policies rather than their social status. More interested in economic welfare than in political abstractions, they have made poverty one of the principal topics of political debate in Latin America.

Because most Latin American voters lack political sophistication and are concerned with immediate objectives, the most successful politicians are often the most reckless. In the time-honored demagogic tradition, they consciously exploit class grievances, they offer simple answers to complex problems, and they promise to telescope the economic process. Often committed only to their own perpetuation in office, they willingly range the political spectrum in search of votes. They intermingle democratic symbols and authoritarian doctrine. When not restrained by coalitions representing the propertied elements or the armed forces, such politicians are strongly disposed, especially when they first achieve office, to support welfare and labor legislation, which they see as advance payment to their constituents for continued support against the onslaught of new aspirants to power. Despite its dubious motivation, legislation of this sort has been a force for good in Latin America. Anti-democratic or not, a number of essentially demagogic politicians—for example, the late Getulio Vargas of Brazil—have been responsible for incorporating the historically marginal elements more fully into the economic, cultural, and political life of the republics.

A number of political parties claiming to represent the popular masses have pitted the city against the country. These parties have been pragmatic: i.e., they have not asked their supporters to accept an ideology. (The Communists and *fidelistas,* by contrast, offer an organization and a body of dogma with which the insecure can identify.) The pragmatic parties, a twentieth-century phenomenon, have been concentrated in the urban centers. Most have depended upon coalitions of intellectuals, professionals, and urban workers for their popular support, although Acción Democrática won the presidency in Venezuela in 1958 by running more strongly in the countryside than in the capital.

The exodus from the rural areas, which in some countries has reached flood proportions, has strengthened the urban-oriented parties at the expense of those parties that traditionally have relied upon the landholders to control the votes of their employees. In Argentina, Brazil, Chile, Mexico, Uruguay, and Venezuela, which together constitute approximately 70 per cent of the area and population of Latin America and produce well over 80 per cent of the gross product, the locus of power now resides in the cities. In these countries, and elsewhere in Latin America, national policies have acquired a strong urban bias. Disaffected urban social groups are in many cases leading the way. Meanwhile, the broadening of the electoral base has led to a splitting of the original pragmatic parties and to the founding of entirely new parties. The new parties invariably demand more radical solutions than the original urban parties, who now find themselves on the right within the urban spectrum and are forced to consider an alliance with the rural-oriented parties to the right of them. Thus Acción Democrática in Venezuela works closely with COPEI, a Social Christian party; and the Radical Party of Chile in recent years has shown a strong preference for the rightist Liberal and Conservative parties over the "leftist" parties.

The very fact that urban parties of the center have survived, often in the face of deep internal dissension, is significant. In surviving they have tended to give continuity to politics, and they have also formed a counterforce to the institution of personalism in politics, a historical feature of the Latin American scene and one still very much in evidence. Moreover, thanks in large part to the influence of these parties, government has become increasingly pluralistic, central governments have grown at the expense of state and local governments, and the state has broadened its social responsibility on a wide front and has assumed primary responsibility for articulating interests.

Unfortunately, these generally desirable developments have their darker side. To the extent that state and local governments have been subordinated to the central administration—as they have been almost totally in Colombia, for example—they have ceased to serve as buffers between the individual and the central authority. This is a serious problem, since only Chile, Costa Rica, and Uruguay, and to a much lesser extent Brazil and Mexico, have developed institutions capable simultaneously of defending individual rights and promoting national interests. Another problem is that the short-range demands of the newly politicized groups, many of which regard democracy with indifference, have led to parliamentary instability at the expense of constructive and orderly administration.

Economic Issues

The leaders of Latin America are convinced, and they have convinced the general public, that only rapid industrialization can provide the answers to the political and social crises confronting their countries. They are therefore quite prepared to make industrial expansion the foremost political issue. Ex-President Juscelino Kubitschek of Brazil went so far as to declare that Latin America will either industrialize or give up democracy.

Politicians and economists have offered impressive arguments for industrialization. The central ones are as follows:

(1) The "collective humiliation" accompanying economic dependence, which most Latin Americans equate with production of primary commodities, contrasts sharply with the prestige that the modern world associates with advanced technological capabili-

ties. President Kubitschek once said, "We want to be on the side of the West, but we do not want to be its proletariat."

(2) Only industrial plants can safeguard the republics from the calamities they suffered as a result of the breakdown of normal international trade channels during the two great wars and the worldwide depression of the 1930's. More generally, as long as the republics remain essentially agricultural or mineral producers, their economies will be attuned to international markets and subject to the vagaries of an economic system over which the Latin Americans have very limited control. They will, as a consequence, be required, as they have been historically, to make adaptive responses to external stimuli.

(3) Industry—by spreading buying power, promoting the growth of strong, independent middle sectors, and providing for the systematic development of markets based on mass demand—offers the greatest prospect for a healthy domestic economy. Currently the 50 per cent of the Latin Americans with the lowest income account for only one-fifth the total consumption, while the 5 per cent with the highest income account for one-third the total consumption.

(4) Industry offers Latin America its only hope of escaping the pressure of its exploding population against its limited agricultural resources. This view derives impressive support from recent figures provided by the Economic Commission for Latin America, which show that by 1975 Latin America must increase its industrial production by 400 per cent and its agricultural production by 120 per cent, in order to provide jobs for the more than 35 million persons who will enter the labor market for the first time in the next decade. Of the 35 million new laborers, a maximum of five million will be absorbed by the agricultural sector.

After World War I industrial development was first channeled in the direction of import substitution. More recently heavy industries, particularly iron and steel plants and heavy chemicals, have received considerable attention in Argentina, Brazil, Chile, Colombia, Mexico, and Venezuela. The growth of industry already has brought about a marked shift in the Latin American import pattern, away from consumer items and toward capital goods. By 1960 industry and commerce accounted for over 50 per cent of the gross national product in Argentina, Brazil, Chile, Colombia, Mexico,

Uruguay, and Venezuela, and industry could be credited almost entirely with Latin America's 5.3% average annual rate of growth, one of the highest in the world between 1947 and 1957. The proportion of industrial workers in the total labor force has increased rapidly almost everywhere. The income of industrial workers is approximately four times as great as that of agricultural workers.

Industry achieved its current strong position despite questionable national policy decisions, and at the price of considerable sacrifice on the part of the workers and the nonindustrial sectors of society. More problems lie ahead. Two basic ones may be mentioned. First, planners have been more concerned to project for the future than to determine how existing resources might better be utilized and integrated. Second, the domestic capitalist class has weak propensities to accumulate, and a pronounced tendency to invest in real estate rather than industry. One finds everywhere indecision born of the desire to use new wealth to sustain old privileges and investment habits.

With the above guidelines in mind, one can perhaps understand why Latin America's industrial development has not lived up to expectations. Regressive taxation has limited capital accumulation to a very few savers, and they tend to invest as their fathers invested; legislation designed to direct savings into basic industries has been ineffective. Planning has been carried out without prior compilation of the statistics that are required to determine the needs of a country and the desires of its people. Despite the claims made for it, industry simply is not absorbing a satisfactory share of the labor force; surplus workers continue to take refuge in occupations of low productivity. As the lines of workers waiting for industrial jobs grow longer, the patience of the workers grows shorter. There has been a general reluctance to invest in the infrastructure. Power and transportation, as a result, are undercapitalized; nonetheless, revenue from them, instead of being invested in their improvement, often is transferred to other sectors of the economy. Progress in a given field is typically attained by shot-in-the-arm methods—arbitrary allocation of the state's limited foreign exchange or of funds from public credit agencies—rather than by deliberately balanced development. Technically trained men and skilled labor of shop-foreman caliber are in extremely short supply. Literacy rates remain low—approximately 50 per cent for

Latin America as a whole, and less than 10 per cent in many rural areas, including parts of northeastern Brazil.

Industrial development, far from contributing to the internal economic equilibrium, ordinarily has in fact distorted the economy by contributing to regional concentration of income. Industries producing construction materials and consumer goods—the great majority of all Latin American industries—have inevitably grown up in the main urban centers, where a steady demand for such commodities originally existed. Thus Celso Furtado has demonstrated that São Paulo's share of Brazil's industrial workers rose from 29.1 per cent in 1920 to 38.6 per cent in 1950, while the share of the economically depressed northeast, including Bahía, declined from 27 per cent to 17 per cent in the same period. In Mexico, the Federal District has one-third of the nation's industrial enterprises and two-thirds of its industrial workers; if present trends continue, the Mexico City metropolitan area will account for 60 per cent of Mexico's industrial production by 1985. Until economic growth has made urban labor considerably more expensive than it is at present, there is almost nothing to induce industry to leave the traditional urban centers.

Much of Latin America's industrial expansion has been and continues to be financed through inflationary borrowing. An intermittent phenomenon in Latin America since the late nineteenth century, inflation surged upward in the late 1930's, and since World War II has spiraled in several countries, notably Argentina, Brazil, Chile, and Bolivia. The Chilean peso, trading at 30 to the U.S. dollar in 1945, plunged to over 1,000 to the dollar by 1960; and the Brazilian cruzeiro dropped from 20 to 1 in 1949 to 1,250 to 1 on the open market in 1963. Many economists feel that further inflation in Argentina, Brazil, and Chile can only bring disaster, but others point to Brazil's spectacular economic growth since World War II *despite* runaway inflation. Nearly all economists agree, however, in deploring the tendency of inflation to direct capital toward short-run, speculative ventures, rather than basic industries requiring relatively long maturation periods. Also, it seems clear that inflation, by eroding the wages of the workers, has kept them from gaining ground—if they have not in fact lost ground—in their struggle to increase their share of the national income.

State intervention in the social and economic areas has been a major corollary of industrial expansion, to the dismay of a small but influential property-owning, free-enterprise element. Today approximately 40 per cent of fixed investment (social as well as economic) in the republics is subscribed through the public sector. In Mexico, the public sector provided over 50 per cent of the total in 1961.

State support for industrialization has proved necessary for a number of reasons. Private investment capital has been in short supply, and private investors have shown a preference for real estate and enterprises promising a quick profit. Foreign capital has been discouraged by the threat of expropriation. This has been a particularly important factor in keeping private foreign capital from contributing to the development of the infrastructure. A few leaders, for example Lázaro Cárdenas in Mexico and Fidel Castro in Cuba, have been committed ideologically to state sponsorship of social welfare and economic growth. In most states, however, the decision has been made on other grounds. For one thing, the nation, because of its tax powers and its ability to borrow abroad, has been the agency most capable of accruing capital rapidly. For another, the emerging classes have accepted the state as the appropriate vehicle for furthering their goals. And finally, unlike Anglo-Americans, who by tradition have enshrined private property, Latin Americans tend to stress the social function of property, and thus have little trouble accepting controls over property by an instrument of society as a whole.

The commonly heard argument that state participation in industry has deprived domestic capital of investment opportunities seems wrong. Except in Cuba, there are more promising investment opportunities in production and distribution than there are investors prepared to risk their capital. Certain other charges have more validity. State welfare agencies, for example, have been given insufficient funds to alleviate the social tensions that state-sponsored industrialization has created. High government officials have typically responded politically to what are essentially economic and social questions. They have been less concerned with effective performance than with public pressures, and they have delegated key administrative decisions to the public bureaucrats, many of whom have proved inefficient and lacking in vision.

Industrialization has few opponents. Even the large landholders view it with favor, since by drawing off farmhands to the cities it serves to hold down pressures for agrarian reform. But the urban-oriented policies inherent in an industrialization program have nonetheless resulted in a dangerous neglect of the rural areas and the agricultural sectors. In some instances, as for example in the highlands and the *montaña* (eastern lowlands) of Peru, the old colonial relationship of *hacendado* to *campesino* persists practically unaltered, and almost nowhere have the traces of feudalism completely disappeared. Provincial towns remain under the domination of neighboring haciendas, and Juan Pueblo remains overworked, underfed, and undereducated. Communication is not complete. Space and time, two great enemies of Latin America, still have not been conquered.

Since World War II farm productivity has hardly kept pace with population growth. The caloric intake of Latin America's multiplying millions (the current population increase is approximately 3 per cent per year) has been maintained, and even slightly raised, only by some shifting from commercial to subsistence farming. There are a number of reasons why this situation has developed. One is that the tax system, which taxes the product of the land rather than the land itself, has favored the accumulation and holding of large properties by relatively few persons. For Latin America as a whole, perhaps 90 per cent of the arable land is held by 10 per cent of the farm owners. In Brazil, half of the farm land is held by 1.6 per cent of the owners. In Chile, three-fourths of the cultivated area is controlled by 2.2 per cent of the farm owners. In Guatemala, approximately 40 per cent of the cropland is held by 500 landholders. The same tax policies permit inadequate use, and even non-use, of the land. Since the land itself is not taxed, there is no need to increase its productivity by introducing improved agricultural methods, and no need either to accept the social responsibilities that go with keeping an efficient labor force on the land. The landholders themselves complain, at times with good reason, that they have been discouraged from modernizing and diversifying their operations by the constant threat of state expropriation.

Three other difficulties are perhaps more central to the agrarian problem:

(1) Given the depressed state of agriculture, few large landholders have the capital or credit to make their operations economically viable even if they should choose to do so. This means that regardless of whether the large landholdings are left intact or subdivided, only the state can launch a major agricultural program aimed at increasing and diversifying production.

(2) Purely economic considerations are of greater consequence than ever before. All but five of the republics derive an overwhelming share of their foreign exchange from the sale of agricultural products.* But with overall population increasing and agricultural techniques changing slowly, farm commodities will inevitably be driven from the international market and retained for domestic consumption, and the foreign exchange required to continue industrial expansion will accordingly not be forthcoming. And efficiency in this context is a matter not just of quantity, but of price. Cotton and wheat can be produced on modern, well-equipped United States farms, where laborers are paid about eight times as much as Latin American farmhands, more cheaply than they can be in most regions of Latin America. Low-cost African coffee and cocoa pose a permanent threat to the Brazilian economy. And as European countries continue to increase their agricultural output, they will have under constant appraisal the financial advisability of substituting locally produced commodities, or alternatively commodities from their former colonies, for those historically imported from Latin America. Finally, the European Common Market may well have an unfavorable impact on Latin America's export markets.

(3) The demands for land reallocation, charged as they are with psychological and political overtones, can no longer be ignored. The revolutionary governments of Mexico, Bolivia, and Cuba have seized land with little regard for the original owners. The Venezuelan government, somewhat better endowed financially than the other governments, has paid for land that it has acquired for distribution to the peasants (three million acres up to the end of 1961). Elsewhere national and international experts and legislators have searched for legal means of dealing with the large land-

---

* The exceptions are Bolivia (tin), Chile (copper), Mexico (tourists), Peru (industrial ores), and Venezuela (petroleum).

holders, who, like their counterparts in the United States, exercise a legislative influence out of proportion to their economic contribution. Agrarian reform has been made the cornerstone of the platforms of the Christian Democratic parties of Chile and Venezuela. The Catholic Church has swung to the side of those urging governments and landowners to find socially tenable solutions to the land problem before solutions are imposed by force.

Latin America's ten super-cities—Rio de Janeiro, São Paulo, Montevideo, Buenos Aires, Santiago, Lima, Bogotá, Caracas, Havana, and Mexico City—are the most visible monuments to the neglect of agriculture and the growth of industry and government. This urban bias is nothing new. Throughout the colonial era and the nineteenth century a disproportionate share of public revenues was lavished on the city (usually the capital) in its capacity as a political, cultural, spiritual, and artistic center. More recently industry and commerce have taken advantage of the city's wealth, skills, and purchasing power, with much of the last being provided by the burgeoning payrolls of the new "service" governments. Now the major centers are growing at an annual rate of 5 per cent or more, in part for mundane economic reasons (the flight from rural poverty), but also in part for what might be called psychic reasons. The super-cities have become great suction pumps, drawing to themselves brains, skills, and wealth from all quarters of the nation as Paris once drew the heroes of Balzac. As in the colonial period, so today: when one leaves the capital, one leaves the center of power, wealth, culture, and sophistication. Only Brazil (São Paulo), Colombia (Medellín), and Ecuador (Guayaquil) have cities at all capable of challenging the capital as a cultural center.

As might be expected, urbanization of this sort has its drawbacks. For one thing, the super-cities have failed to relate themselves to the rural areas they presumably serve; they are glittering demographic nodules, isolated from their dark surroundings economically, politically, and psychologically. Although correlatives of industry, they have grown faster than industrialization. On the average not more than 7 per cent of the population in the major cities is employed in industry. The rest find employment in the services and in other activities of rather low productivity, or find no employment at all. Urban unemployment is an increasingly serious problem.

The urban centers have grown in a haphazard manner as the millions from the rural areas have flooded into them, and the price in human suffering has been high. Ten per cent of all Latin Americans now live in urban slums—the *favelas* of Rio de Janeiro and São Paulo, the *callampas* of Santiago. The social and personal disorganization of these slum dwellers has helped to make the cities fertile ground for the diffusion of extremist ideas.

Nationalism, especially in the negative sense of a tendency to hold someone else responsible for a people's past failures and current difficulties, runs like a bright thread through the complex pattern that has been developing in Latin America since the end of the nineteenth century. Prior to World War I there was little fertile soil in Latin America in which nationalism could develop. The inhabitants of the republics were sectional in their loyalties; their parochialism was reflected in government, where regions competed with one another for control of the nation. Few participated in the cultural and economic life at the national level. The politically powerful landholders, dependent as they were on international trade, were internationalist in their outlook; so were the intellectuals, whose eyes were always on Europe. An occasional intellectual expressed concern lest the culture and sovereignty of his nation fall victim to "the ravages of United States materialism and imperialism," but this uncoordinated and individualistic nationalism had almost no political impact.

Nationalism, whose political possibilities became apparent in Europe during and immediately following World War I, underwent its first major modification in Latin America during the 1920's. After a profound social revolution, Mexico had given nationhood a high priority; and elsewhere, as a result of improved transportation, historically isolated regions began to be coordinated. Politicians began to win votes by associating the traditional ruling elites with a decadent European culture and with foreign business elements who were "victimizing" Latin America. This line led inevitably to exalting the common man, from whose ranks the voter came. As a consequence of this new attitude, politicians repudiated the prevalent notion that the offspring of mixed marriages tend to inherit the worst characteristics of both parents; miscegenation, which was widely practiced in Latin America, was now held to be the key to the spiritual and cultural attainments of the future. Nationalism received further impetus when it became evident that France, the cultural cynosure of Latin America, had declined as a military power, while the United States, often distrusted and despised by the intelligentsia, had almost simultaneously established itself as the undisputed financial and technological capital of the world—as well as the primary purchaser of Latin American export commodities. Nationalism provided a partial barrier against the constant jostling of a world torn by strife, and uncertainty and solace from the distress born of the realization that the republics must be more dependent upon the United States.

The new leadership of the 1930's, sensing the political potential of nationalism, stripped the concept of its intellectual abstractions and offered it to the masses in a concrete and politically charged form. It quickly became clear that under the exhortation of political leaders, nationalism could produce in the masses a hypersensitivity to any slight, real or imagined, to their country's political or economic autonomy. Legislation was passed restricting European and Asiatic immigration to Latin America and regulating the employment and pay of foreigners in administrative posts and in local industry, commerce, and agriculture. For the first time serious attention was directed to safeguarding natural resources.

Nationalism in contemporary Latin America, particularly the more modern republics, bears little resemblance to the nationalism of the interwar years. The old nationalism was defensive: anti-clerical, anti-Yankee, anti-exploitation. The new nationalism is more aggressive, and, in a sense, constructive. Today, more than ever before, nationalism is being used to furnish guideposts for those living in the vacuums produced when old values are surrendered before new fundamental standards have been determined upon. Brazil and Mexico stress national pride and national accomplishments. Chile, Peru, and Ecuador keep alive nationalist sentiment by pressing for control over their adjacent waters and submerged lands. The new nationalism less often seeks respectability in the world and more often stresses the domestic scene. It opposes colonialism in any form and in all quarters. It makes "equality"—the equivalent of esteem and prestige—the highest objective of foreign policy. The search for equality has led inevitably toward neutral-ism, since equality could not plausibly be claimed in an alliance with either side in the present world struggle.

*   *

To this point I have sought to establish in general terms some of the main forces now at work in Latin America. Of course, Latin America is not a single unit, and much of the past—personal-ism, monoculture, gross inequalities—remains even where progress toward a better life has been greatest. The imprints of old atti-tudes and values can be seen on the most modern of institutions. At every turn the impulse for change confronts inhibiting forces. Schools are not producing enough leaders, or enough technicians, to shape the new order in all of its dimensions. In short, change and constancy are in conflict everywhere; it is only a question of intensity.

Not institutions, but people, sometimes individually but more often collectively, will determine, in the final analysis, whether the forces at work in Latin America will retard or promote social de-velopment. With that thought in mind, eight social groups are ex-amined in this volume. Two main questions are considered: (1) What are the main problems and the aspirations of each group? (2) To what extent are each group's goals realistic in terms of its own capabilities and the national interest? These questions involve a number of subsidiary questions: how members enter the group, how leaders are chosen, to what degree group consciousness exists, in what ways the character of the group is changing, how the group reconciles the requirements of its individual members with its own requirements, by what channels members of the group communi-cate with one another (and the group with allied groups), where the group now fits into the power structure, and what it thinks about current major national problems and international issues.

If the volume as a whole appears to stress change instead of con-tinuity, it is because more people in Latin America are concerned with the future than with the past. The authors share this concern. They do not all touch all the bases above: some questions were found irrelevant to some countries or social groups, and others, though relevant, could not be answered owing to sheer lack of the necessary information. Not everything has been said, but what has been said can be trusted to represent much discernment, insight, thought, and conviction.

In Charles Wagley's contribution on "The Peasant," Santiago Chimaltenango, an essentially Indian community of Guatemala, and Itá (the name is fictitious), a mestizo settlement in the lower Amazon valley of Brazil, become the centers from which the author projects of broad view of peasant life in large parts of Latin America. Particularly significant, it seems to me, are the subtle, and sometimes not so subtle, differences Wagley draws between the Indian and mestizo peasants and how they respond to the "larger society." His discussion of the cultural "brokers," a term he has borrowed from Eric Wolf, deserves especially close attention.

The countryside is restless in nearly all parts of Latin America, and where apathy exists one cannot but wonder to what extent it conceals extremely complex emotions. Richard Adams's article deals with the most depressed sector of rural society, "Rural Labor." Rather than a homogeneous group, the rural laborers in Adams's hands are almost infinite in their variety. Their ties with their past are being sundered, but they are not quite ready permanently to join the unscrubbed, unschooled, unskilled masses of the urban areas. One must follow the author's argument closely to avoid the erroneous conclusion that he is disproving the thesis of the volume.

Latin Americans are discovering themselves, but none more so than the men of letters, whose self-confidence has been rising steadily since World War II. Fred Ellison, in "The Writer," explains why this has been true. But he goes on to point out that despite their apparent assurance they are torn by many self-doubts. For example, shall they follow the tradition of their past and be writers and politicians simultaneously, or shall they jettison politics and become "professional" writers? Which is the best way to win the struggle against outworn cultural restrictions and unrealistic legal regulations? The question becomes almost academic when Ellison discusses the increasingly left-of-center orientation of Latin American writers, and their use by extremist political organizations since World War II.

Gilbert Chase combines political and aesthetic understanding to produce a highly illuminating article on "The Artist." I would call the reader's attention especially to two of the several aspects of art that Chase explores: (1) the relationship of artistic trends to ideological attitudes, and more particularly to the effect that "nationalism" has had upon the arts; and (2) the extent and implications of state patronage of the arts.

Lyle McAlister, in his article on "The Military," provides a valuable synthesis of what is known about the armed forces of Latin America from a social point of view. In discussing civil-military relations, the military as a modernizing institution, and the possibility of the armed forces' being made more socially responsible, McAlister offers a new approach to the study of the military question. His propositions and counterpropositions regarding the future of the military in Latin America are both novel and challenging.

In an era of sustained economic growth throughout most of the Western world, Latin America has not lived up to expectations. Argentina and Chile have stagnated for more than a decade. After several years of rapid economic expansion, Brazil's pace of development began to slump in the early 1960's. Mexico has made important gains since World War II, but its further progress is being hindered by the inflexibility of politicians and bureaucrats. Colombia moves ahead slowly. Venezuela has not recovered from the era of economic irresponsibility during the regime of Marcos Pérez Jiménez. Why? W. Paul Strassmann, in "The Industrialist," lays a good part of the blame at the doorstep of the industrial community, which he sees as seeking utmost security while generally refusing to take risks. Many readers, I suspect, will find Strassmann's analysis of the businessman's mentality convincing, and scholars will applaud him for exploring practically unknown areas.

Urban laborers are the fastest-growing social group in contemporary Latin America. Although up to now the workers in the cities have been essentially ex-peasants, with a dependency complex not unlike that of the peasants, they have supported social and political reform. Their organizations tend to be weak and to be dominated by politicians, but they have helped to bridge the cultural gap between the feudal values of the countryside and the impersonal values of the modern metropolitan center; they have also provided a medium for the orderly channeling of protest. Frank Bonilla, who writes on "The Urban Worker," stresses the failure of the cities and the politicians to understand the drives and aspirations of the workers. Bonilla's brief discussion of the strategic position that urban labor must assume in any successful program of "planned change," including change under the Alliance for Progress, is of considerable interest, as is his observation regarding withdrawal of labor organizations from politics.

It is widely accepted that students in Latin America engage in political agitation because they see no hope of acquiring wealth or power so long as the present system obtains. Not so, says K. H. Silvert, who knows the students of Argentina, Uruguay, and Chile from prolonged firsthand contact, and has investigated student activities in a number of other republics. "The University Student" of his essay is the child of his parents, except that he is often more socially responsible than his parents. Being sons of their parents makes the students traditionalists rather than modernizers in the true sense of the term. They will leave the universities certified in their elite status, and become a part of the privileged element.

R. P. Dore's wrap-up for the volume is a "think piece" in the finest sense of the term. A British sociologist specializing in Japan, Dore was asked to provide an "outsider's" view and he carried out his assignment admirably. His paper candidly compares Japanese and Latin American studies as they are being undertaken by both nationals and foreigners, and Japanese studies seem to come off a bit better. Latin American scholars and Latin Americanists in the United States would do well to ponder Dore's remarks. Passing from the methodological to the substantive, Dore introduces the exciting proposition that Japan's cultural separatism and early industrialization (as against Latin America's cosmopolitanism and late industrialization) may explain why Japan has been more politically stable than Latin America, and also why Japanese nationalism differs from the Latin American brand.

In Latin America society remains strongly polarized. There are extremely few commonly shared objectives, and all along the line people are being forced out of their conventional roles and fitted, however imperfectly, into new situations. Historically privileged minorities not only no longer enjoy unchallenged power, but are being driven to accept varying degrees of political and social subordination. At the other extreme are the people who live on the edge of civilization, who feel change only in an attenuated form and have no true perception of its meaning. One step removed are the people who have felt the transition enough to become interested in the future; it will be difficult to persuade them that the present should shape the future to the same extent that the past has shaped the present. The middle sectors, from which the current leadership is drawn, are not tightly organized or fully self-conscious, or even sure of their social identity. The complex interplay between groups with new hopes and groups with old ways is always subject to manipulation by men whose commitment to change at times may be more apparent than real. For all these reasons, Latin America currently oscillates between the extremes of liberalism and collectivism, capitalism and communism, free enterprise and statism. The range of oscillation must narrow if Latin America is to enjoy greater democratic stability and social equality. The groups discussed in this volume will have a lot to say about how, when, and how fast the narrowing process shall take place.

1. The Peasant

Charles Wagley

The population of Latin America is predominantly rural. Well over 60 per cent of approximately 200 million Latin Americans are classified as rural in accordance with the census criteria of various countries.[1] Many Latin Americans live in small towns of less than 3,000 people. Many others work on large pastoral or agricultural establishments such as Argentine cattle *estancias*; Brazilian coffee *fazendas*; banana plantations in Caribbean countries such as Costa Rica and Honduras; sugar plantations in Brazil, coastal Peru, and other tropical countries; and other large-scale monocultural farms producing cash crops such as cacao, henequen, and cotton. Perhaps the largest number of these rural Latin Americans, however, are "peasants," that is, "agricultural producers in effective control of land who carry on agriculture as a means of livelihood, not as a business for profit."[2] They are the Indians living in scattered homesteads or small hamlets in Mexico, Guatemala, Ecuador, Peru, and Bolivia. They are also the small "farmers" of Costa Rica, Chile, Colombia, and most other Latin American countries. But they must not be confused with European or North American family farmers; for the Latin American peasants retain almost everywhere indigenous traditions of swidden or "slash and burn" agriculture. They are generally poor, illiterate, in poor health, out of touch with the modern trends of their nation, and looked down upon as "rustics" by the town and city people. Yet, in some countries, they have a voice. They are sought out by politicians, who realize that at least potentially, political power is rooted in the peasants. They are the people who stream into urban centers, causing the problems concomitant to rapid and unplanned urban growth. They are also evolving rapidly within their own communities, and becoming an important social and political force on the national scene. They are an important sector of the Latin American population, providing many examples of continuity and change.

The Latin American Peasantry

The peasants of Latin America are perhaps the best-studied segment of the population. Some time ago, anthropologists and sociologists became interested in the Indians of Mexico, Guatemala, and Andean South America, who were descendants of the Aztecs, the Maya, and the Inca. In Brazil and the Caribbean lowlands, scholars were attracted to the study of the survival of African traits among the descendants of slaves. From these humble beginnings, motivated by ethnographic and historical interests (i.e., what had survived of Maya culture in Yucatan or Guatemala, or of African culture in Haiti or Brazil), there developed a long series of community studies. As anthropological and sociological theory and technique became more sophisticated, such studies focused increasingly on communities that were considered highly representative of specific subcultures, regions, or nations. The result was a large number of individual community studies and several very persuasive theoretical syntheses of Latin American community life. Robert Redfield's classic work, *The Folk Culture of Yucatan*,[3] stimulated a series of general articles on the relationship of peasants to the larger society of which they are a part.

Latin America is not a particularly fortunate laboratory for these theoretical formulations. It does not have the long cultural and social continuity of Sweden, Greece, India, or West Africa, to cite but a few examples. One cannot trace the development of the Latin American peasantry directly back to the Middle Ages and further back to the Neolithic. The Spanish conquest of Mexico, Guatemala, Peru, and other countries, and the introduction of Negro slavery, were violent revolutions that broke the continuity of New World history more decisively than any political, industrial, or social revolution in the Old World. The Spanish conquest, in its broadest sense, modified profoundly the lives of well over twenty million American aborigines, and slavery transferred to the New World at least ten million Negroes. Everywhere in the countries of Latin America, these two cataclysmic processes created a peasantry that is analogous to the European and even the Asian peasantry only in a formal sense. Its relationship to the local elite is similar to that of its European counterpart, and its land tenure situation is roughly the same; but it is part of a relatively recent society, which took form only after 1500 without the long continuity of Old World history.

The peasants of Latin America comprise a broad spectrum of peoples. They include the rural Indians and mestizos of Mexico, the descendants of the Maya of Guatemala and Yucatan, the Quechua-speaking Indians and Spanish-speaking *cholos* of Peru and Ecuador, and the *caboclos* of the Brazilian interior. They nonetheless share certain traits and a position in the national social structure that allow us to classify them generically as Latin American peasants. First of all, they all live in rural areas, usually quite removed from the modern national life of their country. In one way or another, they have control over the land they cultivate. They may be members of communal landholding villages, individual landowners, sharecroppers, or even mere squatters on the lands of others. They generally plant subsistence crops such as maize, manioc, potatoes, or wheat, but as a rule they must sell surplus food or cash crops to make ends meet. Some of them are artisans producing home wares, and some are traders selling local foods and articles at regional markets. Sometimes, they must seek seasonal wage labor on plantations because their local economy does not provide an adequate income. Thus, the Indians of highland Guatemala work on the coffee *fincas*, and many *caboclos* of Northeast Brazil go to work on the sugarcane fields of the coast each year to supplement their income.

Unlike tribal people, these Latin American peasants are an integral part of their nation and of their regional, if not national, economic system. In some cases, however, peasants are not even aware of their status as nationals and as participants in a larger economic system. They often think of themselves as members of a separate group who must work for outsiders from time to time. Their point of view is analogous to that of a Mexican bracero going to work on a farm in the United States. This is true of many Indians who seek seasonal employment on plantations in Guatemala, Peru, or Ecuador. Others who are fully aware of their economic and national status may be equally distressed about their need to seek employment outside the community, if it separates them from their families and from their normal sphere of social relations.

Generally speaking, all Latin American peasants share what might be called a colonial Iberian culture. This is a New World culture based chiefly on Iberian institutions and patterns of thought, but mixed with traits retained from the American Indian, from the African slave, or from both, depending on the region involved. The peasant's way of life was set in the early colonial period, when the Spaniards and the Portuguese actively attempted, with only partial success, to remake the Indian and the Negro in their own image. Since then, most Latin American peasants have lived in relative social and cultural isolation. Only recently have they been aware of, and subject to, the larger society of which in fact they have always been a part. Latin American peasants are Catholics, but their Catholicism has absorbed so many elements of sixteenth- and seventeenth-century European folklore, African belief, and American Indian religion that it often seems strange to the more orthodox Catholics of the great metropolitan cities.

The peasants' ideal patterns of behavior, their motivations, and their world view are "conservative"—that is, they reflect periods in the past when they were more attuned first to the colonial, and then to the national way of life. Their agricultural methods are "primitive," and peasant markets generally involve primarily local products and transactions between local producers and local buyers. They tend to retain old and traditional institutions and customs. They take seriously the obligations of the *compadrazgo* system; they join and serve in *cofradías* or *irmandades* (religious brotherhoods) in their own communities; and they fulfill their vows to the saints. Whatever small economic surplus they have is often drained by expenditures in their local prestige system, which involves the financing of fiestas, and time off from productive activities for religious and public service to the community. Thus, wherever we go in Latin America, the peasant is a recognizable social type, although he may share many characteristics with other depressed groups such as hacienda workers, or even inhabitants of newly formed city slums.

This generalized characterization of the Latin American peasantry hardly does justice to reality, since there is a considerable variation in the peasant populations of different Latin American countries and regions. The peasants of Mexico or Peru are very different from the *caboclos* of Brazil, and the Indian peasants of Mexico, Guatemala, Ecuador, Peru, or Bolivia differ from the non-Indian peasants of those same countries, although, as noted above, all these groups do share common characteristics and problems. Broadly speaking, one must take into account at least two subtypes, namely the Indian and the mestizo peasants, although a much larger series of subtypes may be distinguished.[4]

Throughout the highlands of Mexico, Guatemala, Ecuador, Peru, Bolivia, and to a certain extent in Colombia, a large number of Indian villages managed to weather the Spanish conquest and to reorganize along lines imposed by the Spanish rulers. Characteristically, these free Indian communities were found in high mountainous areas where the land was marginal and ordinarily too high for cash crops. Under Spanish rule, and perhaps even before, the community was a landholding corporation. While individuals and families might exploit the land (and indeed they generally did), ultimate title belonged to the community. Such Indian peasant communities were closed, for members belonged to them by birth and married within their own group. Each of these closed corporate communities regarded itself as a separate and distinct entity. Its saints were local saints and were unlike those of other communities. Men were obligated to participate in local political and religious affairs. The social world of the individual in such communities was bound intimately to his local group, although he might be forced to leave it periodically to work on a coffee *finca,* on a sugarcane plantation, or even in the city in order to supplement his income. As stated above, these corporate villagers were generally Indians. Their habitual language was Nahuatl, Zapotec, Maya, Quechua, Aymara, or some other aboriginal tongue, and this was another barrier separating them not only from the Spanish-speaking nationals of their countries but sometimes from one another. As a general rule, the people of each community wore a distinctive costume, and it was easy to recognize a man or woman from Santiago Chimaltenango (Guatemala), Chamula (Mexico), Otavalo (Ecuador), or a thousand other communities.

In the nineteenth century, under the guise of ideological liberalism, Latin American governments passed a number of laws aimed at the substitution of private property for communal holdings. Many Indian communities lost their lands and became integral parts of large haciendas, thus in a sense disappearing as free peasant groups. Other such communities divided the communal lands among their members (sometimes preserving a small area of common lands) but retained a strong taboo on alienation of land to outsiders. This allowed them to survive as free Indian villages into the twentieth century. Still others, with aid from the *indigenista* groups and the rise of twentieth-century liberal thought, were able to retain or even re-establish their communal holdings, allocating parcels to their members periodically. These, of course, are the groups that today most markedly retain their characteristics as Indian peasants separate from the nation of which they are a part.

The mestizo peasant community, on the other hand, has always been more closely identified with and related to the nation. Mestizo peasants generally, but not always, speak the national language, whether Spanish or Portuguese. They are the rural mestizos of Mexico, the rural ladinos of Guatemala, the *cholos* of Ecuador and Peru, and the *caboclos, tabareus, caipiras,* or *matutos* of Brazil. Such people may be biologically Indians, Europeans, Negroes, or mixtures in various degrees of the three racial groups. Their biological heritage is not important. What is important is the fact that they are consciously aware of their identity as members of a nation. They participate in national affairs as closely as their isolation, their limited income, and their literacy will permit. They tend to look outward to the region and the nation rather than inward to their little community. If they are literate and if there are elections, they sometimes vote and participate in political affairs as they have in Bolivia since 1953. Although as a rule they marry locally, as most country folk do, there is no rule of endogamy as in the corporate-type Indian communities. They wear western-style clothes, although these may be old-fashioned or ragged. They play soccer, and, in some Caribbean countries, baseball. They respect and celebrate the religious and civic holidays of their nation, and they are familiar with its heroes, both past and present.

As Eric Wolf has pointed out, open-community or mestizo peasants are more closely tied to the wider economic system than

Indian peasants. Many of them live by selling cash crops, which constitute from 50 to 75 per cent of their total production.[5] In the lowlands of the Caribbean, they grow cacao and bananas for sale. In many cases, they grow coffee or tobacco, crops that lend themselves to both large and small holdings. In Brazil, these peasants produce manioc flour, maize, and other food staples for sale at local markets.[6] But, as noted above, the Latin American mestizo peasant is not analogous to the European farmer or peasant. In the transfer of culture from the Old World to the New, the European mixed-farming tradition somehow was lost. The Latin American peasant seldom combines agriculture with stock raising. He may have a few chickens, a pig, and now and again a cow or two, but meat is a rare item on his table. He seldom makes at home butter, cheese, or any of the common farm products of Europe and North America. To buy such foods as well as other necessities, the Latin American peasant must have some sort of surplus to sell at market—or he must sell his labor on plantations or in the city.

The mestizo peasants, as stated above, share some characteristics with Indian peasants but differ in many important respects. Mestizo peasants are generally just as poor as Indian peasants. They are often just as illiterate. Their health is no better. But unlike Indian peasants, they actually prefer to accumulate valuables or land rather than spend their surplus income on service to the community. They are also more highly commercial; almost any mestizo home may also be a shop, with a few eggs, some matches, soft drinks, or other items for sale. Likewise they are aware of and eager for material objects of all kinds (transistor radios, better clothes, better housing, and the like). They are also more apt to migrate in the hope of acquiring such objects and of improving on their miserable rural conditions. They seem to have a stronger desire for education for their children than the Indians. Land is, of course, owned privately, if there is title at all. Mestizo peasants show less cohesion or esprit de corps among themselves; in fact, as we shall see, mestizo peasants usually belong to a community split by class, racial, and even political lines.

The Peasant and the Community

Thus far, Indian and mestizo peasants have been discussed as if they lived apart in small, self-contained communities. In reality, few peasant villages are full-fledged communities, if one defines a community as the minimal local unit that can carry and transmit a culture.[7] Several writers have stressed the structural dependence of all peasants upon the town, the city, and the larger society.[8] Few Indian corporate groups are actually full communities, but some closely approach the abstract model described above. Most Indian villages also include mestizos who are not only peasants, but traders, bureaucrats, and artisans. True, the non-Indians who live in Indian villages may be considered outsiders, despite the fact that they often serve as teachers, government officers, commercial traders, and other capacities essential to the local society. Furthermore, these quasi-Indian communities are often dependent to a large extent on the mestizo towns and cities around them.

The case for mestizo peasant groups functioning as a community seems even less valid. Lacking the unity derived from communal land holdings and from taboos against the alienation of land to outsiders, mestizo peasants generally form mere neighborhoods or a social stratum within a larger community, centered upon a town that serves as their market and bureaucratic center. Most of them live in communities that also include non-peasant storekeepers, government officials, artisans, and even landowners who do not work the land themselves. Sometimes, mestizo peasants may be part of a local community that also includes a hacienda or plantation on which they seek periodic work for wages. One community may include in addition to mestizo peasants, plantation or hacienda *colonos* (permanent wage workers), middle-class elements, and even a landowning aristocracy, as did Vila Recôncavo in the sugarcane-growing region of North Brazil.[9] Or, a community may be composed of both Indian and mestizo peasants and of middle-class town folk as well, as was San Luis Jilotepeque, in eastern Guatemala.[10]

Thus, it is difficult to speak of a homogeneous corporate Indian peasant community or a homogeneous mestizo peasant community, although examples of both may be found. However, it is possible to think of these two peasant types somewhat independently of the communities in which they live. An Indian peasant may live in a corporate community, and his behavior will be conditioned by the current social sanctions of the community; yet, as a rule, if he migrates to a plantation, to a mestizo town, or even to the city, he does not change his behavior abruptly or drastically.

He may no longer spend any surplus he may acquire on community fiestas, for example; but he is apt to look back to his community, to celebrate its saints' days, and in a hundred other ways to behave like the Indian peasant he is. Similarly, the mestizo peasant who has migrated to the city tends to retain his rural behavior patterns as far as this is possible in the urban environment. These two abstract models, the Indian peasant and the mestizo peasant, whether they are considered in terms of homogeneous communities or of social types, can be useful in discussing recent social and economic changes and future trends in the peasant sector of Latin American society.

Although such abstract models as Indian peasants and mestizo peasants can be useful tools of description and analysis, the social anthropologist is most at home when working with concrete cases, namely, specific local communities, attempting as he does to relate his community to a broader frame of reference. For the purpose of this paper, two communities—Santiago Chimaltenango, a community of Indian peasants in Guatemala, and Itá in the Brazilian Amazon region, in which mestizo peasants predominate—will be examined in some detail.[11] Neither community is a truly representative example of its respective peasant subtype. Both are somewhat outside the mainstream of social change among the peasantry of their respective nations. Perhaps this is for the good, for they reflect basic changes in a less dramatic manner, and their future is portended by the changes that are taking place more rapidly elsewhere.

Santiago Chimaltenango: The Indian Peasants

Santiago Chimaltenango is a community of Mam- (Mayan-) speaking Indians situated high in the Cuchamatán mountains of northwestern Guatemala. In 1937, it had a population of approximately 1,500 people. About 900 of these lived in the pueblo, the seat of the county-like *municipio*; the others lived in isolated homesteads or small hamlets (*aldeas*) scattered over the countryside. It was almost a homogeneous Indian peasant community, for only three families (i.e., 37 people) classified as ladinos (non-Indians) lived there. All Chimaltecos spoke Mam habitually, although a small minority, chiefly men, also spoke Spanish. They regarded them-

selves as different from the people of San Juan Atitán and San
Pedro Necta, communities bordering their territory, as well as from
the Indians of all other *municipios* and from the non-Indian nationals of Guatemala. They wore a distinctive costume which set
them off from other Indians and from ladinos. With rare exceptions, they married only among themselves. Individuals who had
entered the community through marriage were considered outsiders for life, and their children were known as the offspring of
mixed marriages.

In the nineteenth century the lands of Chimaltenango were held
in common, but by 1937 all tracts, except a very high and rugged
piece of *ejido* (common land) had been reduced to individual
tenure. Yet at that time community sanctions were still strong
against selling land to outsiders, and the community retained its
corporate character to a large extent. There was a marked difference, however, in the size of individual holdings, which ranged
from over 500 *cuerdas** to less than ten. Most landholdings were
so small that men had to seek wage labor from more fortunate fellow villagers or from coffee *fincas* to provide for their families.
Each year a few families who were landless or whose plots of land
were so small that they provided little income remained permanently on the *fincas* as *colonos*. Such people, living away from their
community, became in time what has been called "transitional
Indians"—people of intermediate status between the "traditional
Indian" of the community and the ladino.[12]

Chimaltenango also retained its traditional political and religious hierarchy, with *principales* (elders), *alcaldes* (mayors), *regidores* (town councilmen), and others, although at the time these
Indian officials were not recognized by the Guatemalan federal
government. Still, most males served at least one year in these
public offices without remuneration, donating approximately half
their time during the year. Many served several years, rising with
age through the hierarchy. The expenditures of office and the
time off from productive work acted as economic leveling factors
that reduced the accumulated wealth of the individual. The officials were selected each year by the *principales*, who had themselves served in several important offices. A man's financial status,

---

* A *cuerda* is 68.6 feet square; there are 9.2 *cuerdas* to the acre.

his age, and his record in lower offices were important criteria in these selections.

Political life in a western sense did not exist in 1937. The Guatemalan dictator, Jorge Ubico, was a face in a picture that hung in the town hall. People were subject to "vagrancy laws" requiring them to give proof of full-time agricultural or wage activities—or be subjected to labor on the roads. A tax was levied on the family sweatbath, but it was seldom collected. The ladino officials were irritants to community cohesion, but their intrusion into community life was minimal. Recourse to such officials took place only if the efforts of the Indian officials failed.

In 1937, all Chimaltecos were Catholics in the local sense of the term, and religion was a community affair fostering considerable esprit de corps and cohesion. Catholic saints and the "Owners of the Mountains" (aboriginal deities) were worshiped equally; prayers and ceremonies in honor of the saints and the aboriginal deities were led by native priests, the *chimans,* who had a knowledge of the Mayan calendar system and of the appropriate prayers and rituals. A Catholic priest came perhaps once a year, chiefly for the baptism of children—the only sacrament of the Church almost universally received in Santiago Chimaltenango.

National institutions were already impinging on the isolation of Santiago Chimaltenango in 1937. There was a school for boys and one for girls in the pueblo-center, but few families sent their children to them. With minor exceptions, Chimaltecos were farmers specializing in maize production. They sold their surplus at local Indian markets, or to ladino merchants in the city of Huehuetenango. They were subjected to national fluctuations in price, and thus participated in the national economic system. Yet, in 1937, Santiago Chimaltenango retained its identity as an almost homogeneous Indian peasant community to a remarkable degree.

By 1956, Santiago Chimaltenango had changed both internally and in relation to the nation. In two decades Guatemala had witnessed the fall of the Ubico dictatorship, the relatively democratic government of Juan José Arévalo (which reorganized the municipal structure), and, finally, the rise and overthrow of the left-wing regime of Jacobo Arbenz. In the years following the fall of Ubico in 1944, there was an official interest in Indian affairs, an attempt at agrarian reform, and an intrusion of national politics into the peasant communities. National programs in public health and education, often with United States aid, were felt in Santiago Chimaltenango. The social changes that had occurred in this one community were similar to those taking place even more drastically in other Guatemalan Indian communities, and in broad terms they were similar to those that have taken place in similar groups throughout Latin America.

The total population of Santiago Chimaltenango grew appreciably between 1940 and 1950,[13] approximately at the same rate (25.6%) as the total population of Guatemala during this period. This population growth, which in itself would have meant less land per capita, was by 1956 combined with a trend for the villagers to sell plots of land to ladinos and to Indians of neighboring *municipios*. Population expansion and land diminution forced more villagers to migrate permanently to coffee *fincas* or even to the cities seeking work. Simultaneously, the sale of land to outsiders brought individuals into the community who were largely unversed in community traditions such as service in the politico-religious hierarchy, celebration of saints' days and the local norms of interpersonal relations. Thus, the shortage of land and the changing pattern of land tenure in such corporate Indian peasant communities have the dual effect of forcing many individuals into new social and economic systems and destroying the community's cultural and ideological homogeneity. This is a basic trend working slowly toward the "ladinoization" of whole communities.[14]

Other changes resulted indirectly from the change in land-tenure pattern in Santiago Chimaltenango. The outsiders brought national politics into the community. Political activity was felt in the village as early as 1944, when the villagers voted solidly for one presidential candidate, Arévalo, who had promised to reestablish them as a separate *municipio*.[15] Arévalo's regime was at first "democratic in orientation and program and solicitous of bringing the Indian component of Guatemala into national life in a meaningful social and cultural manner."[16] But, as political life in the nation became intensified with the appearance of a multitude of political parties and the rise of active left-wing movements, political strife began to be felt even in this isolated community. Political parties and labor unions throughout the country became active not only among the ladino population, but also among the Indians.[17] Some Chimaltecos were driven to Guatemala City in trucks to take part in gigantic campesino rallies, and in 1956 Indians were pointed out to me as "Communists."

This intrusion of national politics and the concepts of western elective democracy proved upsetting to the traditional community government. The *alcalde* and several of the *regidores* were now elected by popular vote. The man elected as *alcalde* was an Indian and acceptable to the *principales,* who had formerly selected this officer. But both this *alcalde* and the "first" *regidor* refused to carry out the religious ceremonies traditionally incumbent upon such officers. Another elected *regidor* had never served in any lower office of the politico-religious hierarchy. He was, in fact, a "party man" much too young for the office. The more conservative members of the community feared punishment from God as a result of these infringements. Such political factions had not as yet divided Santiago Chimaltenango seriously, but the process was under way.

In other corporate Indian communities, the intrusion of politics had already taken on a more serious character, especially in those communities which contained a larger ladino population.[18] In some communities, young Indian men fully aware of national party politics were elected to office and ignored the traditional powers of the *principales* and the old hierarchy.[19] In others, ladinos manipulated the electoral system without regard to the local system.[20] Much of this political activity in the Indian communities ended with the overthrow of the Arbenz government in 1954, but the stability of the traditional politico-religious community system had already been irrevocably disturbed. Today as never before in Latin America, national politics are being felt in these formerly isolated and inward-looking communities.

By 1956, the larger society had also begun to intrude upon the religious life of Santiago Chimaltenango, bringing factionalism to what had been a remarkably united community. There were fifty to sixty *Evangélicos* (Protestants) who had built a temporary church.[21] Furthermore, North American Maryknoll Fathers had established themselves in San Pedro Necta, only ten kilometers away, and were active in Chimaltenango. They considered the traditional Catholicism of Chimaltenango to be "pagan" and condemned the activities of the native *chimans,* the fiestas of the *cofradías,* the use of alcohol in ceremonials, and the prayers at mountain shrines. These missionary priests evidently attempted to maintain close control over the community, teaching people to become orthodox Catholics and forbidding the *chimans* to carry out their ceremonies in the church. Even older persons who were old friends of the author were secretive about *costumbre* (traditional ritual). The orthodox Catholic group were said to go to confession and to attend Mass, and to be married in the church. The community was thus divided into three religious factions: traditional Indian Catholics, orthodox Catholics, and Protestants. The Chimalteco religious experience during the last two decades can be generalized to include all of Guatemala, and perhaps Latin America as a whole.

The development of public services has contributed further to the awareness of the national scene and to the loss of internal unity in Indian communities. In 1937, Santiago Chimaltenango maintained communications with the state capital through weekly messengers on foot. By 1956, there was a telephone that connected the town hall with the capital and neighboring municipalities. Motor roads had not reached the village, but the Pan American Highway was only a few kilometers away, and already jeeps had come over the mountain trails into the village center. The federal government, with United States aid, had installed a water system that replaced the open springs and the fountain in the central plaza. Some houses had water in their kitchens, but most were served by conveniently located public outlets. Many families had privies in 1956; they were unknown in 1937. The market place now had been roofed to protect customers and merchants during the heavy rains. The Chimaltenango school had been enlarged and three schools had been built in the rural districts. The number of teachers had grown from two to six, two of whom had attended special courses on the problems of teaching Indians, offered by an international organization. Although as late as 1950 almost 90 per cent of school-age children in Guatemala did not attend school,[22] the opportunities for education in Santiago Chimaltenango were infinitely better than in 1937. The inhabitants were interested in schools and many more children were attending them.

The changes in Santiago Chimaltenango between 1937 and 1956 were not dramatic, primarily because the community is a rather isolated one. But the forces of change were at work in more intense form in other isolated areas. Few corporate Indian peasant communities survive in Mexico, and each year the Indian peasants come closer to resembling the mestizo peasants. In Ecuador and in Peru, language barriers and caste-like social barriers divide the Indian peasants from the mestizo peasants, as well as from other sectors of the population; but even in these countries, better communications, frequent migration to coastal plantations, and intrusive national institutions and politics are involving the Indian increasingly in national life. And in Bolivia the Indian peasant or so-called campesino is now the locus of considerable political power.[23]

Despite all this, it is commonly observed that the Indian is the most conservative element in Latin American society. The tenacity with which he clings to traditional ways of life continues to amaze observers. Ruben Reina, for example, in his study of the Indian peasants of Santa Cruz Chinautla, located just nine miles from Guatemala City, concludes: "Chinautlecos remain in spite of political or non-political orientations with Chinautla as the locus of their world view." He goes on to say, "It appears that Guatemala City has not seriously influenced the mode of life of Chinautla. Actually, the city is important only as it offers services instrumental in the preserving of the traditional ways."[24] During the Arévalo regime, before Reina's study, the Indian peasants of Chinautla had received land that allowed them to re-establish their traditional fiesta patterns and to regain to some extent their economic independence.

William Stein describes a similar situation among the Indian peasants of Hualcán in the Andes of central Peru. About half of the men of Hualcán own enough land to be independent of the surrounding haciendas. But many Indian landowners must supplement their income by day labor in nearby towns and on the haciendas. A large proportion of the people of Hualcán are forced to migrate to the coast, where they work on large sugar plantations for periods ranging from a few weeks to years. Most of them, however, ultimately return to Hualcán, especially those who have earned a "stake" with which to buy land or animals. Motor roads and the railroad make the coastal plantations easy to reach. These outside contacts and the frequent migration to the coast have set off a series of social changes in Hualcán; yet Hualcán retains most of the quali-

ties of an Indian peasant community. Those Hualcainos who accumulate any economic surplus derived from agriculture or outside
wage labor choose to expend it on the community prestige system
of fiestas and in greater participation in the politico-religious system.[25] In a sense, the income from outside wage labor allows the
people of Hualcán to maintain their traditional institutions and
values, and to remain relatively insulated from national society.

As long as Indian peasants can retain control in one way or another over their minuscule plots, and particularly if they receive
additional land, they will resist change. This will be especially true
as long as the alternative offered them is bare subsistence as second-
class citizens in the larger society. Curiously, this conservatism,
born in large part of a self-protective separatism and of the need
of the *hacendados* to have a readily available pool of free labor,
owes much to the idealistic *indigenista* movements and, surpris-
ingly, to the agrarian-reform programs of various governments, in-
effectual as most of them have been. By adding to the land available
to Indian peasants, the process of integration of the communities
into national life would seem to be at least delayed.[26]

On the other hand, governmental land-reform programs also
mean increased encroachment of outside influences upon Indian
community life. Restored land generally must be registered, and
it must be used, at least theoretically, in a manner that conforms
with federal codes. Agronomists, educators, and other non-Indians
inevitably become part of community life under such circumstances. Furthermore, unless such land-reform programs are more
drastic and provide increasing amounts of land, their stabilizing
effect upon Indian peasant communities can only be temporary.
They provide a solution for the present generation, but as the population grows (and it is growing), the man–land ratio will fall
again. People will continue to be forced out of their communities
to seek employment on plantations and in cities.[27] The trend, then,
seems apparent. The Indian peasant will in the long run disappear
from the Latin American scene, however slow the process. Communities with collective land-tenure systems may be formed under
revolutionary governments, as they have been in Bolivia. In time
these communities will not resemble the traditional, endogamous,
inward-looking corporate Indian communities of the highlands of

Central and South America that have persisted from the colonial period into the present. They will be communities of people fully aware of their status as members of a nation.

Itá: A Mestizo Peasant Community

Itá is a small town and a large county-like municipality, located in the lower Amazon Valley in the state of Pará, Brazil.[28] Like Santiago Chimaltenango, it is an isolated community where social and economic change has been slow and where national crises are felt only in attenuated forms. Yet many of the trends current among Latin American mestizo peasants are to be found there.

In 1948, the town of Itá had approximately 500 people, and was the seat of a local administrative unit almost as large as the state of Rhode Island, with a population of about 5,000. Not all of these people could properly be called members of the Itá community, however. The community was restricted to about 2,000 people who lived in the rural neighborhoods adjacent to the little town. These were the people who looked to the town as the center of their economic, social, and religious life. Individuals and families in more remote rural neighborhoods turned to other small nuclei. Like most open communities, Itá is not sharply defined. It is similar in many respects to the market-town-centered communities of the rural United States.[29] The residents of Itá and surrounding neighborhoods are quite conscious of being members of a single community, but in certain respects they are not sure where the community's boundaries begin and end.

Physically, the majority of the inhabitants of Itá are mestizos in the broadest sense of the term. A few are phenotypically white or Negroid, and some seem to be Amerindian in physical type; but most are mixtures in varying degrees of these three racial types. Most, but not all, of the people of Itá are peasants. In town, there are government officials serving the municipal, state, and federal governments. There are also tradesmen and a few artisans. Some earn their living entirely from manual labor. In the rural neighborhoods dependent upon Itá, there are many people who earn their living entirely from the collection of wild rubber. If the definition of the term "peasant" set forth above were strictly adhered to, only about one-third of the rural population of Itá might be regarded as peasants. These are the people who are full-time agriculturalists planting manioc, corn, and other garden products for their own use and for sale at the local market. The majority of the rural population combine agriculture with collecting.

In Itá, the line between the peasant-planter and the collector of products for sale is a matter of degree—of the percentage of time spent on one or the other activity. Economic activities, furthermore, may vary from year to year; depending on the prices paid for rubber and food products, the same family may emphasize one or the other at different times. This same phenomenon holds true for all of Latin America. Mestizo peasants are often at the same time agriculturalists producing food for their own use and for sale, collectors of native products, fishermen, wage laborers, and even artisans. But, as noted earlier, they share a peasant-type subculture that is mainly agrarian in focus, and they are isolated from the literate mainstream of national life.

Itá peasants do not form a community apart from that of non-peasants. In fact, Itá contains at least two social classes—a town white-collar elite, and a town and rural lower class of which the peasants are an important segment. This is generally true of communities containing mestizo peasants throughout Brazil and in most of Latin America. Such communities might best be termed "town-peasant communities," to indicate their characteristic internal subcultural and class differentiation. But despite this internal differentiation, the two classes in communities like Itá share a diffuse but ever-present feeling of identity. They are all Itaenses, while in Santiago Chimaltenango only the Indians are Chimaltecos, and the ladinos are considered outsiders merely residing within the community. Such town-peasant communities, divided as they are by lines of social class and by differences in wealth, lack the strong esprit de corps of Indian peasant communities. People are not so tied to the soil, and they are more outward-looking and sensitive to national trends.

Unlike so many mestizo peasants throughout the Americas, the residents of Itá in 1948 considered themselves Brazilians in the full sense of the term. Everyone in the community spoke Portuguese. Although the great majority of them were illiterate and therefore could not vote, they were nonetheless aware of and interested in political events. The peasant sector of the community had vague ideas about the size and complexity of their nation. They knew something of its national political figures, its national heroes, past and present, and its national symbols such as the flag and the Seventh of September (Independence Day). They shared with the townsfolk an intense interest in soccer, and they celebrated with the townspeople such Brazilian festivals as St. John's Day, Carnival, and the local community saint's day (St. Benedict's). Their ideal patterns of behavior, which they seldom managed to live up to, were those of the local elite. All of them felt that they ought to be married according to the civil law and the Church, but many of them were not, for one reason or another. They aspired to the traditional Brazilian forms of religion, of family life, of etiquette. Both the peasants and the townspeople, however, retained in varying degrees a belief in concepts of American Indian origin, such as the treatment of illness by the *pagé* (shaman). The peasants of Itá were interested in schools for their children and eager for them to be as well trained as the better-educated Itaenses, whom they respected. The town had only one government-supported school, with two teachers. Only 61 students attended it. And, in the rural zones, there was but one school with an average attendance of twenty to twenty-five pupils.

The mestizo peasant of Itá, like his counterparts throughout Latin America, shares the ignorance and poverty of the Indian peasant. His agriculture is often just as primitive. His agricultural techniques are not far removed from those inherited from the American Indian. In Itá peasants do not plant coffee, cacao, bananas, or sugarcane as cash crops, as do mestizo peasants in other parts of Brazil and Latin America; but they sell manioc flour and wild rubber, hides, *timbó* vine (used as a base for insecticides), and other native products in order to buy manufactured articles and other necessities such as kerosene. Like peasant producers of cash crops elsewhere, they are vulnerable to the rise and fall of prices, which they do not understand. They value the accumulation of property. They are less inclined than Indian peasants to gain prestige from the community by spending their surplus on community service or feasting a saint.

Itá peasants control the land on which they live and work, but few have outright title to the land. In the eyes of the law, they are squatters, occupying land to which either traders or absentee land-

lords have some sort of title. Unlike mestizo peasants in many parts
of Latin America, the peasants of Itá do not have to give days of
labor as rent for their land. They are, however, generally tied by
debt to certain traders to whom they must sell their products and
from whom they must buy their necessities. Each has a *patrão*
(boss), a person to whom he is tied by debt, land-rent obligations,
and traditional personal ties. Throughout Latin America, this
patrão (Portuguese) or *patrón* (Spanish) system relating the mestizo peasant to the landowner, the trader, the employer, or the
political boss has survived as an important relationship.

In 1962, although calm and orderly compared to other places in
Brazil, Itá was feeling the pressures of national economic and political instability.[30] There had never been much food in Itá, but
there was a shortage of some basic foodstuffs such as rice, beans,
and sun-dried beef. Rampant inflation was upsetting the local
credit system. Storekeepers and rural traders did not want to sell
merchandise to agriculturalists or rubber gatherers in June and
wait until December to be paid in produce whose price would have
risen tremendously. Business, consequently, was in the doldrums.
Traders did not solicit new customers, and in fact some of them
were concealing their wares so as not to attract credit buyers. Once
the debt-credit system failed to function normally, the total commerce of the region was jeopardized to the extent that it theoretically could grind to a halt.

Social as well as economic changes were immediately discernible
in Itá. For example, the population of the town had doubled between 1948 and 1962. There were more than a thousand people in
the town. Where there had been three streets parallel to the river,
in 1962 there were four, and a fifth was forming. Itá's population
expansion reflects the remarkable growth of the Brazilian national
population, but it is also the result of a staging process of rural-
urban migration, by which rural Brazilians in ever-increasing numbers are migrating to major cities after first living in small towns
such as Itá.

"The rural *caboclos*," the author was informed, "want to move
to town." They are "disillusioned" (*desiludido* was the exact term)
by prices paid for rubber and other native products of Amazonia
and by the difficulties involved in educating their children and receiving adequate health protection. The people from the country-

side are indeed moving to town. They are planting gardens along the new road that penetrates inland from the river. In the town, they have a school for their children and enjoy the protection offered by a federal health clinic. They have the luxury of electric lights. They like the general *movimento*—the noise of the radios, the daily buying in the few stores, the political campaigns, the gossip, and other business of town life. By 1962 the local economy in Itá could hardly support a larger urban population. Under present circumstances, there is a limit to the amount of arable land that can be worked by agriculturalists living in town and walking to their fields. There are but a few private employers offering wage labor, and highly sought-after employment on the public works projects (a small hospital and the clearing of an airstrip) is quite limited. There is no industry at all. Thus, it is clear that within a short time peasant migrants to the town will be induced to move along to the city, to be replaced by others from the rural zone. The Amazonian cities Belém and Manaus are thus growing more rapidly than the back country and have large shanty towns of recently arrived peasants.

Although this process of emigration to the city is discernible in Itá, it does not reach the same proportions as in northeastern and southern Brazil, in central Peru, in Ecuador, and in other regions of Latin America. The situation of Itá, however, helps us to understand that mestizo peasants do not generally go directly to the great cities. They migrate to plantations that grow coffee, sugarcane, bananas, and other cash crops. They move into small towns from the surrounding rural zones. Then they go to cities and swell the shanty towns.

A great majority of the Latin American population is in the lower age levels. Itá and other Brazilian small towns seem literally to swarm with children. It cannot be stated as fact that mestizo peasants are increasing more rapidly than any other sector of the Latin American population, but in all probability they are. Not only are mestizo peasants multiplying rapidly, but they aspire to a better life. For example, they want their children to have some education. In Itá, as in most town-peasant communities, the educational facilities are swamped. The 1948 school building was still the only educational establishment to be found at Itá in 1962. But then there were nine teachers instead of two. There were over three hundred pupils rather than 61. Furthermore, there were four schools instead of one in the rural zones of the community. These schools offered only four years of primary education. In order to provide as many children as possible with some schooling, they functioned in five shifts of two hours each between 7 A.M. and 7 P.M. The teachers were better trained, but they were not better paid in terms of their buying power. With only two hours per day of classes six days a week, it is doubtful if the education received in 1962 was any better than that received in 1948. And while more mestizo peasants than ever before are being exposed to formal schooling, the illiteracy rate seems to remain stable. Illiteracy, of course, extends beyond the peasant groups to the towns, plantations, and cities.

In 1962, Itá's communications with the outside world were markedly improved over those of 1948. There was an airstrip (called magnificently the "municipal airport") at which "air taxis" landed from time to time. A commercial airline, flying amphibian planes, made unscheduled stops on the river. Boat traffic on the river was heavier. A telegraph (radio) station had been installed. But, above all, there were radios—both battery- and electric-powered—which brought daily news of the outside world. The peasants of Itá, both in town and in the rural communities, were able to follow national political events and, more important to them, the progress of the international soccer games in Santiago, Chile, where Brazil again won the world championship. They knew about satellites. The new awareness of the outside world was illustrated dramatically by a barely literate Itá peasant. As he conversed with the author, while his wife squeezed *assái* (palm nut) juice with her hands, he asked if the satellite that could be seen in the skies in the evening was *"russo"* or *"americano."*

But Itá is still isolated as compared with other town-peasant communities. In other parts of Brazil, and in Latin America as a whole, such communities are generally found on motor roads rather than on rivers. In these localities, truck and bus drivers have become agents of change, transmitting outside influences from village to village and from the town to the countryside. Peasants now cover by motorcar in a few hours distances that in the recent past would have taken them days by donkey or on foot. Furthermore, outsiders, including traders, missionaries, and politicians, now come to them with greater frequency. Rural peasants can migrate to a distant city and return. The result has been that isolation of the town-peasant community is beginning to break down, and its inhabitants, more than ever before, are becoming members of regional and national societies.

Despite the shortage of land adjacent to the town, the agriculturalists of Itá do not suffer from a chronic peasant ill, namely *minifundio*. In much of Latin America Indian and mestizo peasant landholdings have been subdivided by sale or inheritance until they are below the minimum size sufficient to provide a living for a family. "In Guatemala," Thomas F. Carroll estimates, "97 per cent of all farms are less than 20 hectares.* The corresponding figure for Peru and Ecuador is 90 per cent; for the Dominican Republic, it is 95 per cent; for Venezuela, 88 per cent and for the private sector of the Mexican farm economy, 88 per cent. In Colombia some 325,000 farms average 2½ hectares."[31] In all these countries, the land shortage of the peasant is aggravated by the presence of large commercial holdings—*fincas,* haciendas, *fazendas,* or whatever they may be called. Even in Brazil, with its immense territory, many peasant groups suffer from land shortage and from the pressure of latifundios.[32]

Where peasants suffer from the extreme parcelization of land and from lack of land resulting from the pressure of large commercial holdings, land provides the basis for tension and even violence. Northeastern Brazil, the Cochabamba region of Bolivia,[33] and highland Peru[34] are among the best-known current examples of regions of peasant unrest resulting mainly from land problems. In some cases, this unrest has taken the form of forceful invasions of large plantations or forceful resistance to eviction. Mainly as a reaction to land problems, peasant leaders have appeared, and peasant organizations, such as the rapidly growing Peasant Leagues of northeastern Brazil and the campesino "syndicate" (*sindicato*) in the department of Cochabamba in Bolivia, have taken form. Although not unknown among Indian peasants, such peasant leaders and organizations are more common among mestizos. With more frequent relations with the outside and greater awareness of regional and national issues, mestizo peasants are becoming an in-

* One hectare is two and a half acres.

creasingly articulate sector of Latin American society. Even more than the Indians, they are at least potentially a focus of widespread social and political change.

The Peasantry and the Nation: A Conclusion

Two types of Latin American peasantry have been described, and each must be considered separately in terms of its relationship to the nation of which it is a part. The Indian peasant remains outside the nation in many ways, although often providing a necessary labor force for the national economy. Indian peasants tend to be conservative, are sometimes resistant to change, and value continuity of their traditional forms. They are not eager to exchange their community world view, their own prestige system, and their separate identity for a place on the lowest rung of the ladder of the national social and economic system.[35] Still, there is a marked trend throughout the highland Latin American countries, where Indian peasants still form a significant segment of the national population, for them to become mestizos, plantation laborers, or members of the urban poor. This process is stimulated by internal changes within the Indian peasant groups themselves, but just as often they are forced to migrate by the lack of land and the absence of other economic opportunities. Efforts to retain and to reform the Indian corporate community may for a time delay the process, but in time Latin American countries will cease to be pluralistic or dualistic societies divided into Indians and mestizos (or ladinos, cholos, and other nationals). Eventually, all the population groups in these countries will fully identify themselves as members of a national system.

Everywhere in Latin America, the mestizo peasants are more open to social change than the Indian peasants. They are often economically as badly off as the Indian peasants, but they have linguistic and cultural advantages. They speak the same language and they share the same ideal patterns of behavior as the middle- and upper-class townspeople and urbanites of their nations, although their accent, grammar, and actual behavior may seem even comical to their more sophisticated countrymen. Mestizo peasants are more apt to have higher material and educational aspirations, and are thus more vulnerable to political ideology, than Indian peasants. Because they have aspirations they cannot afford, they are more often frustrated than their Indian counterparts. They are thus more sensitive to outside leadership, and more apt to develop their own leaders in protest against their low position in the national society.

Both Indian and mestizo peasants are now, more than ever before, influenced by the national society.[36] In most Indian peasant villages, and certainly in all small towns where Indian and mestizo live together, there are individuals who may be described as cultural "brokers" to use Eric Wolf's term. In all small peasant communities, Indian, mestizo, or mixed, there are "individuals who are able to operate both in terms of community-orientation and national-oriented expectations. . . . They become the economic and political 'brokers' of nation-community relations, a function which carries its own rewards."[37] These people derive their power from a simultaneous understanding of the local culture and of the national culture; they are a bridge, so to speak, to the outside. As Wolf states it, "They stand guard over the crucial junctures or synapses of relationships which connect the local system to the larger whole."[38] They know how to manipulate personal and traditional ties in the peasant village, but also know how to translate these into a different kind of power on the outside.

Who are these cultural brokers? As yet, little is known about this important group, or better, these individuals, for it would seem that they generally operate as individuals. To date, most sociologists and anthropologists who have studied Latin American peasant societies have concentrated upon the internal structure of the local community, rather than the relationship of the local community to the larger society. Tentatively, however, it would seem obvious that such individuals fall into two general types, which might be called "traditional brokers" and "new brokers." The traditional broker is an individual whose role derives out of traditional and internal relationships within the peasant community, while the new broker's role relates to the larger society and the new influences from the outside upon the local community.

Traditionally, of course, the broker was a *patrón*. He was the local trader upon whom the peasant depended for credit. In many Indian peasant communities, brokers were the recruiters for work on coffee *fincas* (Guatemala), on coastal sugar plantations (Peru), and in the United States (Mexican braceros). In many peasant communities, the local padre was a traditional cultural broker, although the shortage of clergymen throughout Latin America meant that few Indian peasant communities had a resident priest. In mestizo peasant communities and in mixed communities, the traditional cultural broker has generally been the local upper-class politician, a man whose power depended almost entirely upon his role as a broker. Whoever he was, the traditional broker maintained his position through traditional roles—through his family, extended kinsmen, and *compadres,* through favors extended to the members of the community, and through an intimate knowledge of the local social scene and custom. His relationship with the community always had an element of noblesse oblige; and he depended upon tradition and established economic relations with the larger society for his position. The traditional broker is an influence for continuity, not for change.

The new cultural broker works generally for change. Some new cultural brokers are native sons of the community in which they live, and thus are fully aware of the traditional values and of the local social system. But even these native sons have lived in and learned something of the larger society, and they have accepted the values of the outside world. Throughout highland Latin America, there are a growing number of bilingual Indians who have spent considerable time on plantations and in large cities, and who have returned to live in their native communities. Many of them reject what they saw and learned while away from home, and attempt to reintegrate themselves into the local community. Others become innovators and cultural brokers. They have learned of the power of labor unions, political parties, and the judicial process. The young Indian political leaders who appeared in so many Guatemalan communities after the revolution of 1944 are a good example.[39]

Among mestizo peasants, cultural brokers originating in the community are, of course, more numerous, since there is a greater awareness of the outside world and no linguistic barrier. Yet it would seem probable that few potential cultural brokers with experience outside their local communities actually return to perform that role in mestizo communities. The mestizo peasant community lacks the distinctive set of values and integration that encourage so many Indians to return. Mestizo peasants, already consciously a part of the larger society, are more likely than Indians never to return home, especially if they are successful in the larger society. As in the United States, every village and small town in Latin America has its native sons who were successful in the city and never returned. Still, there are a few who do return, and they are important in interpreting the outside society to their compatriots.

Finally, one must consider the new cultural brokers who come from outside the local community. As national institutions penetrate peasant communities, they bring cultural brokers from the outside—teachers, agronomists, public health officers, Peace Corps personnel, Protestant and Catholic missionaries, and politicians. Most of these people cannot fulfill the role of a cultural broker, for they do not understand the local society in which they are assigned to work. But, increasingly, they are being taught to be cultural brokers—by UNESCO in its school at Patzcuaro, by the Peace Corps, and by Latin American governments, which realize the great gulf that exists between technically trained personnel from the cities and the mass of people with whom they must work. Important among the new brokers from outside the community are, of course, politicians, labor leaders, and others who are deliberately attempting to awaken political consciousness among peasant groups. More and more, politicians find the peasants ready to listen and to participate. Often the peasants do not fully understand the leaders from the outside, and, in many countries where literacy is a requirement for voting, they have no recourse to the polls. The time may not be too far off, however, when nationally organized peasant groups will wield decisive political power in many nations of Latin America. Already in several Latin American nations, such as Venezuela, Colombia, Bolivia, and Mexico, the peasant is considered an important locus of political power. Crucial to the form and direction that such political movements will take are the people we have called the new cultural brokers.

The source of change for peasant communities of Latin America must be the larger society of which they are now parts. Change will probably originate in the political process, and economic change will follow. Land reform, technical assistance, credit, and education for the peasants will be part of the platform of political parties seeking their support. Such change may be slow, unequal, and painful, but it would seem to be inevitable if Latin American societies are to enter the modern world. Latin American nations cannot continue with a large segment of their people neglected, impoverished, illiterate, and living in isolation but inside their frontiers. The peasants may not be the wave of the future in Latin America, but certainly they are the material, the human mass, out of which the future will be made.

2. Rural Labor

Richard N. Adams

Latin American rural labor has attracted little attention from social scientists. Within recent years, the first forays into the subject have been made in community studies involving people playing wage-labor roles, studies of a few plantation situations, and extremely committed, normative expositions.

One problem in discussing "rural labor" is the wide variety of forms covered by the rubric "rural." The following kinds of rural labor have been mentioned in different contexts: (1) *reciprocal labor* (including festive labor), occasional exchange labor with peers; (2) *peasant labor,* part-time wage labor, part-time independent farmer; (3) *plantation proletariat,* full-time wage labor on large-scale agricultural enterprises (this is Sidney Mintz's "rural proletariat"); (4) *hacienda colono* or *corvée labor,* usually resident labor enjoying use of land in return for labor, or for share-cropped produce; (5) *mining proletariat,* full-time wage labor in mines; (6) *forest labor,* the collectors of rubber, chicle, lumber, etc., working full time, but sometimes for limited periods; (7) *rural-industrial labor,* the laborers from rural communities who maintain their rural way of life, but commute to a city or work in a rurally located industrial enterprise. Applying the term rural to these types obviously involves divergent criteria. Rural varyingly refers to (1) a non-urban way of life, (2) a non-urban work location, or (3) an agricultural work situation. To avoid haggling over definition, the present chapter will draw on one or another of these criteria, depending upon the particular phenomenon under discussion.

Although the use of group typologies has been popular and has a preliminary utility in ordering materials,[1] an attempt must sooner or later be made (and the sooner the better) to analyze the variable properties of the subject scientifically. This is particularly important in the present instance, since a dominant characteristic of rural labor in Latin America is that few individuals depend entirely upon a single source of wage labor. Furthermore, it is increasingly the rule among peasant groups that at some point part of their income is derived from wage labor. An adequate discussion of wage labor must, then, refer to population groups considered elsewhere in this volume.[2] The population under consideration here is that which provides labor in exchange for any combination of wages, goods, services, and privileges, and specifically meets any of the three criteria for rurality just mentioned.

Although rural laborers are clearly important in Latin America, the available statistical data are too incomplete to be satisfactory. Table I arranges 17 countries according to the percentage of the total economically active national population classified as "agricultural workers." Central American countries lead all the rest in this respect, followed by three Andean countries and Brazil. Panama is in last place, since most of her agriculturalists are squatters

TABLE I

Percentage of All Salary and Wage Earners
Employed in Various Classes of Activities

Country	Agriculture	Service	Mining
Honduras	65.4 (1956)	14.8	0.6
Nicaragua	58.8 (1950)	——	——
El Salvador	56.2 (1950)	19.6	0.6
Guatemala	50.0 (1950)	——	——
Costa Rica	49.2 (1950)	20.4	0.3
Peru	49.2 (1940)	7.8	4.0
Colombia	43.0 (1951)	25.4	1.8
Ecuador	42.5 (1959)	19.8	0.6
Brazil	41.0 (1950)	23.4	——
Haiti	40.5 (1950)	33.5	0.1
Mexico	37.3 (1958)	19.8	——
Cuba	36.0 (1953)	0.1	0.6
Chile	28.1 (1952)	26.5	6.2
Venezuela	26.9 (1950)	35.1	4.6
Bolivia	22.7 (1950)	20.2	12.7
Argentina	21.2 (1947)	26.7	0.7
Panama	13.4 (1950)	34.3	0.2

SOURCE: University of California, *Statistical Abstracts of Latin America* (Los Angeles, 1961).

on government land. Why Bolivia falls so low is hard to determine, unless the figures omit the *colono*-type population.

Rural labor is growing more slowly than urban labor, and the total rural population of some areas is now on the decline. In Venezuela, one of the countries in which the agricultural labor force is smallest in relation to the total labor force, nine states showed an absolute decrease in the rural population between 1941 and 1950.[3]

Table I does not, however, account for all the people being considered here, since the independent agriculturalists are excluded. Well over half of the so-called self-employed in agriculture probably work for wages at times. Even with part-time laborers excluded, Table I indicates that the agricultural labor force is larger than any other category of wage labor in all countries except Panama, Argentina, and Venezuela, and possibly (no data being available) Uruguay and Paraguay. Except in Argentina, where manufacturing accounts for more labor than agriculture, only the category of services has outstripped agriculture in these countries.

If it may be granted that rural labor is important, there still remain a number of problems in conceptualization. Eric Wolf recommended taking an ecological view to avoid a surfeit of typologies.[4] He suggested that human groups, like biological forms, are more or less specialized in terms of specific environment. He further suggested that many Latin American rural populations are somewhat generalized, with their sustenance coming from at least two major sources, wage labor and individual farming. Unfortunately, Wolf set up yet other types to account for some of the alternatives he found.

Here an effort will be made to avoid typologies, and to concentrate instead on (1) the operation of the labor market, as it affects the status of the rural laborer; (2) the impact of areas of power control, here called power domains, on the situation of the rural laborer; (3) the adaptation of social structures and attitudes to the environment in which the rural laborer lives and works.

The Labor Market

Observers of Latin America have pointed out that the distribution of natural resources makes economic utilization difficult. In modern times, commercial or large-scale agriculture has thrived in the lowlands, the hilly piedmont, and intermountain valleys. The most important is the lowland—either coastal or inland subhumid areas—on which cotton, rice, corn, sugar, and other less important market crops can be cultivated. Two, three, or even four crops may be harvested per year. Irrigation is often crucial for development of these regions, since some, such as the Peruvian coast, have almost no rainfall. In both Middle America and the Andes, the lowland potential has periodically drawn considerable numbers of people in search of work from the highlands. In the hilly piedmont and some intermountain areas, crops such as coffee are produced. Higher mountain areas have relatively little commercial agriculture potential.

Another "resource" that historically has made certain rural areas desirable for commercial exploitation is the availability of labor that is tied to the land.[5] The encomienda of the colonial period and its successors were based on the availability of labor, and, until recently, debt peonage and anti-vagrancy systems perpetuated this practice. However, while it persists in the Andes and elsewhere, the low yield resulting from hand technology and highland climate and soil has made commercial enterprises so economically undesirable that owners are increasingly willing to break them up. Gathering and semi-cultivation of forest products have long been alternatives available to laborers in Latin America, although they have usually lived far from these resources. Chicle in Yucatan and Guatemala, rubber in the Amazon, and hardwood in the tropical forests have been gathered by limited local labor, supplemented by imported labor. Wages are usually above average, because living conditions are harsh and the laborers ordinarily must be away from their families for extended periods.

As industrialization comes to rural regions, power resources become increasingly important. The location of a textile plant in the Guatemalan Indian community of Cantel, for example, was determined by the fact that the flow of the Samalá River was sufficient to turn a turbine to power the spinning machines. Since labor is relatively mobile, it seems likely that power resources will play an increasingly important role in the future.[6]

Certain general patterns have emerged in resource availability. As agriculture becomes more and more commercialized, lowlands are more intensively exploited. The spread of industrialization dictates that power resources become increasingly important. Resource location both forces migration and draws people away from wage labor into individual agriculture. A study of migrants in Nicoya (Costa Rica) showed that 63 per cent of them had formerly been wage laborers, whereas at the time of the study, 92 per cent had become independent agriculturalists. They had migrated to Nicoya because public lands were available.[7] Finally, there are areas suffering from soil depletion and subsequent emigration. It is not possible at this time to estimate what portion of those affected become independent agriculturists in a new location and what portion enter the labor force.

Most major changes in the labor picture involve migration. The declining death rate, due in great part to public health efforts, has created a man-land pressure that lies behind most migrations of the type being discussed here. Furthermore, even though the urban increase may be relatively larger than the rural, the absolute increase in the rural areas is still generally greater than the urban.[8] The rural population is actually decreasing in a few areas, such as the nine Venezuelan states already mentioned.

While it is easy to establish that man-land pressure stands behind migration, it is much more difficult to produce a simple, usable formula that will tell us when an area has been demographically saturated. In some instances, economic factors will be painfully evident; in others, they may be masked by aspirations that gradually come into play as the local situation deteriorates.

An understanding of migration has been inhibited by a tendency to classify migration as either "temporary" or "permanent." Such a distinction can only be made after the fact, because few migrants really know if their move is permanent. Thus, seasonal highland-lowland migration often leaves a residue of laborers who remain more or less permanently in the lowlands. Similarly, there are many instances of migrants who have, after a long period as wage laborers, returned to their original home to take up farming again. This certainly has been true of many Mexican migrants to the United States, and it has also been reported in Peru.[9] There are at least two situations that help fix a migrant in a new locale. One occurs when an individual commits himself to a long-term job on a large plantation; and the other when a wage earner turns to independent agriculture. Encouraging the latter with planned colonization efforts has not proved easy. Undirected migrations generally have been more satisfactory.

We are still far from defining all the kinds of migration patterns that can occur. It is possible here only to suggest a few patterns evident from the present literature. The already mentioned migration from the highlands to the lowlands, both temporary and permanent, is among the most common. Another pattern is stepmigration, whereby people move from small population centers to the next larger one. George W. Hill, José A Silva M., and Ruth Oliver de Hill have reported this for Venezuela in general,[10] and material from the plantation Central Tacarigua and Sucre State confirms the generalization.[11] On the other hand, there is ample episodic evidence from Peru and Central America that migrants make longer jumps. The problem here is to ascertain the varying conditions leading to one or another of these.

There are indications that much rural wage labor is of recent origin, resulting from the sharp increase in population since World War I. Eric Wolf reports that it is very common for laborers to be only one generation removed from the private farm in Puerto Rico,[12] and this impression is given in a number of other reports. Of even greater importance is the fact that one hears little about rural labor shortages today. In the latter part of the last century, the labor shortage contributed to the continuation, and in some instances reconstitution, of forced and debt-based labor. The shift of free labor in almost all areas, with few complaints about shortages, suggests that a significant stage has been reached in the rural labor picture. The implications of this need further evaluation. Formerly, the peasant sold the time left over from his own subsistence production, thus earning the income to carry him through the year. With the increase in wage labor, the potential competition between the peasant part-time laborer and the landless fulltime laborer has increased. Not only are peasants being forced into the wage-labor force, but the growth of this force places the peasant in an increasingly marginal position. There are, at times, other alternatives. Ruben Reina reports that many Indians of Chinautla, who live close to Guatemala City, prefer to go seasonally to the coast and rent land to extend their private agricultural production.[13] A similar seasonal migration is described for the Guatemalan community of Palo Gordo.[14]

Seasonal and permanent migration to other rural areas has been a standard answer to local population pressures. Today, this safety valve does not always work, since rural commercial agriculture is not expanding in such a way as to absorb the ever-increasing population. Indeed, many large landholdings have been sloughing off excess population for some generations. Much of the Chilean *roto* (urban poor) population originated in this way.[15] The increased rural-urban migration may be due in part to the growing impossibility of moving to other rural areas, and the big city becomes the only visible alternative. Indeed, not only migration to rural wage labor, but migration from rural wage labor has been specifically reported from Puerto Rico, where plantation labor, facing a shortage of work, tends to move into non-manual labor positions.[16]

Change in rural-labor status is only one aspect of mobility that directs attention to the role of varying aspirations. There is little systematic material relevant to rural-labor mobility in Latin America, but Melvin M. Tumin and Arnold S. Feldman have done a suggestive analysis of the intergenerational shifts among various classes of occupations in a Puerto Rican sample (see Table II).[17]

TABLE II

Changes in Occupation in a Selected Sample from Puerto Rico

Occupation	Fathers	Sons of farm owners or managers	of farm laborers	Totals
Non-agricultural		689	462	1,151*(55.3%)
Farm owner or manager	276 (49%) 1,126 sons	167	61	228 (10.9%)
Farm laborer	286 (51%) 958 sons	270	435	705 (33.8%)
	562 fathers	2,084 sons		2,084 (100%)

SOURCE: Tumin and Feldman, *Social Class and Social Change in Puerto Rico* (Princeton, 1961).

* Of the 1,151 sons in non-agricultural positions, 81.7 per cent were engaged in manual labor and 18.3 per cent in non-manual labor.

The number of farm owners and managers declined about 18 per cent, and the number of farm laborers increased 146.5 per cent. The largest single group, however, comprised the 462 farm laborers' sons who left the agricultural field entirely. Of these, 81.7 per cent continued in manual labor. In this particular case, half the second generation left agriculture entirely, the rural labor force grew significantly, and the farm-owner and management population declined slightly. Besides presenting a microcosm that conforms to our general picture of much of Latin America, this case points up the problem involved in understanding the relationship between desires and mobility. Given that in many countries there is land pressure, how can the varying response be explained? And given that there may not be land pressure in all instances, how is migration to be explained at all?

Easiest to understand are the extreme cases when the alternative is death. In such cases, it seems unnecessary to look far for reasons for migration and taking whatever steps may be available for survival. In the Guajira peninsula some years ago, a fierce drought reduced the livestock from over a million head to barely 30,000; almost half the population of 56,000 people migrated to neighboring Venezuela to seek whatever form of support they could find.[18]

In more ordinary cases, aspirations that bring people into the rural labor force should be distinguished from those that make them leave it. Wage labor provides one of the most common possible sources of income for the peasant or sharecropper, the land-poor individual who wishes to cultivate land independently and pay for it in labor, crops, or cash. The historical background and evolution of the relationship thus established between the peasant and the large operator has been traced by various students.[19] Essentially this attraction operates on a local scale. The peasant is relatively uninterested in, or at least effectively separated from, rewards beyond the local area. The Indians of Chiapas, for example, seek seasonal labor to provide the necessary cash for their annual fiesta and annual reclothing.[20]

When outside contacts are more extensive, the demand for industrially produced goods increases the demand for cash, and the appeal of a center where these goods may be obtained. The studies of Puerto Rican plantations by Sidney Mintz and Elena Padilla Seda provide a graphic view of the dependence on commercial

outlets.[21] Studies of the process called "proletarization" suggest
that this change in orientation occurs after labor has been on the
plantation for an extended period. The actual rate at which this
occurs is still very unclear, as are details as to what hastens or slows
the process. Both Mintz and Padilla reported a decline in gardening, and Mintz elsewhere recorded how uncomfortable a lowland
laborer felt during a visit with highland relatives. On the other
hand, Henry F. Dobyns has pointed out that there are many
places, such as the W. R. Grace sugar plantation at Paramonga
(Peru), where the laborers use a variety of devious and ingenious
methods to continue their garden-cropping, even in the face of
restricting edicts from the management.[22] Some adjustment to
wider material wants evidently need destroy neither gardening
interests nor the community as a whole, if there continues to be
some base for coherence. Thomas McCorkle's description of the
Guayquiri of Margarita Island (Venezuela) indicates that many
keep up ties with their community while engaged in outside wage
labor, and Richard N. Adams and William Mangin provide parallel evidence from Peru.[23]

In general, rural wage labor rewards those whose knowledge of
the outside is widening, and who can find no other occupation to
provide access to needed goods. The development of new aspirations does tie in with the loss of rural labor to the cities and to a
variety of non-manual occupations. A small but significant percentage of rural migrants to major cities have cited a desire for education as a principal reason for migration.[24] What portion of these
people came from the rural labor force is not known. Padilla's Nocorá material confirms this tendency. World War II veterans particularly wished to avoid labor in the sugar fields, and therefore
tried to become chauffeurs or truck drivers, enter small enterprises,
go to school, work as clerks, and so forth.[25] This swing to non-
manual labor, of course, was also significant in the Tumin and
Feldman study cited earlier.

Among many farm laborers, the desire for commercial products
has not overcome the aspiration to be a private operator. In the
study of Nicoya migrants, 63.2 per cent were formerly salaried employees.[26] Seventy per cent of the labor force (those working on the
plantation or for small local operators) wished to own land in the
sugar-growing Central Tacarigua. By contrast, only 32 per cent of

the factory workers and business operators in the same population had this wish.[27] Furthermore, 62 per cent of the Central Tacarigua agricultural labor had small pieces of land that they planted.[28] The people of Chinautla clearly preferred farming rented coastal lands to commuting to the city for wages, but this was, of course, a peasant population to begin with.[29] In this connection it is interesting that in the Turrialba region of Costa Rica, though farm labor was able to produce three times as much per capita as the smallholders, the latter had a higher standard of living in almost every index used.[30]

The kind of generalizations possible from these data—that aspirations change as knowledge and experience broaden, and that step-migration and step-mobility are common—are likely true, but hardly helpful. We need propositions that pinpoint the characteristics of people who will prefer landholding to urban living, or vice versa; or who prefer wage labor to private enterprise, or vice versa, etc. Henry Dobyns, for example, cites the case of the cattle-raising Indian community of Catac, Peru.[31] When enclosure forced a reduction in its livestock, the surplus population sought work in the mines. Together with other reports, this suggests that marginal livestock producers will seek wage labor as an alternative to destitution.

Another popular generalization of relatively little usefulness is that civilization follows the roads, i.e., that physical feasibility is a prerequisite to migration. But since roads usually go in two directions, we need hypotheses to help us predict which direction a migration will take. To formulate these, we must know what alternative sources of subsistence or income are really available. This problem involves the question of power domains, which will be discussed later. Of concern here are first, the division of labor, second, principal and supplementary occupations, and third, typical combinations and their explicit conditions.

Usually, the head of a household (whether male or female) is its economic mainstay, either cultivating land, selling goods, or working for wages. Where the income from this effort is not sufficient, the other family members will also work. Particularly in *colono* and sharecropping situations, the wife and children may have to supplement the family income. Among peasants, labor is sold by the individual, not the family as a whole. In Central America, for

example, wives and children earn additional money as seasonal
coffee pickers. When a peasant's land becomes insufficient to support both him and his children, generally the sons must seek an
alternative. If they do not marry into a family with land, and even
in some cases where they do, they will enter the labor force. Later,
when the parent is incapacitated or dies, one or more of the sons
may return to take up agriculture again.

Where wage labor is the principal mainstay of the family, the
roles are reversed, but the pattern remains the same; the father
stays in the labor force, and the son is forced out, either to find
a job elsewhere, or, in some instances, to undertake independent
agriculture. Such is the case of the major plantations described in
the Steward studies.[32]

The division of labor may deviate from the above pattern if the
head of the family is a woman and the family is poor. In these instances, there are a variety of economic support mechanisms, most
of them marginal. The ambiguous role of women in these circumstances drives many of them to the cities. Rural areas hold few
opportunities for families without a male breadwinner.

The Latin American rural worker is notable for the diversity of
his sources of income. Even the simple, concrete distinction between the independent operator and the wage laborer has become
meaningless.[33] An extreme case in point is the peasant. Although
this term once referred only to an independent operator, now it
is much more commonly applied to an individual who must spend
part of his time working either for his peers or for large landholders. Although peasants usually prefer to depend on produce from
their own land, inflated prices and the scarcity of land have made
it impossible for most of them to continue independently. The
peasant will usually sell his labor only if there is no possibility of
surviving on his own production. Thus, a drop in market prices, a
drought, or some other equally severe crisis must occur to force
him on the market.

The term *colono* (and a number of local and regional variations)
refers to a person who is dependent upon a large landholder for
his residence and land, in return for which he must provide certain services. The central and southern Andes probably harbor the
harshest surviving *colono* systems. Personal servitude includes the
entire family, which must work the owner's land for extended pe-

riods and pay in produce for the privilege of grazing their live-stock on the owner's land. The *colono* system is undergoing a number of significant changes. Its manifestly uneconomic returns, together with the strong movement for social justice, have led to such efforts as the Peru-Cornell project in Vicos, the provincially sponsored agrarian reform of Bolivia, the establishment of rural labor unions in Peru, Mexico, and Guatemala, and agrarian reform and the establishment of *ejidos* in Mexico.[34]

The *colono* system is a product of the cultural isolation of the *colono* on the one hand, and the political dominance of the landowner on the other. The first of these is increasingly giving way before political and social propaganda, and the second is being undermined by the gradual nationalization of the Latin American countries. The *colono* system is, however, far from dead.

The rental and sharecropping system is similar, but much more flexible. Although sharecropping is evidently disappearing from areas of subsistence crops,[35] it is still of considerable importance in the production of tobacco in Puerto Rico and Colombia, of cacao in Brazil, and of other suitable commercial crops.[36] The nature of the market accounts for the perpetuation of sharecropping. In a good market year the landowner prefers wage labor, but in a bad year he prefers sharecropping, trusting a greater part of the loss to fall on the cropper. The owner's ability to enforce his wishes in this matter reflects, of course, his local political dominance, or at least the absence of legal protection for the laborer. The rental system of Argentina has also developed to the exclusive benefit of the landowner.[37] The tenants are generally held to limited production, and uncertain, short-term tenancy. The fact that only a small percentage of the population of Argentina is rural has led to the contention that there is no agrarian problem in that country. Nothing could be further from the truth; the juridical and social status of the tenant is little better than that of the Andean *colono,* although his European background may make his way of life appear somewhat less exotic. He is as effectively blocked as the *colono* from access to land for his own use. The tenant's major advantage over the *colono* is his greater mobility; there is in fact a regular migration to major cities, particularly Buenos Aires.[38]

Steward and his students applied the term rural proletariat to confirmed wage laborers in rural areas. Padilla felt that confirmation in this status was not complete among the workers on the government-owned sugar plantation she studied, since they were still personally dependent on their supervisors and since gardening, fishing, and other alternative sources of income persisted. Data from the Venezuelan sugar farm, Central Tacarigua, indicate that laborers there also prefer a semi-peasant status. We might call these rural laborers a semi-proletariat, to distinguish them from the extreme cases such as the workers in Cañamelar,[39] who were almost completely cut off from traditional alternatives.

There is another proletarian group that has never, so far as I know, been adequately studied, probably because it is hard to follow. This is what might be called a mobile rural proletariat, a population that is probably growing in size. The efforts of large rural commercial enterprises to rid themselves of responsibility for their labor,[40] and of entrepreneurs to initiate short-term (often only one year) speculative agriculture, have produced a rural population that must drift from one agricultural venture to another.[41] Just who these people are is not known. They seem to be ready to adopt any expedient economic alternative, be it rural labor, independent farming, urban labor, or the like, without reference to political consequences.[42] Many communities in commercial agricultural areas house countless numbers of such individuals, who are generally at the bottom of the social heap.[43]

The demand for a product, and the level and kind of technology involved in its production, are central to understanding the labor market and the consequent behavior of rural laborers.

The larger the enterprise, the more catastrophic a drop in a long-term market can be for the rural laborer. The fall in the chicle market after the switch to artificial chicle is only one of many cases in point. The introduction of aniline dyes destroyed much of Guatemala's and El Salvador's external market in the last century, and coffee was force-fed into the economies of those countries to provide a national income. The Brazilian rubber boom of the nineteenth century, and the wartime boom in quinine, are other historic examples. Currently the swelling of world coffee production threatens a familiarly destructive process, and, with the growing ranks of rural labor as dependent on coffee as they are, the impending consequences are dark.

The simultaneous increase of rural labor and competitive sources of supply is guiding many a large-scale producer toward speculative agriculture and evasion of responsibility to his workers and his land.[44] Similarly, the continuation of tobacco sharecropping in Colombia and Puerto Rico is the producer's direct response to the vagaries of the market. The fact that the laborer does, one way or another, adjust to many of these changes indicates how delicately responsive to world market conditions are the peasant laborer's work patterns and opportunities.

Another market change has made cattle an increasingly valuable commodity. A widespread enclosure movement has taken place in Peru in recent years, and there has also been a sharp increase in the dispossession of Argentine tenants in favor of cattle.[45] This process usually reduces both the number of jobs for rural laborers and the land available to peasants for agriculture and grazing.

Essentially the Latin American rural laborer is a manual laborer, and it is primarily in the processing of local agrarian products that industrialization is appearing. There is some, although irregular, growth in field technology. Few countries have seriously begun to introduce the mechanization characteristic of North American agriculture. For the most part, the manual field laborer finds it possible to move between peasant agriculture, wage labor, and urban unskilled labor, because the level of knowledge required is relatively constant. For this reason, the general level of rural income remains roughly the same, although there are regional differences, and, of course, urban labor tends to receive somewhat higher wages. The peasant may have a slight standard-of-living advantage over the laborer, but the two are in the same category when compared with the rest of the population.[46]

The level of technological knowledge affects the laborer profoundly in a number of ways. First, his standard of living cannot rise appreciably until his technology is substantially bettered. Second, a sudden advance in technology can cause serious dislocation throughout a society, unless the fruits of improved technology are shared in some equitable way.

Aside from the fact that control over superior technology is usually restricted to a few, improved technology differentiates individuals according to their position in the production process. Skilled labor may develop, but unskilled rural labor continues to be a mass of interchangeable parts. The reduction of both wages and the work week following mechanization of the Nocorá sugar plantation is a telling example.[47] The threat of technological unemployment in rural Latin America is not yet widespread. There is, however, no question but that increased mechanization will cut the agricultural labor force at the very time that the population is increasing sharply.

Despite the obvious importance of these problems, there are studies of economic development that all but ignore labor in all of its aspects. The studies of the International Bank for Reconstruction and Development on Guatemala and on Mexico, for example, restrict their concern with labor to pious observations on the apparent virtues of increasing per capita production.[48]

With unemployment a major consequence of technological improvement in agriculture (as elsewhere), it is not surprising that the peasant laborer prefers a return to peasant status to conversion to urban labor. This alternative, as we noted earlier, is both physically and psychologically often closed to him. There is little land to which to return, and his adjustment to full-time labor makes it increasingly difficult to satisfy his demands with the handicraft of the peasant.

Demand and technological dislocation are two major variables that no one has found a way to control. The striving of socialist countries for equality has not altered the fact of scarcity, nor the concentration of wealth in the hands of those who control production. Whereas in the capitalist countries the largesse falls to the independent producers, in the socialist countries it falls to the government. The fact is that the solution of the basic problems of rural labor can come only with its virtual disappearance.

Power Domains

Every society operates according to systems of power distribution. We are concerned here with suprafamilial organizations, such as communities, commercial enterprises, governments at various levels, which may be termed "power domains." A power domain or, simply, domain refers to such an organization when it has (1) a distinctive resource base; (2) an authority (however it may be organized) that determines the use of the resources; and is based on (3) control of force and sanctions; and (4) a consequential set of social relations and cultural forms. Domains may have tighter or looser control of the resources; they may be dominant, subordinate, or coordinate in relation to other domains. They are intrinsically destructible and should the resource base disappear, the authority crumble, the network of relations disintegrate, the domain would no longer exist. Domains try to perpetuate themselves. When perceived by their authorities to be threatened, they become competitive for survival, and, in some instances, predatory.

Domains affect rural labor in a number of important ways. The domain in which the laborer finds himself determines the kinds of things he is forced to do, the kinds of rights and privileges he may anticipate, the relations he has with superiors and, in some instances, with peers and subordinates as well. Some of the major changes that have been reported in rural labor's behavior can be attributed to changing domains.

The crucial question that must be asked about each rural labor population is: What domain or domains does it fall within? For it will always fall within at least one, which will determine its behavior, structure, and relations. In order to best see how these behavior changes come about, I will explore factors that operate through domains to affect rural labor—the control of sanctions and force, labor relations, provision of services, and the strategic position of domain—and briefly describe the major types of domains.

The ultimate control of force, whether to enforce commands or exercise sanctions, is a principal factor in rural labor behavior, with extensive ramifications responsible for many of the changes underway.

Through the earlier republican period, and still today in some areas, the hacienda controlled the behavior of rural laborers. Control over large pieces of land carried with it the right and power to set local labor relations and determine labor's privileges. The local hacienda was stronger than the provincial government, and if left alone might become the center of revolt against the national authority. This pattern paralleled (but was not "caused" by) the older encomienda pattern and its successors, wherein distances and poor communications permitted the provincial landholders to effectively run their domains as they saw fit.

Many haciendas of the Andes and some in Meso-America still exercise the right of corporal punishment of recalcitrant laborers.

The laborers on Hacienda Capana who sought aid in forming a union were triggered by corporal punishment inflicted upon one of them.[49] It is not at all unheard-of for an owner, administrator, or renter of a hacienda to call in local troops or police to disperse discontented labor, as a number of instances in the Peruvian highlands testify.[50] Much of the civic violence in Colombia in recent years also stems from the use of force against agrarian people.[51]

Similar to the hacienda control is that exercised in some isolated areas by labor contractors and agents, notably the agents for rubber collection in the Brazilian Amazon. During the earlier period of the rubber boom, when the Brazilian government exercised no effective control in the region, agents and their parent companies were able to keep the rubber collectors in line simply by refusing them supplies should they fail to bring in the rubber. Today the situation is modified by the decreased demand for rubber, and the penetration of the interior from coastal areas is offering the collectors alternatives.[52] In the Meso-American highlands during the early part of this century, labor contracting was carried on by individuals who used the cover of the government forced-labor laws to bring Indians out of the hills to work on the developing coffee farms. The contract situation specifically had government support, and could not operate without it.

The development of an independent labor force in Latin America has caused some concern among North Americans interested in labor movements, because the rise of trade unionism has often been closely identified with, if not controlled by, the government. Unlike another observer,[53] I do not see this condition as a passing phase. Rather, the situation is one in which the government, in centralizing its control, has gradually switched from support of regional land-based entities or income-producing entities to control over the individual's productive capacity. Labor unions are fostered or discouraged, depending on whether they enhance or threaten government strength. The general rapport between political operators and union leaders reported in Cantel, Nocorá, and Mexico clearly indicates that the unions were strengthened by government support.[54]

This does not mean that there is no attempt to create independent trade unions in Latin America, or that there has been no attempt to establish company-controlled or Communist-dominated ones. At present, however, a national government's interest in trade unionism reflects the political nationalizing process. The strong encouragement of the trade unions by the Mexican government, coupled with their very strict control, is a current example. Mexico is regarded as the most rapidly developing country in the region, and its success is due in part to government control of the labor force. The degree to which unions are encouraged depends also upon the relative strength of the landholding domains. In Brazil, where landholders have exercised great power, the constitution of 1946 expressly required agricultural workers' unions to have sufficient membership to assure their success. In other words, the government could not, in itself, assure their success.

In contrast to the rural labor unions are the peasant confederations. These have generally formed somewhat independently of the government, but not necessarily in opposition to it. The Cochabamba peasant confederation in Bolivia organized independently of the revolution's political leadership, but they grew from the same seeds and joined in making the revolution.[55] It is worth noting the independent character of the confederation; it has its own arms and is superior in numbers, and probably in firepower, to the miniature Bolivian army. For this reason, it is by no means an arm of the government, but rather directs the government to act in its best interests (as it perceives them). Guatemala offers a somewhat different case. There the government established the Unión Campesina in the early 1950's in an effort to control the peasant vote. The organization was, from the peasants' and laborers' viewpoint, a device for fulfilling their own needs. The Unión failed to become a military force because the government did not arm it. Members of the Unión were held responsible for much of the sporadic burning of crops and hacienda facilities during the 1953–54 period, and their activities were regarded by many Guatemalans as a show of force that needed to be countered.

The exercise of force is not limited to governments or government-supported domains. In the smaller domains of corporate and *ejido* communities, collective control over the land may, in some circumstances, take the form of murder by witchcraft or in retaliation for witchcraft. In corporate communities members cannot easily be removed, and most corporate communities rely on informal mechanisms to handle differences. Mexican *ejido* communities differ, since they operate under the mantle of the national government and, presumably, the power of the national government may be called upon. Thus the *ejido* administration does not act as the corporate representative of the *ejido* members alone, but also as a local arm of the national government.

The interest of the state or national government in these situations is sometimes expressed through the operation of sympathetic or subservient local groups, e.g., labor unions and political parties. These seldom have power themselves, but may call in the power of the government. In Chiapas, Mexico, positions in the union are regarded as stepping-stones to political power,[56] and in many parts of Mexico the *ejido* committee is more powerful than the local town government.

Studies of two large plantations in Puerto Rico contrast the roles of unions and political parties. In Nocorá, the union is the most effective local power, and has displaced the dominant political party in local control.[57] In Cañamelar, the political party has taken the dominant position.[58] The authors of the Nocorá and Cañamelar studies concluded that Nocorá represented a transitional stage, and Cañamelar the culmination of a switch away from an older, paternalistic, localized, small-capital hacienda, to the newer, larger, highly capitalized, semi-industrialized corporate plantation. It might be more useful, however, to regard both these cases simply as effective adjustments to the growing concentration of power in the hands of the government, differentiated by the presence of private corporate management in one case.[59]

The establishment of rules, in the last analysis, resides with those who have the power to exercise sanctions. This power may reside in the population within the domain, as in corporate communities, or it may lie outside the domain but be available to it. The apparent shift from hacienda control, to transitional state, to corporate plantation, might better be described in different terms. In competing for control of the haciendas, the central government tried to devise institutions through which the laborer could appeal directly to the government for support. Two such institutions were unions and political parties.

Whether a domain—be it peasant organization, labor union, or political party—receives its support simply from the national government or from foreign domains is of crucial importance on the local scene. There is reason to believe that the developing confederations in northeastern Brazil are receiving support from Cuba, which hopes to extend its domain, just as military and economic aid provided by the United States is directed to the same (but competitive) goal. Latin American nationalists periodically insist that they wish to be under neither Cuba nor the United States, nor under Germany, Russia, or China, because their own national domain remains most closely associated with the population involved. There is little evidence that the rural laborer from northeast Brazil, the Peruvian highlands, the Puerto Rican plantations, or the Guatemalan coast really cares about the distant issues of competing, internationally predatory domains. Nonetheless, his way of life, future relations with the state, and rights and privileges as a laborer clearly are going to be determined not only by the competition of domains within Latin America, but also by the complex international struggle. Unions and political movements can draw power not only from their own governments, but from any goverment, and indeed, many other sources.

One aspect of the very difficult position of the United States today in the Alliance for Progress is that it publicly advertises that development will only be achieved if the older local domains are destroyed or weakened (e.g., if the latifundios are broken up), but the greater amount of investment must be made through government agencies that are, of course, concerned with the integrity of their own domains. And since many Latin American governments are still controlled by partisans of the older domains, it is not reasonable to anticipate official programs calling for rapid change. Cuba, in its efforts to extend a domain of international scope, overtly bypasses the domain of the national government. It does this by offering services that national governments are not providing, promising land, which is increasingly scarce, and guaranteeing the removal of the old local domains, in some instances explicitly including the governments that have controlled the status of the rural laborer for so long.

For present purposes, the rural labor situations surveyed here can be classified in terms of the rights or privileges of the employer and labor. Where labor and employer have mutual privileges with respect to each other, the relationship is "personalistic." Where the employer has rights against labor but labor has only privileges against the employer, the relationship is "paternalistic." And where labor and employer each have rights against the other, the relationship is "impersonal."[60] It is noteworthy that the impersonal relationship exists by virtue of lying within a larger domain. Each party has rights because each can refer to a stronger power. The principal kinds of domains of concern to us here are haciendas, communities, unions, political parties, and governments.

Within peasant communities work relations are almost always of a personalistic nature. An illustrative form of this (but by no means the most common) is exchange labor, wherein a specific amount of work, usually in terms of so many work days, is exchanged for the same amount on another occasion.[61] Although labor exchange is being replaced in most peasant communities by wage labor, the nature of the exchange tends to remain essentially the same. The employer has no special rights over the laborer, nor does the laborer have any over the employer. So it is that in Tobati, Paraguay, the wage laborer believes he is doing the employer a favor.[62] As soon as he has earned the money he needs, the laborer stops; as a result, raising wages merely serves to increase labor turnover. Similarly, but to an even more extreme degree, the laborer in the Colombian town of "Aritama" maintains he is doing the employer a favor and publicly rejects the notion that he needs the work.[63] He does everything he can to demonstrate his superiority to the employer, and, since labor is hard to come by, the employer must watch his own behavior carefully. This kind of relationship is altered when national labor legislation becomes effective, and both labor and employer regard themselves as having legal rights. For the most part, rural communities have ignored any such legislation to date, and nations have not had the power to enforce sanctions in such relationships.

Perhaps the most publicized kind of labor relationship in Latin America today is paternalism. This category, in which the employer has rights and the laborer only privileges, occurs most frequently on the haciendas in the Andean highlands of Peru, Ecuador, Colombia, and Brazil, the *estancias* of Argentina, the *fundos* of Chile, and the *fincas* of Guatemala and Chiapas, Mexico. The *colono* pattern dominates here. Laborers are required to provide a wide variety of services, including domestic and personal service in extreme Andean cases, and in return they are permitted to use a piece of land for crops, and, with restrictions, to pasture a limited number of animals. However, labor's privileges vary widely; it is apparent that "services" are provided by the *patrón* only at his discretion. The elimination of paternalistic relations is thought by some to be desirable.[64] However, where the change means merely a loss of privileges by labor, with no concomitant gain in rights, the problem is obviously more complicated. This is the case in many speculative agricultural situations; something of the kind, for example, is in the balance in Tabara, Puerto Rico.[65]

The owners of latifundios began to see the handwriting on the wall at the time of the Mexican Revolution. The Catholic Church in Peru seriously tried to rid itself of uneconomic holdings before World War II,[66] and landowners in various areas have indicated willingness to convert their land to cash. However, a number of conditions make this difficult. Buyers in these areas are few. Indeed in many, like Vicos, Peru, lands were held for rental and exploited in a manner essentially similar to the speculative agriculture of Guatemala in recent years.[67] The difference between the two is important, however: in the Peruvian case the land carried with it the rights to the services of the resident *colonos,* whereas in Guatemala speculative agriculture developed so as to rid the employer of responsibility for labor.

A reversal has occurred where labor legislation, aimed at establishing rights for labor, has so fixed responsibilities that the employers cannot now rid themselves of resident labor. This turns the tables so that, in practice, the farm owners are unable to exercise their rights. Although this type of situation needs much more analysis, it is clear that despite the "socialist" label often applied to it, the allocation of rights to labor is resolving many problems, even though new ones are created in the process.

The exercise of rights by labor to counterbalance employers' rights has been seen by many as the end of personalism and paternalism. While this is clearly the case, the new relationships sometimes retain paternalistic or personalistic qualities in new forms. Padilla holds that the paternalism and dependency formerly characteristic of the hacienda situation is still to be found in Nocorá, but that it has been displaced to the agents of the political party. She sees this as an incomplete transition to the full-blown rural proletariat of Cañamelar.[68] As noted earlier, however, Nocorá belongs to the government, and, while a labor union actually runs the plantation, the workers' needs above the subsistence level and special favors are referred to a political party. Cañamelar, by contrast, is privately owned, and it is the labor union that dominates the laborers' organization and provides them with the strength to fight for better conditions. The labor union in Nocorá cannot effectively combat the government, because the major power it exercises is derived from the government. Thus, the Nocorá worker still essentially has no rights against the employer (the government), whereas the Cañamelar worker can turn to the government to support his rights against the plantation corporation. Paternalism continues at Nocorá because the relative allocation of rights and privileges is essentially unchanged.

There are other situations that can be similarly analyzed. The medium landholder of Tabara still has labor in a semi-paternalistic situation, though the clear-cut hacienda situation is no longer operative. Essentially, however, the landholders have not given up their rights; they have simply switched to a system where they determine whether they will let their land out for sharecropping or for rent, whichever promises the greatest profits. The only right a worker has in this situation is to refuse both alternatives; he has no right to select the one advantageous to him. Restricted though they may be, labor's rights are beginning to be exercised, and Robert Manners noted that the younger men tended to assert their rights more than their elders.[69]

In Guatemala under the Arbenz "law of forced rentals," a man who had more land than he used but less than the amount affected by the agrarian reform could be forced to rent it for 5 per cent of the produce of the land. This essentially reduced the sharecropping system to the point where it became economically advantageous to the sharecropper rather than the landowner. It can well be imagined how long paternalism persisted under these circumstances.

The centralization of power by the national government has been responsible for bringing about changes not only in certain areas of labor relations, but also in the immediate conditions that have made those changes feasible. But meanwhile, national income ordinarily has been insufficient for the state to underwrite either the protection guaranteed by labor codes or the benefits promised by welfare legislation. The resulting plight of the workers is further aggravated by the hacienda and plantation owners, who continue to use all the resources at their command to retain their traditional autonomy.

Furthermore, since many governments are not able to act consistently on behalf of labor, effective rural labor unions are rare, and many political parties that appeal to rural workers are transitory. As a solution to the pressure of growing population on restricted resources, peasant and labor confederations are beginning to appear on a regional basis, as in Bolivia and northeastern Brazil. Rural Colombians have formed numerous smaller bands that have had marked political and agrarian effect. A less flamboyant measure has been squatting on private latifundios. This has been observed on an increasing scale in many areas, and efforts to resist the movement have turned out to be both explosive and only temporarily effective.

Government's increasing power has not yet been sufficient to displace completely the competitive haciendas and to provide labor with alternative sources of income. The question of the development of labor leadership has, therefore, become crucial. Where local labor unions have developed, an organizational agent is usually responsible. In Guatemala under the Arévalo-Arbenz regime, the Indian farm laborer showed no interest in union activity.[70] Yet by 1954, many Guatemalan farms were unionized, and the United Fruit Company hosted the best-organized rural unions in the country. The role of labor leadership elsewhere has fallen variously to unions, political parties, political movements, peasant movements, and, as often as not, no one at all. But a large population under land pressure will turn to those who promise help. Such leadership is appearing, and usually educated. A study of members of rural labor organizations in Guatemala immediately after the 1954 revolution found that of the people who had held office in the labor unions, peasant confederation, political parties, or agrarian committees, 70 per cent were literate, as opposed to approximately 28 per cent in the population as a whole. The officeholders also, as might have been expected, showed a significantly heightened degree of political articulateness.[71]

North Americans tend to both overestimate and oversimplify the role of personality and ideology in rural Latin American leadership. The successful leaders are those who have provided for the ever-increasing wants, and, indeed, desperate needs, of the growing rural population. It is not easy to sell a peasant a nonexistent product.

Social Structure and Attitudes

A study of this scope cannot undertake an analysis of the internal structure of rural labor societies. The interested reader might well refer to the few original sources.[72] Two questions, however, can be dealt with here: the essential flexibility of Latin American laborers and their attitudes toward themselves and their work.

The previous section emphasized the restrictions and obligations that power domains impose on rural laborers. Of equal importance are the ability of rural laborers to adjust to a variety of conditions in the world about them, and their success in surviving despite their growth in numbers. Rural labor, like most of Latin American society, is generalized in its adaptation. Only in extreme situations, as Wolf points out about Cañamelar, has the society become highly specialized in a limited niche.[73] The typical peasant laborer is capable of working his fields, renting land, sharecropping, working as a day laborer and as a seasonal laborer, or converting to permanent wage labor. Furthermore, he may migrate either to frontier areas or to the urban centers without too much concern for carrying many worldly goods with him. He is able to adapt to the unskilled labor force of the city with almost equal alacrity. While any specific laborer will face many restrictions, there are multiple niches that a peasant may occupy without a great deal of learning. Of course, few areas provide all the alternatives cited above. The change from primary dependence upon natural or cultivated resources to dependence upon more indirect channels of income requires increasing specialization, especially as one moves up the economic hierarchy. Similarly, the simultaneous presence of both personalistic and paternalistic relations provides comparable socio-economic flexibility. When the laborer achieves a fully impersonal relationship vis-à-vis his employer, such flexibility is considerably reduced. Loss of flexibility is the price paid for development and a rising standard of living. Higher levels of per capita production and consumption can only be achieved by increasing specialization in all phases of economic activity.

Another aspect of the adaptability of the peasant and rural laborer is revealed in his lateral relations. In great part these operate through a kinship system, and, as in other expanding societies such as Japan, fictive kin ties and unusual kin extensions have grown in importance. The principle of reciprocity, central to the labor relations within the domain of a community, extends to many relationships and serves in many capacities. The extensive system of *concuñados* and *parientes* provides the laborer of the Argentine pampas with an almost infinite set of relations through which he can seek aid in time of need.[74] Strong reciprocal bonds provide for exchange labor, gift giving (especially gifts of food), and hospitality, and generally guarantee a wide range of friends one can depend upon.[75] Reports from Puerto Rico and Argentina suggest that these relations may not generally extend across generations. It is assumed that sons will take care of themselves, and that such ties must be renewed every generation. Children of a migrant to the city "tend to be sloughed off the countryman's list of relatives," even though the parent retains his own lateral relations. Among Guatemalan ladinos a strong *compadre* system appeared in situations that regular kinship ties were unable to cope with.[76]

The important feature to note here is not the specific role of kinship, but rather the factors at work that confirm old lateral ties or create new ones, which may be based on kinship, *compadrazgo*, friendship, neighborliness, or economic advantage.[77] That this is by no means restricted to rural laborers, but also includes migrants to the city, was first made explicit by Oscar Lewis, and has since been reaffirmed by various other investigators.[78] The adaptive advantage of this kind of lateral system of relations is great, for when a rural worker's immediate source of income fails, he must either find an alternative resource in his immediate environment or migrate. A worker involved in personalistic, rather than paternalistic, relations must seek help within this framework. It is therefore crucial for the migrant to move where he may expect initial aid in finding his bearings, obtaining employment, and so on. Different generations have dissimilar relations in part because there is nothing—neither goods nor status—to inherit in these societies. Essentially, each generation must supply its own needs. Another aspect of this lateral emphasis is that the creation of new occupations in the urban areas is not necessarily producing new kinds of mobility; rather, the tendency is toward diversification within the present hierarchical structure.[79]

The last observation throws light on the nature of the developing class system in rural Latin America as well. Though to a lesser extent than urban industry, the mechanization of agriculture is calling forth new skills. The new occupational statuses of tractor driver, truck driver, mechanic, and the like are allocated to what had previously been a very small class of farm supervisors who, socially, fell between the laborer on the bottom and the owners or administrators on the top. Thus, in Aquiares, Costa Rica, the four daughters of the coffee-mill foreman married, respectively, an overseer's brother, a fireman in the capital city, the son of a shop foreman, and a chauffeur; the two sons married the daughters of a shop foreman and an overseer. Other cases duplicate this pattern.[80] There is no profound alteration in the class structure, no evidence of great mobility, but rather an expansion of the kinds of categories occurring within a specific social range.

Aside from Mintz's biography of a Puerto Rican cane laborer, there are few detailed data on how the rural laborer in Latin America sees himself and his opportunities. Peasants and rural laborers, irrespective of their particular social relations, regard themselves as a part of "the poor." This is particularly true in the pure wage-labor situation, but also is found in communities and in *colono* situations. From place to place, however, there are differences in how laborers occupying different niches see each other. The wage laborers of the sugar plantations of Nocorá and Cañamelar look down on the laborers and peasants of the hills. But the peasants of Chinautla regard their independent status as vastly superior to that of a wage laborer. The Costa Rican study of immigration to Nicoya showed, it will be remembered, that most of the migrants had formerly been wage laborers, but moved to get land for themselves. A generalized hierarchy, which reflects the attitudes of the people involved and is applicable to all the situations reviewed in this essay, would look something like this:

(1) Wage laborers in an impersonal relationship with their employers and independent peasant producers who need not resort

to wage labor to supplement their own production tend to stand on a par. One or the other may be considered superior in a particular place, in reflection of special factors.

(2) Both the above consider themselves better off than peasants who must supplement their independent production with seasonal and periodic wage labor (a judgment these peasants concur in).

(3) Wage laborers in a paternalistic relationship with their employers, including those who use land provided by their employers when the use of this land is a privilege, not a right, consider themselves and are considered inferior to the two above categories.

(4) Among wage laborers with no rights, those with a permanent privileged position on a hacienda are considered better off than those without such a position.

There is no evidence for such a systematic ordering of the more standard categories of wage labor, such as "sharecroppers," "renters," "tenants," and "*colonos.*" Within any given locale, where people in one of these categories share essentially the same rights and privileges and are distinct from other groups in this respect, they can be classified accordingly. But in another locale the same rights and privileges may not coincide with the same categories. Also, within any given locale when the rights change, views of relative status will change, too. So it was when the "law of forced rentals" was established in Guatemala; previously "inferior" renters rapidly came to regard themselves as superior to the landowners from whom they were able to force the rental of lands.

Ethnic differences—e.g., descent or color—sometimes superficially confuse the picture. It is generally accepted that the mestizo in Meso-America and the Andes looks down upon the Indian. However, this does not seem to change attitudes about labor status, which form the structure of rights and privileges. Thus in Guatemala, a dispossessed ladino without steady employment can disparage, and at the same time envy, the Indian who is a fully independent producer.

The rural laborer's attitude toward work as such is a frequently raised issue. We often hear that Latin Americans lack the "proper work attitudes," the "necessary motivation," etc. Indeed, there is little evidence that the rural worker (either independent or wage-earning) is singly devoted to work. In studies of Puerto Rico, Mexico, Colombia, Peru, Paraguay, and Brazil, the story is the same,

differing only in emphasis.[81] The most positive attitude reported
is that of the Cañamelar worker: "He will be . . . hardworking,
but not to the extent that it interferes with his social obligations."
The most exaggerated attitude is that reported from the Colombian town of Aritama, where, as noted above, work is openly despised and even the implication that one is engaging in it is regarded as an insult. Instead, leisure is the goal. As Wolf points out,
leisure is not equated with idleness, which is roundly condemned;
leisure is something to be savored and appreciated. Incidentally,
this attitude toward work is closely coupled with distrust and envy
of anyone who is economically aggressive. Various devices are used
to discourage the individual from showing too much success.[82]
This negative attitude toward work is not universal in rural Latin
America; in rather integrated communities in the Peruvian highlands and in Guatemalan Indian communities, at least, a strikingly
different one prevails. Muquiyauyo and Huaylas in Peru are both
communities in which the Indians and the mestizos tackle common problems together.[83] In both places work is greeted with considerable enthusiasm, and in both instances this is attributable, at
least in part, to an identification of common purpose that occurred
at least as far back as the nineteenth century. The degree to which
this attitude extends to wage labor is not certain.

An extremely positive attitude toward work is found in many
Guatemalan Indian communities. Nash reports that "hard work,
sweat on the brow, and calluses on the hands are valued in Cantel
culture, and a man grows up expecting to work hard. . . . It is
wicked to be idle."[84] In the community of Magdalena, the good
man was the one who was good with the hoe; the reader of newspapers, the discusser of current events, would be roundly scolded
by his wife. The contrast here may be, of course, between two quite
distinctive cultures, between the Guatemalan Indians and the
other Latin Americans. The question therefore remains: do Latin
American rural laborers generally manifest a distaste for work?

There is, at present, no satisfactory answer to this. It is likely,
however, that attitudes toward work reflect the conditions of survival in a given society. An attitude that discourages the worker
from exerting himself excessively may be disturbing to anyone interested in entrepreneurship or economic development, but it is
not necessarily inimical to survival. To survive one requires a wide

variety of alternatives, and this the rural Latin American laborer seems to have. On the other hand, the almost compulsive efforts at hard work characteristic of many Guatemalan Indians have not brought them superior adaptability. If a guess were to be made, it would be that merely to survive, the Indian has had to develop a much higher evaluation of labor, at least for himself, than the mestizo. Both colonial and republican society have forbidden the Indian access to certain alternatives open to mestizos, unless he gives up his Indian way of life, and in fact becomes mestizo. Indian survival has, therefore, generally required careful managing of natural and cultivated resources; a switch to the extended lateral relations of the mestizo and the related access to wider socio-economic resources may have implicit in it the devaluation of hard work.

This brief excursion into attitudes is stimulated by a tendency of North American social scientists and politicians to place inordinate faith in analyses of group attitudes. The obviously limited and defective material from Latin America suggests that attitudes may be descriptively useful, but must be seen in relation to social structure and, more important, in relation to the conditions that help account for them. For, whether we like it or not, children of Guatemalan Indians devoted to work often become Latin Americans devoted to leisure.

3. The Writer

Fred P. Ellison

The writers of Latin America are, like their counterparts everywhere, intellectuals, who, in Edward A. Shils' definition, are particularly "enquiring, and desirous of being in frequent communion with symbols which are more general than the immediate concrete situations of everyday life, and remote in their reference in both time and place."[1] Such men have social influence out of proportion to their relatively small number. They may be members of the liberal professions, educators, priests, administrators, lawmakers, historians, writers, artists, or musicians. Here, attention will be directed to the writer as creator of *belles lettres,* be he poet, novelist, dramatist, or essayist.

The last category may include philosophers, educators, historians, political writers, journalists, and others not ordinarily associated with *belles lettres,* provided they have literary style—that is, a way of writing that pretends to beauty. Stylistic distinction is highly valued in Latin America.[2] The pervasive influence of literature and related stylistic preoccupations on Brazilian education has been noted by the sociologist Fernando de Azevedo: "Literature is but one of the elements of general culture; but, because of the specific conditions of our formation, which was almost exclusively literary, it was the first, the strongest, the most persistent, the most expressive element of our culture."[3] K. H. Silvert has emphasized style in speaking of the entire Latin American intellectual community: "To be counted in this prestigious company the individual must manipulate ideas of a philosophical nature and communicate them in an artistic fashion."[4]

Here, however, the emphasis will be not on evaluation of individual works or the creative process, but on the sociology of the writers: their social provenance, their economic situation, and their status and role in society, particularly in politics. Literature, after all, is a social institution, and its creators are members of society. Admittedly there are inherent limitations in such a generalized approach, especially in a field so vast and relatively unexplored.

Group Consciousness

The existence of a national group consciousness among writers is attested not only by the statements of literary historians and sociologists, but also by the existence of numerous nationwide professional organizations, such as the Sociedad Argentina de Escritores, the Asociación Venezolana de Escritores, and the União Brasileira de Escritores. It is not uncommon for the writers to compare their own national standing with that of their opposite numbers in the United States. From such comparisons emerges a generic profile: the Latin American man of letters has high social prestige as an artist, but is ill rewarded for his creativity; he may, as a writer, hold the highest positions of public trust, usually as a result of a well-developed political aptitude, but in most cases does not enjoy independent professional status as a writer; he is frequently entrusted with the loftiest educational, political, and cultural responsibilities, and even more frequently must live in exile, see his books burned, or face arrest or economic reprisals for his views.

Continental group consciousness is more tenuous. Latin American writers know each other's work less well than one might think, and there is truth in the quip that the concept of Latin America exists only in the United States, where "Latin American studies" are pursued. The Argentine novelist Jorge Luis Borges offers this explanation: "We feel that we are very much alike in the various regions of Latin America, and for that reason, the work of a writer from a given region does not arouse much curiosity among the writers of another region. . . . On the other hand, if we read European writers we think we're going to find something different."[5]

Improved transportation and communication are changing the situation, but even now it is possible to speak of a continental spirit, to refer, as Alberto Zum Felde has done, to the "continental literary unity upon which Spanish American criticism is based."

He sees this as a consequence of the countries' common language, common cultural and historical origins, and common concern with what he calls "telluric" problems.[6] The Mexican critic José Luis Martínez has justly observed that "the poetry, drama, and novel of the countries of America have crossed their own borders to make us conscious of the peculiar meaning of their ways of life, their ideas, and even their dark infamies; and because of these worthy efforts at friendly interchange, it may be possible to speak of the existence of an American consciousness."[7] Literary historians have begun to include Brazilian literature in their panoramas, and since the last presidential term of Getulio Vargas, Spanish American writers are being studied in Brazilian universities.

The radical left, especially the Communists, seek to encourage this latent continental consciousness among the writers of Latin America through writers' congresses, publications, and so forth. A significant gathering of Cuban and Latin American writers was the First Congress of Cuban Writers and Artists, held in Havana on August 17–22, 1961. On its agenda were: "The creative responsibility of the writers and artists vis-à-vis the Revolution and the Cuban people"; "Exchanges, contacts, and cooperation of Cuban artists and intellectuals with those of Latin America and all other countries, in defense of the people's culture, national sovereignty, and universal peace"; and "Organization problems of Cuban writers and artists."[8] Among the principal speakers were the poet Nicolás Guillén, the novelist Alejo Carpentier, and the critics José A. Portuondo and Roberto Fernández Retamar. In his speech, Carpentier commented on the sense of community that existed among many of the Latin American writer-politicians in the nineteenth century, their intercommunication and shared values, especially their hatred for Spain. He chided present-day writers for their failure to take political action in concert. "We Cubans are more like the nineteenth-century intellectuals," he said, proclaiming a national and hemispheric group spirit he hopes to see increase throughout Latin America.[9]

Education and Social Class

Changes in educational practice inevitably have been reflected in literature. Certain literary concerns identifiable with nationalism in nineteenth-century Brazil can be attributed directly to the growing prestige of Brazilian educational institutions. Because of its Jesuit heritage the Brazilian educational system long maintained an aura of humanism and aristocratic values, which was reflected in Brazilian literature until quite recently. Since the 1920's and early 1930's intellectual activity has taken on a distinctly anti-traditional and anti-academic tone, in response to major social and economic changes. Speaking of Brazil, Fernando de Azevedo said that new social forces "contribute to breaking the hold of the traditional school, inaugurating . . . an era of restlessness, and the tapping of sources of the most modern and singularly fecund inspiration to the literary milieu. Now, it is not through its direct influence, but outside the school, and in opposition to it, that criticism, fiction, poetry, and the theater revive and develop."[10] And elsewhere in Latin America, as a consequence of the University Reform movement, members of the working classes and lower-middle sectors receive higher education and join the literary force.

Speaking at the Congress of Cuban Writers and Artists, Nicolás Guillén berated the colonial system of education in Cuba for what he called its stifling effects on literature and general culture and its alienation of the writers.[11] He promised that the new Marxist-Leninist system would be "of positive value for the intellectual worker. Ahead of him looms a reality different from the one in which he lived until now—a reality not only different, but superior, because his work will stop being profitable principally for the capitalist, who under other regimes, in diverse and subtle ways, lives off the intellectual production of others."[12]

In his speech Guillén reflected the Marxist thesis that intellectuals cannot be identified with a single social class. Similarly, the sociologist Karl Mannheim holds that intellectual activity is now the domain of "a social stratum which is to a large degree unattached to any social class, and which is recruited from an increasingly inclusive area of social life." While this may be true in Europe, Silvert has accurately observed that, socially, the Latin American intellectuals "are invariably rooted in middle or upper classes."[13] In literature, the distinction between middle and upper classes was not important, for many aristocrats of Spanish America who made important contributions to letters in the nineteenth century defended the liberalism of the middle groups.

During the nineteenth and early twentieth centuries in Brazil, literature was primarily the province of the aristocracy; but especially during the reign of Dom Pedro II, himself an amateur writer and generous patron, writers from the middle sectors profited from literature's great prestige. Until the end of World War I, the rising group of writers from the middle sectors tended to emulate the literary values of the elite that were perpetuated by the Brazilian Academy of Letters. Many Brazilian writers still represent traditional ruling families who, if no longer affluent, own distinguished names. The situation in Chile, however, is more typical of Latin America; there "literature is no longer the province of the ruling class; . . . it no longer has anything to do with military and political power; and . . . there is now a lively sensitivity, an alert literary consciousness that contemplates its own universe, whether to express disapproval or delight."[14] Though literature itself may have little direct connection with political power, literary men may have a great deal, as will be shown later. Suffice it to say here that we can expect fresh and often strong points of view from the writers of the lower-middle strata.

The Trend Toward Professionalism

The current trend toward professionalism among writers reflects new economic circumstances. Literary men in the nineteenth century undoubtedly had little professional status *qua* writers; literary activity was a sideline of politicians, journalists, members of the liberal professions, and so forth. There was prestige, glory, and power to be had through writing, but little pecuniary reward and hence no professional status. Men of letters belonged to the aristocracy and upper middle classes, which monopolized positions of affluence. Many writers treated creative writing as an incidental activity to be pursued until they became established as lawyers, politicians, or bureaucrats. In the view of Brazilian critic Nelson Werneck Sodré, only with the rise of the middle class in Brazil at the close of the nineteenth century did it become "possible to distinguish literary activity from some of its earlier nonspecific manifestations, in which it appeared as an ornamental or auxiliary element. Among the lists of authors, it is possible henceforward to separate those who utilized the spoken or written word merely as a vehicle, within specialized and even professional activities, from those who used it for artistic creation."[15] There were similar developments in the Spanish-speaking nations, led by the Nicaraguan poet Rubén Darío. Literature now ranked with diplomacy and politics as a career, though there were still few literary men who could support themselves by their writing.

This remains true even today, despite the demand of a wider literate public and technological advances. Contemporary writers are perhaps more sensitive to their economic plight than ever, since a good many come from the lower classes and lack the support available to their more well-to-do predecessors. The following is typical of complaints heard throughout Latin America:

Writing is not remunerative work. It becomes impossible for intellectuals to concentrate the best of their energies on such work, since they must cling to bureaucratic and other jobs for the sake of their own livelihood. As a rule Brazilian writers are dilettantes—that is, they compose their novels and poems in moments stolen from their normal rest, often by dint of anti-sleep stimulants and gallons of bitter black coffee.[16]

The high illiteracy rate, prohibitive costs of paper and equipment, ineffective distribution of books (especially to the interior), the low purchasing power of the populace, and inflation all contribute to the financial insecurity of the writer. Recent studies of the book trade in Argentina, Chile, Peru, Colombia, and Brazil confirm the jeopardy of writing as a career.[17] And fragmentary research on the reading public in Rio de Janeiro, where the rate of illiteracy is less than 10 per cent, established that books are "strange and unknown objects to the vast majority of *cariocas* [residents of Rio]."[18]

Propaganda of the extreme left has been aimed at the writers' dissatisfaction with their economic situation, and it has stressed defense of professional requirements. The Communists have been alert in subsidizing writers whose works have propaganda value, with translation royalties and expense-paid trips to Russia, China, and other Iron Curtain countries. The United States, too, would like to play host to Latin American writers, but, to our embarrassment, immigration regulations have barred many highly respected writers suspected of Communist sympathies. The exclusion of novelist José Lins do Rego, who wanted to visit his daughter in Washington, D.C., caused a furore in Brazil, where critics have always considered him politically moderate.[19]

As one might expect, there are signs of an eventual improvement in the writers' financial situation—expanding mass media, government subsidies, and professional movements in Brazil, Argentina, Venezuela, and Cuba. The União Brasileira de Escritores, for example, is working toward the adoption by the publishing industry of advanced methods of marketing and distribution, and toward legislation protecting writers' contract and copyright interests. The federal government supports the writers' organization and a similar association of Brazilian playwrights.

The French tradition of state patronage has undoubtedly served as a model in many Latin American countries. The governments of Venezuela, Colombia, Ecuador, Mexico, and Brazil have sponsored publications, the building and maintenance of theaters, libraries, archives, and academies, as well as cultural campaigns designed to enhance the professional status of the writer.[20] But most intellectuals find the government's support insufficient, particularly those who favor state intervention in many areas of national life. The writers' economic well-being has not been substantially improved by these state-supported measures, though their indirect influence on culture should not be underestimated.

Considerable expansion in education and mass communications characterizes almost all Latin America.[21] One might expect the writers to have benefited from the expansion of the reading public and from the financial rewards of radio, television, and mass-circulation newspapers and magazines. This is not necessarily the case, however, to judge from the apprehension of, and outright hostility to, the newer media on the part of many noted writers. Despite the possibilities of increased earnings, such writing lacks the value and prestige associated with more traditional forms.[22]

Journalism deserves special mention, for now, as in the past, it is closely tied to literature. The distinguished critic Baldomero Sanín Cano proudly called himself a "journalist." Rubén Darío and many of his followers, though poets of the most refined taste, were also newspaper correspondents, columnists, and editorial writers. This is partly because, as one critic notes, "The newspaper continues to be the ordinary citizen's library as well as news headquarters. Almost invariably literary works have appeared in newspapers long before their advent in book form."[23] Brazilian critics have debated the question and are apparently agreed that journalism is in many respects a literary activity.

In Brazil, beyond a doubt, those who have created the most legitimate and authentic literature were, are, and will always be journalists. In a land without cultural periodicals, the literary supplements of the great

Rio newspapers are true literary journals. They have, for example, an extraordinary importance and usefulness, and, with contributors of the highest category, are truly precise and faithful mirrors of Brazil's cultural panorama.[24]

While writers have yet to make a satisfactory adjustment to their changing social and economic circumstances, they continue in their traditional role as the creative and critical conscience of society. Success in serving the nation as intellectuals and artists compensates for shabby treatment in the market place. John Gillin observes that it is their quest for ultimate values and ideals "that in large measure makes life worth living for many Latin Americans of middle status."[25] The *pensadores* carry on the tradition of nineteenth-century political theorists and social philosophers (Simón Bolívar, José Bonifácio, Esteban Echeverría, Domingo Faustino Sarmiento, Joaquín Montalvo, José Martí) in their concern for national and continental problems. The Mexican government has recently summoned the philosopher and writer Leopoldo Zea to formulate the goals of the Partido Revolucionario Institucional,[26] and the poet (and industrialist) Augusto Frederico Schmidt received a similar commission from President Juscelino Kubitschek. In government positions of great responsibility and trust, one finds distinguished poets, novelists, and essayists. As Gillin notes, "They receive such posts not only because of their prestige, but also because of a genuine belief that their success in aesthetic pursuits fits them for posts of national responsibility and leadership."[27]

Writers have served not only democratically constituted governments, but also totalitarian ones. As Zum Felde pointed out, "The difference between the 'enlightened' dictatorships and the simply 'barbarous' ones is defined by the attitude of the intellectual minorities with respect to them."[28] In these terms, Porfirio Díaz and Guzmán Blanco would qualify as enlightened and Anastacio Somoza and Rafael Trujillo as barbarous. Clearly, the majority of intellectuals have stood against the most benighted dictatorships. They may have relaxed their usual scruples in the case of Getulio Vargas, himself a literary man of sorts. In his dictatorial phase, Vargas and his infamous DIP (Departamento de Imprensa e Propaganda) burned books and jailed writers of the extreme left; but at the same time he did much to support the writing profession, founding, for example, the Instituto Nacional do Livro (National

Book Institute).[29] The dictator Juan Perón "felt the immediate necessity of having his own ideology, with a respectable philosophical basis, and he surrounded himself with a team of university men under the leadership of Father Benítez in order to create a new political doctrine, which they called *justicialismo,* derived from 'social justice.' "[30]

But most dictators, including Perón, have regarded writers as enemies, and have sought to destroy or restrict their time-honored role as social critics with a heightened sense of responsibility. Censorship, the closing of universities, book burning, arrest, imprisonment, and exile are familiar hazards in mid-twentieth-century Latin America. For Arturo Torres-Rioseco, "the greatest obstacle to the development of art and literature in Spanish America is the lack of freedom."[31] As long as they are not denied freedom of expression, the writers of Latin America may be expected to contribute to national development in its broadest sense.

Naturally, writers have been active agents of intellectual progress, and have shown a remarkable spirit of innovation. The Spanish critic Ricardo Gullón has related Hispanic letters (we can include Portuguese) to the whole complex of new forms and attitudes in western art that arose between 1890 and the begining of World War II, to which he applies the term *modernismo,* giving it broader significance (somewhat like Renaissance or Enlighten-ment) than it had in the earlier—and still current—notion limiting it to the Parnassian-symbolist school. *Modernismo* reflects a widespread quickening of creative vitality, and of receptivity to cultural currents flowing between Europe and America. This concept embraces many disparate and often conflicting artistic movements that have arisen in the last half century, and reconciles such disparate works as the subjective symbolist novel and the naturalist novel of social protest, the escapist poems of a Leopoldo Lugones and the social poetry of a Drummond de Andrade. The fundamental attitudes in modernist literature derive from the unstable, revolutionary ferment of romanticism, and the humanitarian and more tolerant reformist ideals of liberalism. These ideals are expressed in the modernists' "opposition to all forms of exploitation of man by man, and to all political repression"—opposition exemplified by Martí, Unamuno, Díaz Mirón, Valle Inclán, and Antonio Machado.[32]

Because of the preciosity and taste for the ornate of some early modernists, literary historians and critics (as well as many "vanguardist" writers of the 1920's) overlooked their relation to more conventional revolutionary currents. Exoticism and *indigenismo* are, as Gullón observes, forms of escapism that reveal deep dissatisfaction with the late-nineteenth-century world. These escapist tendencies, like the anti-bourgeois sentiments that accompanied them, were assimilated by avant-garde movements in Europe and America during and immediately following the First World War.[33] In the present context, the writers wish to transform society and popularize the best new cultural forms among their compatriots through the education art provides.

Leadership and Prestige

The writers' leadership and prestige stem from their traditional role as men of uncommon vision placed at the service of important national and hemispheric causes. Their special status is due to the rich cultural life of the middle sectors, which, as Gillin notes, "has an aesthetic tone which middle-class North Americans of today do not often permit themselves."[34] Outstanding characteristics of Latin American culture are the persistent esteem for humanistic education, the high regard for poetry and poets, and the comparatively widespread interest in reading literary criticism in newspapers. The public deference shown writers is well illustrated by the success of two Bahian writers, Jorge Amado and Luis Viana Filho, in having writers exempted from the income tax on royalties.[35] In short, as Frank Tannenbaum puts it, the writer in Latin America has "a basis for leadership in the nation which is both admirable and unique. It is admirable because he is independent, and unique because he cannot be deprived of the following that he has, or lose it except by ceasing to write and publish."[36]

This sort of leadership has been exercised by a few Latin American writers who, according to Tannenbaum, "are almost household words among the literate people in the entire area, particularly in the eighteen Spanish-speaking countries." His list comprises names from both the humanities and social sciences: Alfonso Reyes, Germán Arciniegas, Mariano Picón Salas, Rómulo Gallegos, Luis Alberto Sánchez, Gilberto Freyre, José Luis Romero, and Fernando Ortiz.[37] To these should be added the late Nobel Prize win-ner Gabriela Mistral, Jorge Luis Borges, Pablo Neruda, and Jorge Amado. With few exceptions, all these writers have achieved both artistic excellence and consequent European recognition.

This high estimate of the writer's social prestige is not quite unanimous. The most vigorous dissenter is Francisco Ayala, a Spanish writer who has lived in many Latin American countries and in the United States. He laments the disappearance of a "qualified" elite of intellectuals and authors, which in the nineteenth century helped shape the values of the ruling classes, and blames "mass society" for the absence of any group that exercises authority by virtue of its particular qualifications. He concludes that "the proportions and relations within the social framework have been altered to such an extent that [the writer's] figure, once obvious in the foreground, has become insignificant and marginal."[38] Latin America is not the only place, of course, where writers, as bearers of a humanistic tradition, find themselves opposed to many values of mass society and are afraid of losing identity, prestige, and influence.[39]

Political Power and Influence

Writers continue to wield actual political power through public office and party activity, and exert considerable political pressure through their writings. The majority of literary men in Brazil now belong to left-of-center parties. The same is true of most other Latin American countries. However, since there are writers of almost every political persuasion, and precise information is wanting, generalizations on this subject are necessarily impressionistic and tentative.

In nineteenth-century Latin America, writers by and large supported progressive constitutional regimes, opposed the usurpation of power by force, and advocated the extension of social and political liberties. A few rightists—Andrés Bello, Gabriel Moreno, Rafael Núñez, and Carlos Reyes—justified conservative or authoritarian governments. The political role of writers was a great one. In the apt words of Peruvian Luis Benjamín Cisneros, "In Spanish America, where the republican form of government gives each individual a direct role in political life, where truly imperishable literature is still in the process of gestation and therefore subject to the most heightened passions, names abound to confirm this

observation. In the entire chain of republics that extend along the
Pacific, there is hardly a literary name that is not at the same time
a political name."[40] Throughout Latin America there were writer-
politicians or politician-writers in positions of power and leadership. The literary historian Pedro Henríquez Ureña gives an incomplete list of some thirty writers who were presidents of their
respective countries in the nineteenth and early twentieth centuries.[41]

He laments that the Cuban writer and political idealist José
Martí was "the last of the great Spanish American men of letters
who were at the same time political leaders."[42] In his view the so-
called modernists–e.g., Darío, Ricardo Jaimes Freyre, Amado Ner-
vo–accepted a "division of labor" and by choice abandoned politics, at least during the first twenty years of this century.[43]

Though perhaps attenuated, the tradition of writers' intervention in political affairs clearly was not broken even among the followers of Darío. Indeed, some of his contemporaries were deeply
involved in social movements. For example, the literary successors
of Justo Sierra and Antonio Caso in Mexico were challenging positivism, and the little band led by José Ingenieros in Argentina represented an awakening interest in dialectical materialism. Gonzales
Prada, as both man of letters and political leader, contributed to
the rise of the indigenous Marxist movement of the Peruvian José
Mariátegui and his Amauta group.

Later developments that involved writers in politics were the
Mexican Revolution, the beginnings of the APRA movement in
Peru, the rise of the Socialist party in Ecuador, the pre-revolution-
ary ferment of the 1920's in Brazil–to which the "Semana de Arte
Moderna" group in São Paulo and the Regionalist movement of
Gilberto Freyre in the Northeast are both related–and the demand
for social reform from every corner of the continent during the
economic crisis of 1929–30.

Pedro Henríquez Ureña insists that though the writers since
1920 "have begun to return little by little to their traditional
course of participation in public affairs," they have had only limited success in achieving political office, mainly because as revolu-
tionists they challenge the established order. "Men of letters who
take part in our public life rarely manage to get into government:
they belong to the opposition, and customarily spend much more
time in prison than in office, not to mention life in exile, whether

forced or voluntary."[44] Even when their parties achieve power, the writers may hold points of view more advanced than those of their own party. The election in 1963 of the novelist Juan Bosch as president of a free Dominican Republic, as well as the presidencies held in recent years by the novelist Rómulo Gallegos (Venezuela), the poet and essayist Natalicio González (Paraguay), and the political essayist Juan José Arévalo (Guatemala), indicates the continuing role of literary men in high office–and the difficulties they face once they achieve it.

It is difficult to measure the extent of political influence exerted by poets, novelists, playwrights, and essayists in their nonpolitical writings. Certainly most of them joined, if they did not anticipate, the demand for social reform that has been constantly heard since the Mexican Revolution. Though there are many writers whose work has no connection with politics, political import, reforming zeal, and the pursuit of social objectives are fundamental characteristics of Latin American literature.[45]

The high point in combative writing, especially propaganda novels, seems to have been reached in the 1930's, when "socialist realism" in the novel and proletarian literature of all sorts flourished. The battle between literary right and left was perhaps fiercest among the novelists of Ecuador, with the left virtually eliminating the opposition before the war. Literature was closely identified with political participation, as the names Enrique Gil Gilbert, Joaquín Gallegos Lara, Alfredo Pareja Díez-Canseco, Jorge Icaza, and Humberto Salvador testify.[46] An extensive literature in Mexico dealt with the problems of the Revolution, after Mariano Azuela and Martín Luis Guzmán had shown the way. Every Latin American country could offer similar lists, particularly Brazil, where in the 1930's a vital literary movement was headed by the Northeastern novelists José Lins do Rego, Graciliano Ramos, Jorge Amado, Rachel de Queiroz, and José Américo de Almeida. All these writers represented left-of-center political philosophies, and wrote works full of implied or explicit social protest. They wrote in behalf of the Negro, the rural and urban workers, the drought-stricken *sertanejos* (backlands people). They surveyed the social and economic consequences of the latifundia system, which came under attack from a number of directions. And elsewhere in Brazil other voices echoed their protests.

In Brazil as elsewhere in Latin America, proletarian literature continues to be produced, but writers and critics have generally forsaken it for less explicitly propagandistic forms.[47] This generation has been just as relentless in attacking the established order, but the visions of poets, novelists, and playwrights have taken an intensely poetic form that reflects new aesthetic preoccupations. One thinks of parts of Pablo Neruda's *Canto general,* of Graciliano Ramos' *Memórias do cárcere,* Miguel Angel Asturias' *El Señor Presidente,* Carlos Fuentes' *La Región más transparente,* Jorge Amado's *Gabriela, cravo e canela.*[48]

Though the aesthetic value of this literature may have increased, its usefulness as propaganda has doubtless declined. The political and social influence of twentieth-century writing is also limited by the vast gap between the men of letters and the general reading public, not to mention the illiterate masses. Brazilian critics trace the phenomenon to the rise of the Parnassian and symbolist movements at the end of the nineteenth century. Even authors of proletarian novels have lamented that they would never be read by those they were intended to serve. The Peruvian critic Augusto Salazar Bondy has recently observed that in his country there is no "social support" for the arts, and that such pursuits are "a task of minorities for minorities, carried out against the background of a vast illiterate community."[49]

The Writers' Postwar Political Influence

The writers' left-of-center allegiance seems to have become particularly marked after World War II. The rise of *fidelismo,* to be discussed below, is perhaps the most dramatic example. The concept of "littérature engagée," that is, of social and political participation through writing, is still important, though it has been rejected by many.

Robert G. Mead, Jr., found in 1956 that Mexican writers were divided into two opposing factions: a Marxist-nationalist group that proclaimed "Mexico for the Mexicans" in a literary debate, and a more cosmopolitan group he described as "universalists":

Indeed, if we discount certain inevitable differences, this controversy between the two groups can be interpreted as the form that is assumed today by the age-old conflict in Mexican literature, that is, the struggle between the defenders of a narrow chauvinistic nationalism against the universalists, who have defended the prerogative of Mexican authors to enjoy complete freedom in shaping their artistic creations and to undergo the influence of writers and literatures from other countries.[50]

Professor Mead's distinction may well be applied to all Latin America, though subject to the usual limitations of any taxonomic device. In general, the Marxist-nationalists expect the writers to take up social themes and to express, at least by implication, a political point of view. While the Marxist-nationalists can easily be identified with the left, the cosmopolitan-universalists may represent the right, center, or left, without ideological conformity being demanded of them. Perhaps more than the Marxist-nationalists, they seek to harmonize the autochthonous with the universal. The poet and social philosopher Octavio Paz, the critics Enrique Anderson-Imbert, José Luis Martínez, and Arturo Torres-Rioseco prolong the quest for spiritual renovation and beauty undertaken by the followers of Rubén Darío. This group's outstanding representative was Alfonso Reyes, until his recent death Latin America's most distinguished man of letters. Undoubtedly these men have fulfilled their civic and political obligations, but their work has never had to hew to an ideological line.

Since World War II, the chief organization of Brazilian writers has wavered between a strong position on political issues and complete withdrawal from politics. An ABDE (Associação Brasileira de Escritores) congress in 1945 voted a series of strong statements supporting middle-sector reformist principles and opposing the dictator Vargas. Three years later the ABDE split over outlawing the Communist party.[51] A number of anti-Communists withdrew, and for several years thereafter the Association supported radical politics. A reconciliation was reached in 1957 when the two factions were reunited in the purely professional UBE (União Brasileira de Escritores), whose statutes expressly forbid members and officers to take political positions in its name.

There is strong sentiment in Brazil today for a professionalism that will free literature from involvement with politics. This is particularly the position of the so-called New Critics—who have their analogues in other Latin American countries. The leader of the Brazilian group, Afrânio Coutinho, has bemoaned the fact that men of letters must, because of the shortage of intellectuals, fulfill a multiplicity of social functions, especially political ones, with the result that writers become amateur politicians and, as he notes, politicians dabble in letters.[52] In recent years, Coutinho has headed a rather successful movement to liberate critics from all activity that is not essentially literary. A fruit of his campaign was the First

Brazilian Congress of Literary History and Criticism at Recife, August 7–14, 1960. In describing the meeting, Coutinho recently wrote:

Another matter made clear at the Congress was the independence of critical activity, that is, the notion that literary criticism must be, above all, literary—an autonomous activity, with its own individuality, not subsidiary to other intellectual pursuits. Such a distinction will become more and more precise among us: the literary critic can be only that, and his function possesses a high dignity without its being necessary for him to be also a sociologist, a historian, a politician, a journalist, a poet or a novelist, in order to take his place in the intellectual community.[53]

Greater professionalism, however, does not imply a loss of interest in politics. The consensus of center-left and leftist sentiment (leaving aside the question of Communism, which splits the left in many countries) has apparently convinced many writers that they can gain their political objectives in Brazil without concerted campaigns. Since the death of Stalin, militant leftists have soft-pedaled or abandoned the Communist theme. An indication of a developing tolerance of leftist ideas, even in so traditionally conservative a body as the Academia Brasileira de Letras, is the award of the Sylvio Romero Prize of 1959 to Luiz Pinto Ferreira for his *Interpretação da literatura brasileira,* a Marxist history of Brazilian literature.[54]

Fidelismo

The rise of *fidelismo* pinpoints the tendency of writers to coalesce at the left of the political spectrum. Since 1959, the Castro government has boasted of widespread support by writers throughout the continent. Manifestos of adherence to Castro and his movement were given by hundreds of writers, including some of the most noted.[55] A guarded statement by the Mexican Alfonso Reyes shortly before his death was accorded much prominence.[56] Of course, the Cuban government's lists of supporters, published in 1960, do not necessarily include only Marxist-Leninists or even radical leftists. It is too early to estimate what effect Castro's public avowal of Marxism-Leninism late in 1961 and Khrushchev's intervention in Cuba in 1962 may have had on the writers' enthusiasm for the Cuban revolution. Nearly all the leading Cuban writers continue to back Castro—the defection of the novelist Lino Novás Calvo was a resounding exception. Another was the denunciation of Castro by the Argentine Jorge Luis Borges, who was in turn immediately attacked by writers of the left.

John J. Johnson has argued that "the original middle-sector leaders and their successors have tended to assume a centrist position and now face the prospect of being overwhelmed by the forces they fathered in the not-too-distant past."[57] The writers' idealism, civic responsibility, and concern for humane values make it unlikely that they will defend a centrist emphasis on a rather narrow, economically oriented program that, as Johnson notes, tends to exclude "moral values and the dignity of the individual."[58]

Since the 1930's, a small but prestigious company of Latin American writers has placed its talent and influence at the service of international Communism. A list of these should include Aníbal Ponce, José Carlos Mariátegui, César Vallejo, Joaquín Gallegos, Enrique Gil Gilbert, Graciliano Ramos, Astrojildo Pereira, Aimé Césaire, Pablo Neruda, and Jorge Amado.[59] In addition, an impressive array of Cubans actively supports Castro. The best known are Juan Marinello, Alejo Carpentier, Nicolás Guillén, José Antonio Portuondo, and Fernández Retamar. Such respected figures are used by the Communists to foster a sense of Latin American cultural superiority vis-à-vis the United States. They are perhaps more effective in bringing intellectuals into front groups than in getting them into the Party. They also head "cultural" congresses and petition campaigns, and are generally "useful to the Party in establishing Communist influence in professional and other organizations which have great prestige in the national life of the various countries."[60] The Communist writers' role is thus an important one, especially given the Latin American tendency to ignore the international implications of supporting Communist causes and paying respect to distinguished Party members.

The idealistic writers are particularly sensitive to the appeal of Communism and especially *fidelismo* for social justice. Communism invokes seductive visions of a better and happier society. George Steiner observes that "Communism . . . has been a central force in much of the finest of modern literature; and personal encounter with Communism has marked the sensibility and career of many of the major writers of the age." After all, the creed of Marx, Engels, Lenin, and Trotsky "is a creed penetrated from the

96 FRED P. ELLISON

very moment of its historical origin by a sense of the values of intellect and art."[61]

Ideology

Though ideological positions vary, they have many common features. The ten-point plan for the "Second Independence Movement" of the Ecuadorian critic Benjamín Carrión summarizes goals common to many writers of the center-left and left: (1) agrarian reform, "to abolish the feudal system," (2) assimilation of indigenous elements and the rural workers in an improved socioeconomic system, (3) social security, (4) civil liberties, (5) equal rights for women, (6) international equality, (7) revision of political structures, (8) a campaign against underdevelopment, (9) greater inter-American cooperation, and (10) peace.[62]

There has always been agreement on the urgency of improving public education, but in Brazil, for instance, a strong attack has recently been made by the leftist UNE (União Nacional de Estudantes) on the Diretrizes e Bases (Norms and Bases of Education) law of December 20, 1961. And the same organization has recently struck the national universities in an attempt to gain greater student influence in university administration. In addition to attacking "curricular unilateralism," "political-ideological discrimination," corruption, and other alleged evils, the students cite "imperialist infiltration in our educational system, through Point IV and the Ford and Rockefeller Foundations, and even through the Alliance for Progress. These sabotage university instruction through a useless kind of technology [*tecnicismo*]. They do not afford learning that might be useful to students and permit our economic development, because that would merely mean the economic independence of our country from the imperialist yoke."[63] Marxist-nationalist writers have generally supported the students.

Many Latin American writers deplore the masses' nonparticipation in politics and rejoice in the formation of new political parties to replace the old "liberals" and "conservatives."[64] Until recently, on behalf of the Brazilian Communist Party, Jorge Amado worked to instill political awareness in the apathetic masses. There are also left-wing writers like Octavio Paz and Alfredo Pareja Díez-Canseco who unhesitatingly attack "totalitarian socialism" and the police-state morality of Communist Russia.[65]

Paz voices the now frequently heard suggestion that the so-called underdeveloped countries of Latin America join forces with the beleaguered countries of Asia and Africa to promote mutual economic growth.[66] In Brazil, the new Afro-Asian Institute, under government sponsorship, fosters "an effective cultural policy" toward the African and Asian countries. The Brazilian literary critic Adonias Filho mentions important new books by Eduardo Portella, José Honório Rodrigues, and Adolfo Justo Bezerra de Menezes that were stimulated by the Institute.[67] According to many writers, the nations of Latin America must also renew their efforts for hemispheric cooperation, independent, of course, of what is widely considered the economic imperialism of the United States.

The theme of *antiyanquismo* is sounded constantly in Latin American writing today, and no topic could be of greater importance to this country. After enjoying great prestige in Latin America during the early years of the nineteenth century, the United States saw its moral leadership and influence seriously questioned at the end of the century by a number of writers. They admired some aspects of North American civilization, but feared its technological encroachment and scorned its pragmatism, materialism, and apparent disregard for humane values. The Uruguayan modernist José Enrique Rodó gave literary form to this resentment in his artistically written *Ariel* (1900), which Zum Felde has called "the most widely read essay in Spanish America."[68] The influence of this book is still felt, and from it has arisen the name *arielismo*, which has come to mean a refined but critical approach to the United States and suspicion of its role in Latin America.[69] The viability of the image of the United States as the corrupting imperialist exploiter is confirmed by the frequency with which it is still evoked. The writer who attempts to alter its outlines is rare indeed, no doubt because so many are convinced of its essential truth. In 1962 the prestigious *Cuadernos americanos* of Mexico published an anthology, *Hispanoamérica en lucha por su independencia,* a collection of selections from Latin American leaders, beginning with Bolívar and Miguel Hidalgo and ending with Castro and Lázaro Cárdenas, that reinforces this image.

Nationalism may take countless forms, from narrow xenophobia and programmatic *antiyanquismo* to the widest range of concerns considered peculiarly Latin American, especially vis-à-vis Europe and the United States. Literary nationalism dates from the *ameri-canismo* and romanticism of the writers of the Independence move-ment. They considered writing of the people, the customs, the his-tory, the flora and the fauna of their native land a patriotic ser-vice. Since Domingo Sarmiento's day, the men of letters have given increasing thought to the problems of their nation and continent. In his extensive study of the Spanish American essay, Zum Felde has found a preponderant interest in American topics, and the same may be said for the novel.[70] The regionalist concerns of Gil-berto Freyre and his group are but a modern variant. Every Latin American literature has its interpreters of the national "reality," and critics who examine accepted values in an unremitting search for the national identity. The search for *argentinidad* by such writ-ers as Eduardo Mallea, Jorge Luis Borges, and Ezequiel Martínez Estrada is applicable to all America, "because the 'profound' or essential man, whether Argentinian or American, is universal man himself, and universally valid."[71] It should be stressed that this broad kind of nationalism (which does not exclude universal im-plications, as Freyre is always quick to point out) is the most char-acteristic theme of Latin American writing, embracing not only the humanities but the social sciences as well.

At least passing mention must be made of the related theme of the writer's alienation, much discussed in the United States as well as Latin America. Marxist and nationalist writers hold that the intellectual is cut off from reality by a "colonial" mentality that keeps him from seeing himself and his nation as they actually are, and that similar impediments have hindered Brazil's national de-velopment.[72] The opposing argument has been stated thus: "The thinker who hurls the charge of *alienation* against our Nation's entire past, who refuses to take into account the goodly number of national values modeled by time in a long process of sedimen-tation, actually represents an ideological current that can very justly be situated at the antipodes of nationalism. For he rejects out of hand the Brazilian nation and its culture, the only Brazilian nation and culture that really exist."[73]

Since the era of Darío and Rodó, the value of technology and industrialization has been generally accepted, but few well-known writers would endorse them enthusiastically. A modern writer, Benjamín Carrión, is stung by the disparity between technology and ethics.[74] This is because technology, which a Latin American has called the "mystique of today," conflicts with many humanistic values, a conflict well expressed by the critic Enrique Anderson-Imbert:

Our countries of Hispanic tradition have not had an Industrial Revolution nor have we had technical progress or scientific preparation. We are behind the times in comparison with the countries of Western civilization who are leading the world through a tremendous mechanization, one of whose resources is the atomic bomb. On the other hand, we maintain the basic ideas of the older humanism. The individual and his own efforts to express himself still constitute our measure of value. Of course we are becoming modernized. We accept the results of industrial transformation. We indeed slip into the social and political process of our time. But, for having arrived late, we feel keenly the cultural impulses of the past. Our intellectuals have not suffered the devastations of industrial civilization and are in a position to affirm their own individuality against totalitarian cruelty and capitalistic mediocrity.[75]

An extensive study of attitudes of Latin American writers toward technology concludes that hardly any writers treat technology as a legitimate or valuable contribution to Hispanic culture, though it has won a grudging acceptance, particularly by historians and essayists.[76] The high value on leisure and a centuries-old hostility to practical, as opposed to theoretical, pursuits strengthen the resistance. Indicative of a fresh approach to the problems of modern Brazil, with its basic conflict between a static rural order and "a dynamic urban structure impelled and transformed by the process of industrialization," is the young critic Eduardo Portella's appeal to the writers to accept the challenge and creative stimulus provided by "the complexity and dynamism of our contextual reality."[77] His article is significantly titled "The Literature of Development."

By now it should be apparent that the men of letters are powerful agents of political change. One recalls Edward A. Shils' observation that "modern liberal and constitutional politics have largely been the creation of intellectuals with bourgeois affinities and sympathies, in societies dominated by land-owning and military aristocracies." The statement is applicable to most of the writer-politicians and politician-writers of nineteenth-century Latin America. Shils has further noted that there is a close connection between "ideological politics" and the intellectuals. Indeed, "the function of modern intellectuals in furnishing the doctrine of revolutionary movements is to be considered as one of their most important accomplishments."[78] As we have seen, the writers have exercised intellectual leadership not only in the cultural but also in the political sphere, and in the twentieth century their voices most often have been raised to advocate change. They have increasingly aligned with leftist ideologies advanced by the middle sectors. A few of the most outstanding writers in recent years have been Communists, and large numbers have been associated with Communist front activities. Their influence has been the greater because of the widespread respect they command as men of letters.

Creators of change, the writers are also subject to it. Changing patterns of education in the twentieth century, for example, tend to lessen the influence of the traditional school on literary creativity. Educational reform has enlarged the sector from which writers may emerge, and they no longer represent the elite so preponderantly. The rise of the middle sectors has contributed to the professionalization of literary pursuits, although journalism, diplomacy, and the bureaucracy remain essential to the writers' livelihood. Less closely identified with the elite, writers are more sensitive to financial pressures; the majority of writers, despite professional intentions, are still unable to live by writing alone. Governments have lent some material assistance, and the Communists have on occasion ministered to the writers' sense of economic insecurity. The mass media and the expanded general reading public have not been the answer to their quest for professional independence. Paradoxically, the gap between writers and their public has widened since the end of the nineteenth century, when literature became more esoteric. The monolithic works of socialist realism and outright propaganda notable in the 1930's have given way to a more poetic expression of the aspirations of man and society.

The writers insist on performing their time-honored tasks as political and social thinkers, and society, as always, accords them high prestige and great responsibility. In ideological terms, many Latin American men of letters are obviously out of sympathy with some attitudes and values basic to the civilization and culture of the United States. If this country has not been entirely successful in the communication of ideas, it may be because it has not learned to engage in mutually advantageous dialogue with Latin American intellectuals, especially the writers.

4. The Artist

Gilbert Chase

There are no "massive reservoirs of dependable knowledge" upon which to draw in determining the socio-political role of the contemporary artist in Latin America. Only Mexico, in the period from about 1920 to 1940, when the direction of art was decisively influenced by socio-political factors, might provide sufficient data for such a study. But on the whole, a sociological survey of the arts in Latin America remains to be undertaken.[1] This chapter seeks to examine the problems, clarify some of the issues, and, hopefully, lay the groundwork for a more comprehensive study when substantiating data become available.

The term "artists" will here be understood to mean professional practitioners of music, painting, sculpture, and architecture.[2] In respect to music, the composer—the "creative artist"—will be intended, rather than the performer or interpreter (although the latter should not be altogether excluded from the picture).

The professional artist in Latin America is an urban social type. Because of the large degree of centralization, he is also—with few exceptions—identified with a capital city. The most notable exception occurs in Brazil, where São Paulo is an important art center and regional movements, particularly in painting, are fairly strong. The city has always been the center of civilization, and the fine arts are essentially a product of the culturally complex, socially stratified, and occupationally differentiated type of social organization that we call civilization. The city sets the pace in ideas and innovations, provides both the stimulus and the market for works of art, and gives to the artist maximum freedom combined with maximum security.

Within this urban milieu, the artists' socio-economic positions range all the way from a high degree of civic responsibility (in the case, for example, of a government-employed architect) to anti-social attitudes as revealed by the "Bohemian fringe," or, in today's parlance, the "beatnik" artist. In an adaptation of Ogburn's classification of urban social strata on the basis of occupation, Gist places the artists (including sculptors, musicians, architects) among the professionals in the top stratum just below the capitalists, together with physicians, publishers, clergymen, professors, lawyers, judges, etc.[3] John J. Johnson, in his study of the Latin American "middle sectors," places the artists among the "teachers and bureaucrats, lawyers, notaries, newspaper men, publishers," who "had roles to play and tasks to perform" in the formation of the Latin American nations. And he adds, "These functions tended to identify them with the elites and to dissociate them from the laboring groups."[4] Finally, among the six characteristics listed by Johnson as common to the middle sectors in Latin America, at least one is definitely applicable to the professional artists: "They are overwhelmingly urban."[5]

The urban associations of the artists, and particularly their identification with the capitals, are emphasized in Latin America by their frequent economic dependence on the State. This is simply because in Latin America the State is the chief patron of the arts: it commissions murals to be painted in public buildings, supports academies of art and museums, subsidizes opera houses and symphony orchestras, and in some cases provides stipends and cash prizes for favored artists. It also supports the universities, which have become increasingly important as centers of artistic activity, especially in the field of music. Thus, the head of a department of music or the director of a conservatory or a symphony orchestra is a government official as well as an artist. According to the Chilean musician Juan A. Orrego-Salas, over 85 per cent of the composers in his country are dependent on the State for at least 70 per cent of their income. While comparative data are lacking for other countries, the situation would probably be similar.

The folk and popular arts have been excluded from consideration here because they would lead to excessive complications.[6] But even within the fine arts themselves it is necessary to make certain distinctions, since the situation of the artist differs considerably

according to the nature of his art. Consider, for example, the situation of the architect as compared with that of the composer.

It is a truism that the architect has a complex and multiple role
in today's society. As Lewis Mumford writes, "His work now involves more than the design of the isolated building; it includes
planning and coordination, touching factory production at one
end and community planning at the other."[7] Surely a professional
worker who is probably connected with a large business firm, who
may even be a capitalist in his own right, or at least the manager
of an important enterprise, who may deal on the one hand with
factory production and industrial designing and on the other with
city planning and its related problems, will have more in common
with such urban types as the businessman, the industrialist, the
lawyer, and the bureaucrat, than with such artistic types as the
painter, the sculptor, and the musician. His social and political attitudes are more likely to be shaped by his status as a professional
worker than his status as an artist.

At the other end of the spectrum we have the artists who are
most remote from the pressures of society—the musicians. The
American composer Virgil Thomson, writing on the topic "What
it feels like to be a musician," has this to say: "Every profession is
a secret society. The musical profession is more secret than most,
on account of the nature of music itself. No other field of human
activity is quite so hermetic, so isolated." He explains this by adding that music, alone among the great techniques of human expression, is "an auditory thing," hence "comprehensible only to persons who can remember sounds."[8]

Thomson would be the last to deny that musicians have interests
outside of their own "secret society." His book *The State of Music*
deals with a number of these interests, including food, civil status,
sources of income (and their effect on musical style!), censorship,
and politics. One chapter, in fact, is titled "Composers' Politics."
As he explains it: "By political action I mean what he [i.e., the
composer] does in a group to conserve or to improve his economic
privileges." His conclusion is that "The composer's political action
. . . is determined by his source of income."[9]

This line of economic determinism leads to two main classifications for composers: those who live by their composition and those
who live on inherited capital. The former, according to Thomson,

are liberals, "like most small proprietors." They tend to defend themselves "through professional guild-associations against the depredations of finance-capital."[10] It should be added that, except in the field of commercialized popular music, the composers who live by their composition are few in number, whether in Latin America or the United States. But the fact that they are so few gives them additional prestige as an elite group. In Latin America, furthermore, some of the most successful composers have played both sides of the game: on the one hand they have received grants and commissions from private foundations in the United States, while on the other they have received emoluments, cash prizes, and commissions from their own governments. There is a definite relationship between these two sources of income, because a Latin American composer who has received recognition in the United States has a better chance of being rewarded in his own country.

The composer who lives on inherited capital is, as might be expected, "solidly with the investors always." Furthermore, according to Thomson, "In any dispute between the union and the management he sides with the management." Latin America has known a number of composers who lived on inherited capital. In our time the most conspicuous example is Guillermo Uribe-Holguín, member of the coffee-growing oligarchy of Colombia. The Chilean composer Alfonso Letelier Llona belongs to the class of large landowners. Others might be named; but they are a minority that has shrunk in recent years, owing principally to the rise of the middle sectors and the growing emphasis on professionalism in music. (The musician with inherited wealth would be an amateur by definition.) It may be remarked in passing that both Uribe-Holguín and Letelier were at one time directors of the national conservatories of music in their respective countries—which affords a neat example of "government by oligarchy" in the realm of music.

For the situation in Latin America, one would certainly have to add another category to Thomson's classifications: that of the composer who lives from the government's payroll. As indicated above, he does not receive his salary as a composer, but for serving in some administrative capacity, as head of a conservatory, as leader of a symphony orchestra, or as artistic director of an opera house. In any case he is a government employee, of either the State or the municipality. The significance of this situation, from a socio-economic standpoint, is that it creates a system of patronage which, combined with the high degree of centralization, enables certain individuals to exercise a sort of hegemony over the musical activity of a particular country—a kind of musical caudillismo. The extent to which this kind of hegemony can be established and maintained (granted there is a suitable "strong man" on the scene) is in direct ratio to (1) the degree of centralization of cultural activities, and (2) the degree of political stability in the country. The presence of all these factors in Chile (the strong man in this case being the composer Domingo Santa Cruz Wilson) has resulted in the most concentrated and sustained example of personal leadership in music to be found in any Latin American country, for it has lasted some twenty-five years. "Leadership" is to be understood here in its political sense, involving the exercise of power through patronage, backed by public funds.

Just as in the political sphere, the removal of a musical caudillo by death or other circumstances leaves a void in which factionalism flourishes while the struggle for the succession is carried on by contenders who hitherto have been existing in the leader's shadow. This usually results in a condition of crisis, marked by a lack of direction and uncertainty over who the new leader or leaders will be. This was the case in Brazil following the decline of Villa-Lobos as that country's musical strong man and his death in 1959.

Although the musician may have professional interests and political motives that give him a certain solidarity with artists in other fields, the nature of his art—"comprehensible only to persons who can remember sounds"—tends to isolate him from society as a creative artist. The architect, on the other hand, is involved with an art that by its very nature is social, that begins with the idea of being *useful* for a specific purpose related to society's material needs.

What about sculptors and painters? In both cases the degree of socio-political involvement and impact covers a very wide range, extending at one end to an art so remote from common reality as to be "completely impenetrable to outsiders" (as Thomson said of music), and at the other end debouching in "social realism," in which the representational power of sculpture and painting, through the depiction of politically loaded symbols and other equally obvious devices, serves to carry a message. Between these

two extremes there is traditional academic art, which in sculpture
is displayed in the public monuments and statues that adorn most
cities of the Western world; and in painting by works of historical
commemoration, conventional landscapes, official portraits, and
the like. Academic art, like social realism, relies heavily on the
non-aesthetic component in art.

Cultural historians do in fact distinguish a non-aesthetic component in art. As Dilman W. Gotshalk writes: "It is fairly obvious
that educational, religious, commercial, memorial, utilitarian, and
historical values can be derived from works of art without any central concern for aesthetic values."[11] He goes on to say, however,
that "they are not the values most distinctive of art, and they
should not be substituted for the central or distinctive (i.e., aesthetic) values, as they often are in popular thought and superficial
philosophical analyses"—and as they often are, he might have added, in art that aims primarily to serve a social or political cause.
At what point does art become mere propaganda? How much
importance should be given to the aesthetic component in art that
is concerned with achieving social significance? Can a political
cause be most effectively served by an academic art or by an art
that has assimilated the technical and expressive innovations of
its own time? Which kind of art is more valuable, that which por-
trays the issues and passions of the moment and thereby evokes an
immediate response, or that which seeks to transmit to future generations the enduring values of form, style, and expression? These
are not merely rhetorical questions. They lie at the very core of
contemporary art in Latin America. Most of the history of the
visual arts since 1900 could be written in terms of these questions
and the answers that have been made to them—in both theory and
practice—by the artists of Latin America, and most particularly by
the painters.

A brief review of the Mexican muralist movement will serve to
illustrate the foregoing. In 1921, under the Obregón administration, the Mexican government undertook the task of political, economic, and cultural reconstruction to consolidate the gains of the
Revolution. The government at once became the most important
patron of the arts, commissioning, in an epoch-making decision,
several Mexican painters, working as a group, to decorate the walls
of certain public buildings—notably the National Preparatory

School—with frescoes illustrating the ideals and aims of the Revolution. To emphasize their group solidarity the artists early in 1922 organized themselves as the "Syndicate of Technical Workers, Painters, and Sculptors." The Syndicate undertook to propagate its views on art among the people in a periodical published in Mexico City called *El Machete,* which glorified the role of the laboring class in the Revolution. The two leading figures in the Syndicate, Diego Rivera and David Alfaro Siquieros, believed in the principle of collective art and upheld the view that a so-called creative artist was, in socio-economic status, in fact no different from a day laborer. Rivera consequently applied for membership in the most powerful Mexican labor organization, the Confederación Republicana de Obreros Mexicanos, and thereafter, contrary to tradition, artists began to dissociate themselves from the elite minority.

The Syndicate, in its "Social, Political, and Aesthetic Declaration," issued in 1922, proclaimed that "the art of the Mexican people . . . is collective, and our own aesthetic aim is to socialize artistic expression, to destroy bourgeois individualism." To make clear its political ideology, the Syndicate addressed, among others, "the workers and peasants who are oppressed by the rich; and the intellectuals who are not servile to the bourgeoisie." Its aesthetic aims were spelled out in three essential clauses:

"We repudiate the so-called easel art and all such art which springs from ultraintellectual circles, for it is essentially aristocratic.

"We hail the monumental expression of art because such art is public property.

"We proclaim that this being the moment of social transition from a decrepit to a new order, the makers of beauty must invest their greatest efforts in the aim of materializing an art valuable to the people, and our supreme objective in art, which is today an expression for individual pleasure, is to create for all, beauty that enlightens and stirs to struggle."[12]

The implications of easel art as "essentially aristocratic" will be discussed later, in connection with the rise of a middle-class market for easel painting in Mexico. For the present, it should be noted that this declaration definitely advocates change rather than continuity, since it calls for a new order to replace the decrepit

values of the past. The change, however, is specifically proclaimed
to be one of social transition. The argument is that artists must
adapt to the new social order, must repudiate aristocratic associations and bourgeois individualism, for the purpose of creating
an art that will be public property, an art valuable to the people.
The manifesto does not specifically call for a new art in terms of
new techniques or new aesthetic principles, as distinct from political doctrines. This bears out the contention of Marta Traba, the
Colombian art critic, that "Rivera and Siqueiros were 'revolutionary men' not 'revolutionary painters.' "[13] The distinction is crucial
in attempting to answer the question, "Have artists been a modernizing force in Latin America?" It leads us to ask whether this question means a modernizing force in art, or in society. However close
may be the relationship between art and society, it can by no means
be assumed that both types of change are identical. Profound social
changes can occur with very little change in creative art; this is
clearly demonstrated in the case of Soviet Russia, where "modern
art" is taboo, where artistic innovations are systematically suppressed, and where the official aesthetic doctrine of social realism
produces a retrogressive academic art. The innovations in abstract
art that had begun in Russia around 1913 with the experiments of
Larionov, Gontcharova, Tatlin, Rodchenko, and Malevitch—leading to such influential modern movements as Suprematism, Con-
structivism, and Non-Objectivism—were banished when the Communist party decreed that "modern art" was incompatible with the
ideology of the Revolution, and the leading Russian modernists,
such as Gabo and Pevsner, went into exile (the former to Berlin,
the latter to Paris) and continued their *artistic* revolution.

It was because the Mexican mural painters, on the whole, remained unreceptive to the revolutionary innovations of contemporary art that Marta Traba said they were not revolutionary
painters, and accused them of "lack of reverence" (for their art)
in placing painting "at the service of a political cause." Her argument is that by doing this, "the influence of the Mexicans retarded
for many years a comprehension of the artistic language that the
European artists were already speaking freely."[14] Thus, while the
artists who identified themselves with the aims of the Mexican
Revolution called for a new order, the changes they advocated
were social, political, and economic, not artistic. They received

some influence from Cubism and Expressionism, but long after the original movements in Europe had passed their apogee, so that these traits in Mexican painting could not be regarded as artistically revolutionary. The Mexican muralists actually revived an old technique (after numerous material difficulties and some discouraging failures)—fresco painting—and they were much influenced by painters of the Italian Renaissance, such as Paolo Uccello and Piero della Francesca.

Accordingly, our answer to the question "Were the Mexican muralists a modernizing force in art?" would have to be at least partly negative. As will be shown later, the real modernizing force in Mexican art was exercised by the nonpolitical painters, who as early as 1928 associated themselves with a literary group called Los Contemporáneos (The Contemporaries) that was opposed to nationalism and tried to arouse local interest in the international trends of contemporary art. Poets and painters united in this effort, publishing a review that included reproductions of works by Braque, Picasso, di Chirico, and other artistic innovators of the time. Associated with this group was the Mexican painter Rufino Tamayo (b. 1899), destined to become one of the most important figures in modern art after 1940, and at present regarded as the leading modern painter of Mexico.

In his excellent book *Mexican Painting in Our Time,* Bernard S. Myers has shown that the internationally oriented modernist movement in Mexican art was able to make some headway in the decade between 1924 and 1934 because the administration of President Plutarco Calles brought a swing to the right, marked by the abrupt termination of the first government-sponsored mural projects in 1924 and the dissolution of the Syndicate a year later. During the Cárdenas regime (1934–40), however, the ideology of the Revolution was vigorously restored, social reforms were aggressively pursued, politico-cultural groups of radical tendency renewed their activities, and government patronage of the arts was once more the order of the day. Under these conditions, mural painting regained its supremacy, and the individualistic art of easel painting was again thrust into the background.

But the cooperative group spirit that had animated the first mural projects was not renewed. And other significant changes were taking place within the Revolutionary art movement. In 1935

Siqueiros was publicly involved with Rivera in a controversy over the nature of "Revolutionary art."[15] Although Siqueiros has always held to his view of art as a weapon in the class struggle, he differed sharply with Rivera over the kind of art best suited for this purpose. He no longer believed, for example, that fresco was the best medium for such an art, or that the "Revolutionary" artist should exploit the national folklore mixed with remnants of archaeology. "We may be able," wrote Siqueiros, "to play a revolutionary hymn on a church organ, but it is not really an adequate instrument for such a purpose; the fresco, at least technically speaking, does not correspond to the formal and organic quality of architecture . . . of our time; we must turn to materials that correspond to industry, that is, to the society of which we are a part."[16]

Here we have Siqueiros, the incorrigible revolutionary man, adopting at long last the position of a revolutionary artist, calling for technical and formal innovations, for the use of new materials corresponding to the art of our time. Myers attributes this attitude of Siqueiros to his technological experiences in the United States; in the 1930's "he consistently used the Duco paint medium (a Du Pont trade name for all pyroxylin paints) adapted from industrial procedures such as the spray-painting of automobiles." Thus, the first notable influence from the United States on Latin American painting was derived, not from aesthetic sources, but from industrial technology. Siqueiros, with a team of assistants, worked with pyroxylin paints on a mural for the Electrical Workers Union in Mexico City; paint was applied to the wall surface with a spray gun. As Myers observes, "Here in the mural of the Electrical Workers Union, Siqueiros has achieved his first complete synthesis of modern techniques and political ideas."[17]

In a paper on "The Mexican Experience in Art," delivered at the American Artists' Congress in New York in 1936, Siqueiros further emphasized his divergence from Rivera's views by insisting that art intended to serve a socio-political cause ("Revolutionary art," in his terminology) must be concerned not only with the content or theme (the propaganda message), but also with the problem of form. Siqueiros was aiming at a "new realism" in which photographic techniques (still and motion picture) would be combined with new painting techniques and materials. He had an opportunity to apply his ideas in a large mural project that he was commissioned to execute in 1941 for a school in Chillán, Chile. Using pyroxylin on masonite, and applying the photographic techniques with which he had previously experimented, Siqueiros achieved, in his own manner, that prime objective of contemporary artists, the creation of a new kind of space—"a space that results from the multiplication of parts and the cinematic superposition of images that may be viewed from different angles."[18]

At this time Siqueiros was also painting many easel pictures (he completed seventy of these in 1946–47), thereby demonstrating once more his divergence from the muralist dogmatism of the Revolution. He further emphasized the unity of his work as a whole, as well as his refusal to create a doctrinary barrier between mural and easel painting, by also using pyroxylin in the latter. Indeed, commenting on murals done by Siqueiros at the Palacio de Bellas Artes in 1951, on the subject of "Cuauhtémoc Reborn," Myers remarks that in certain panels "the effect is more of easel painting than of mural."

These aspects of Siqueiros' work have not been stressed to establish value judgments, but rather to illustrate ways in which the artist can operate as a modernizing force, and to suggest that he accomplishes this in ways intrinsically related to the specific techniques of his own particular craft, even when he draws upon other areas—such as science and industry—for ideas and materials. Indeed, the fact that he does utilize the resources of modern technology and modern concepts of time-space is precisely what makes him a contemporary artist, a modernizing force in society.

Historical evidence again and again demonstrates that if non-aesthetic components are consistently allowed to prevail over aesthetic components in the work of art, it will eventually lose its effective power, not only as a work of art, but also as bearer of the very extra-aesthetic values it was intended to transmit. A case in point is that of the Peruvian painter José Sabogal (1888–1957), founder and leader of the so-called *indigenista* or nativistic school of painting in Peru. A visit to Mexico in 1923 aroused his ambition to create a "national" movement in Peruvian painting by exploiting indigenous themes and local scenes. As a result, his work was widely accepted and supported by the official establishment, not for its artistic qualities (which, by any severe standards, were very slight), but for its nationalistic implications: in Gotshalk's terminology, it was believed to convey "educational, memorial, utilitarian, and historical values." Appointed Director of the National School of Art in Lima, Sabogal exercised a formative influence over a whole group of younger Peruvian painters. Even such an acute observer as Jorge Basadre (in a very early work, it is true) was taken in by the specious *peruanidad* of Sabogal and devoted a chapter of eulogy to him and his school. But, in the words of the art critic José V. Acha, "In time, the work of Sabogal followed the natural sociological course of any tendency lacking true artistic premises. . . . The initial enthusiasm awakened by such a valiant and promising nationalistic attitude vanished as people became conscious of the absence of aesthetic criteria."[19]

It is perhaps significant that Acha uses the term "sociological" to describe the process whereby, through the attrition of time, works of art not based on aesthetic criteria (i.e., in which the non-aesthetic components predominate) lose their effectiveness. What he probably has in mind is what may be called a law of cultural dynamics. The aesthetic component is constant; but the non-aesthetic components are variable, and thus their effectiveness depends on interests, issues, and conflicts arising from particular social situations in time and place.[20] This is also what Siqueiros may have had in mind when he insisted that the problem of form should not be neglected in "Revolutionary art."

The case of the late Brazilian painter Cândido Portinari (1903–62), without being as extreme as that of Sabogal (for he was a much better painter), is nevertheless illuminating in this context. As a young artist, he received a government stipend to study in Europe, where he appears not to have assimilated the new artistic currents, apart from some influence of Picasso. Upon returning to Brazil, "he joined the group of young intellectuals who, like those in other countries of the Hemisphere, were concerned with social problems and with the realities of life for contemporary man in the Americas."[21] How was this concern reflected in his work? By including in his paintings, we are told, "Negro, white, mulatto, and Indian workers to symbolize his country." But Portinari was never a man of violence, never addicted to ideological extremes. His dilemma was that he could never bring himself to be either a completely "Revolutionary" artist in the political sense or a completely "revolutionary" artist in the aesthetic sense. The first limitation prevented him from being a militant leader like Rivera or Siqueiros, who became heroes of the class struggle; the second limitation caused his artistic influence to be short-lived, for the revolution in modern art bypassed him. By 1950 he had ceased to be an influential figure: he already belonged to the past.[22]

To see this, one has only to compare his murals in the Ministry of Education in Rio de Janeiro with the building itself, which, under the guiding hand of Le Corbusier, marked a turning point in contemporary Latin American architecture. The building was the product of a modernizing force in Brazilian society: that of the new architecture led by Lucio Costa, Oscar Niemeyer, and others. But the murals, although admirable in certain respects, conform to the conventional eclecticism that pervades so much of Portinari's work. The work of Costa, Niemeyer, and their associates would continue to evolve and to have highly important consequences for the modernization of Brazil; but Portinari left no pupils and no followers.

The modernizing influences in Brazilian painting must be sought elsewhere—for example, in the exhibition of paintings by Anita Malfatti at São Paulo in 1916, described by Almeida Cunha as "the first exhibition of a modern Brazilian artist to take place in Brazil."[23] Malfatti, who had exhibited at the famous Armory Show in New York and was a friend of Marcel Duchamp, the most revolutionary artist of his time, introduced Cubism into Brazil. Then, in 1922, the celebrated Week of Modern Art took place in São Paulo, through the united effort of poets, painters, and composers. "Rebellion is our aesthetics," declared one of the group. The establishment viewed this event as a subversive act. A São Paulo newspaper published the following notice: "The columns of the free section of this paper are at the disposal of those who would attack the Week of Modern Art and defend our artistic heritage."[24] The artists, for their part, viewed themselves as victims of a reactionary society bent on stifling all original creative activity. As Almeida Cunha says, "What they all wanted was a change." They might quarrel among themselves and argue about the validity of such terms as "futuristic" or "modernistic," but they all agreed on the necessity for change.

The theme of change keeps recurring like a Wagnerian leitmotiv throughout the contemporary arts in Latin America; with each decade it becomes more insistent—and more effective, as the pressures of the modern world work in favor of the new forces. A recent article on the arts in Latin America was entitled "The Wind of Change": there can be no doubt that the title is apt.[25] The general atmosphere of impatience with the status quo, of determination to break through to something different, is summed up in a statement made by an American cultural observer in Bogotá: "Intellectuals down here are all disciples of change. Most of them aren't sure of what they want to change to, but they are looking for something different. And I'm talking about change in their art *and* their social and political conditions."[26]

The last remark suggests a crucial question: Are changes in art inextricably bound up with changes in social and political conditions? Is the revolutionary artist interested in changes other than those he wishes to bring about in his own art? Another case history may help answer these questions. The Peruvian painter Fernando de Szyszlo, born in 1925, belongs to that generation of artists in Latin America which came of age when non-figurative art was in full possession of the field, both in Europe and in the United States. Convinced that this was the art of their own age, these artists adopted the new techniques and then brought them to their respective countries. After his return from Europe in 1955, Szyszlo gave the first exhibition of truly modern art ever held in Lima. Interviewed in 1962, he said, "We are all looking for new things."[27] He went on to explain that a few years earlier a group of Peruvian artists—painters, poets, architects—had founded a movement called Espacio (Space). Like the Brazilian artists of 1922, the Peruvians were reacting against the status quo. (The time lag is significant, since it points up the difference between a closed and an open society.) "We wanted a change," said Szyszlo. Then he went on to explain that at first "we were just talking about art, but then we got more and more political." Doubtless this shift of emphasis was due to the presence in the group of Fernando Belaúnde Terry, the architect and former director of the National School of Architecture who entered politics in 1955, ran for the presidency in 1956 and 1962, and was finally elected in 1963. According to Szyszlo, Espacio was transformed into the Social Progressive party. "Then the whole thing split over Castro. My group was not for Castro, neither were we against him. But the others went more and more to the left. We dropped out, and they were invited to Cuba and Moscow and China."[28]

How much does this episode tell us about the political role of the artist in Latin America? Actually, not very much. When Belaúnde turned to politics he became a politician, i.e., a member of another social group, and the fact that he had been an architect became little more than part of his personal history. As for Szyszlo himself, he summed up his position by declaring, "I don't like political parties. I think I am too individualistic." Szyszlo happens to be the leading abstract painter in Peru today and one of the foremost artists of Latin America. Clearly, this is of more importance to him than belonging to any political party or taking a definite stand on such a hot issue as the Castro regime in Cuba. Let others go their political way, he seems to be saying, as long as I am allowed to paint the way I want. In the interview quoted above, he made it plain that what he was primarily interested in attacking and overthrowing was not a political regime but a socio-cultural attitude. "The country," he said, speaking of Peru, "was still living in colonial times. . . . We thought this must end, we wanted a change." Having achieved the change—Peru now accepts contemporary art and has a flourishing abstract school of painters—Szyszlo discovered that he was not really interested in political parties. Here, in contrast to the Mexicans, Szyszlo stands for the pure artist, for whom putting first things first means ultimately placing art above everything else. It is precisely for this reason that artists of his type are frowned on by totalitarian regimes: they are too individualistic and too loyal to aesthetic ideals to be useful tools of a political ideology. Freedom and change are their watchwords, and perhaps they will react in concert—unite for political action— only when they feel their freedom to create is threatened.

One more point should be made in connection with the Szyszlo episode. Let us assume that we were to take his painting during the height of his period of political activity with the Espacio group, and attempt a correlation between painting and political action. The result would be negative as far as any distinct social, political, or ideological factors are concerned. True, Szyszlo did combine modern abstraction with pre-Hispanic symbols and motifs derived from the textiles and ceramics of the various indigenous cultures of Peru, such as the Nazca and the Inca. But this involved no program of nationalism, and no manifestation of solidarity with the socio-economic plight of the Indians: what interested Szyszlo was the assimilation of these indigenous traditions, as an aesthetic component, in his painting. This is significant because it illustrates a generalization that can safely be made about contemporary art in Latin America as a whole today: the aesthetic component predominates over the non-aesthetic. This is the real revolution that has taken place in Latin American art over the past fifteen or twenty years, and it was accomplished not only without the aid of the Mexican "Revolutionary" painters, but in spite of their influence.[29]

The new artistic language of the twentieth century was effectively transplanted to Latin America, not through Mexico, but through Argentina, Brazil, and Cuba. Mention has already been made of the introduction of Cubism into Brazil in 1916. In Argentina, the painter Emilio Pettoruti was the initiator of modernism with some abstract drawings executed in 1914; he subsequently became the leading exponent of Cubism. His emphasis on purely plastic values, combined with superior technical ability, exerted a beneficial influence on the younger artists. Ever since the early years of this century there has been a continuously developing movement of modern art in Argentina, largely centered in Buenos Aires, which stands in opposition to the tendencies represented by the contemporary art movement in Mexico. Fernando de Szyszlo, in an extremely perceptive article on "Contemporary Latin American Painting,"[30] speaks of Mexico City and Buenos Aires as the two great and contrasting "centers of influence and attraction" for contemporary painting in Latin America. Mexico City represents the trend toward nationalism based on socio-political and ethno-geographical factors; its influence was greatest in those countries having large indigenous populations: Bolivia, Peru, Ecuador. Buenos Aires represents international modernism, based on sophisticated aesthetic premises, excellence of techniques, emphasis on plastic values, and maximum individual freedom. It is not surprising, therefore, to find that since 1950 contemporary Argentine painters have been attracting increased attention in the art galleries of Europe and the United States, and that today the modern art movement in Buenos Aires compares with that of Paris or New York. This movement, however, remains concentrated in the studios and art galleries, while in Brazil the modern art movement has gained wide influence and international prestige through the enterprise and initiative of its great museums of modern art in São Paulo and Rio de Janeiro.

The modern art movement in Cuba had a relatively late start, since it may be dated from 1934, when the painter Amelia Peláez returned from Paris after having worked there with Juan Gris and other Cubists. The artists who gathered around her formed the first Cuban "school" of modern painting, which succeeded in being contemporary and international (the terms are virtually synonymous) while retaining Cuban traits, notably a great exuberance of color. This is true even of a painter like Wilfredo Lam (b. 1902), who has spent most of his life in Europe without forgetting his Cuban heritage. According to Szyszlo, Wilfredo Lam has exerted an influence on many Latin American painters—always in the direction of contemporary plastic and expressive values.

Although the main trend of Mexican painting from about 1920 to 1950, with its strong nationalistic bias and its exaggerated sociopolitical content, can be regarded as marginal to the mainstream of contemporary painting, it would be a mistake to assume that the muralist movement stemming from the Mexican Revolution was completely unified in its aims, its methods, and its results. The polemic between Siqueiros and Rivera on the nature of "Revolutionary art" has already been mentioned. The third leading figure of the muralist movement, José Clemente Orozco, makes it clear in his *Autobiography* that he did not go along with most of the ideas expressed in the 1922 manifesto of the Syndicate of Technical Workers, Painters, and Sculptors (which, incidentally, was written mainly by Siqueiros). In a summary of Mexican thought about art in the year 1920, Orozco heaps ridicule and scorn upon the current notions, including extreme nationalism, the belief in "natural genius" ("It had come to be believed that anyone could paint and that the greater the ignorance and stupidity of the painter, the greater the value of his work"), and the cult of indigenous crafts. He is noncommittal about such doctrines as "Art at the service of the Worker," active intervention in militant politics (which he attributes to the precept and example of the late Mexican painter Gerardo Murillo, better known as Dr. Atl), and the "passionate preoccupation of artists with sociology and history." He does, however, condemn by implication the excessive emphasis on thematic content that characterized much of the Mexican painting of this period, when he writes that some of the artists "came to cherish the theme of the painting with such passion that they completely abandoned the field of art and gave themselves over to activities no longer bearing any relation to their profession."[31]

In a section of his autobiography dealing with the "socialization of art," Orozco criticizes point by point the manifesto of the Syndicate, and concludes that its validity was almost nil, either because its doctrines remained inoperative or because its concepts were too confused to be useful. For example, the manifesto "promised combat painting, to incite the oppressed to a struggle for liberation." But "instances of the arts exerting a decisive revolutionary influence upon the spectator," writes Orozco, "must be conditioned by some factors as yet unknown and others of a purely fortuitous nature." Hence, "this point remains too obscure for us to ascertain precisely what it means."

Again, the manifesto "laid great importance upon the content of the work of art, that is, upon the sum of ideas and feelings that it expresses." This notion, he continues, is also confusing, "for it leads us down the road to purely illustrative, descriptive painting . . . indeed, to literary painting, which neglects form in order to declaim or tell stories—to anecdotal painting, that is." This is exactly what happened in Latin America wherever the influence of the Mexican nationalistic school prevailed. (The *indigenista* movement in Peru was cited above as a conspicuous example.) It is certainly significant to find this tendency denounced by one of the leading figures of the Mexican Revolutionary movement— and the one who is now generally conceded to be the greatest painter among the "Big Three."[32]

On the question of easel painting versus mural painting, Orozco is categorical: "The repudiation of easel painting did not occur at all"—that is to say, it was repudiation in name but not in fact. He goes on to explain: "Clearly it was unreasonable, for easel painting was in no way opposed to mural painting; it was merely different, and quite as useful as the other for popular purposes. So it was called 'movable painting,' but it remained the same thing." This demolishes the accepted dichotomy of mural and easel painting in relation to the aims of the Mexican Revolution. It also leads to a more critical examination of the thesis that equates the increasing acceptance of easel painting in Mexico since 1940 with the rise of the middle class.[33] The emphasis on easel painting, in this view, is seen as a middle-class symptom, "for easel works could be privately owned, whereas murals were public property." Obviously, murals could be privately owned, too, and many of them are. The issue is not quite so simple as that.

Factors of taste, of fashion, of education, as well as of social structuration, cultural environment, and economic condition, must be considered in trying to determine what kind of art appeals to different social groups. Referring to the so-called "proletarian art" that was advocated by the Syndicate, Orozco observes that "this turned out to be an error, since a worker who has spent eight hours in the shop takes no pleasure in coming home to a picture of workers on the job. He wants something different, which has nothing to do with work but serves the purpose of repose." In other words, he wants "bourgeois art." If the proletariat had no taste for "proletarian art" (and the evidence indicates that they had none whatever), then why should we assume that the middle class has a taste for "middle-class art"? Why should we assume that a social class, as such, has any "taste" at all? Orozco takes up this question, too, when he discusses the notion that the artist, while he is creating, "should have the collectivity in mind, or the society of which he forms a part." We must first know, he says, "which collectivity is in question, which social class, which race, what age, what level of education." But even that information is not sufficient: it leaves out the matter of taste. "Above all," writes Orozco, "we need to know whether the collectivity really has a taste." And he thinks he knows the answer: "But of course it has: it mostly likes sugar, honey, and candy. Diabetic art."

If it is true, as Orozco says, that "the proletarians would gladly have bought bourgeois art if they had had the money," this is probably because bourgeois art is a status symbol for the lower classes, just as certain types of "proletarian art" would be status symbols for the upper classes. "The halls of bourgeois homes," writes Orozco, "are full of proletarian furniture and objects." Nothing is more aristocratic than to patronize the people, nothing more chic than to go slumming. We are led to conclude that both classes would prefer, if left to their own devices, the equivalent of calendar chromos. As Orozco puts it: "Art interests everybody but unfortunately non-art interests everybody equally as much, if not more." If there is any correlation at all between taste and wealth it is simply that the wealthy person has better opportunities for the kinds of experience whereby taste is acquired; but there is no guarantee that it will be acquired merely because the possibility exists. In any case, only a very few persons actually exercise taste and judgment in matters of art; most are content to rely on reputation and/or market value. As the American painter Robert Motherwell remarked, "A Picasso is regarded by speculators as a sounder investment than French government bonds."[34] Insofar as the rise of a middle class in Mexico, or elsewhere in Latin America, implies the growth of a market for sophisticated contemporary art, one may speak of "the rise of a middle-class market for art," but the concept of a middle-class *tradition* in Mexican art appears as dubious as the concept of a proletarian tradition that Orozco took pains to undermine.

Hostility to departures from traditional norms in art is common to all classes, while innovation is always fostered by small minorities.[35] The murals by the Mexican "Revolutionary" painters in the National Preparatory School were attacked on all sides. "Students in the Preparatory School," writes Orozco, "did not take kindly to the painting. It is safe to say that none of them liked it." Finally, "Siqueiros and I were driven out by the students, who badly defaced our pictures with their clubs and knives and the stones they threw." At the Week of Modern Art in São Paulo—held in the same year, 1922, that work was begun on the murals of the National Preparatory School in Mexico—"gentlemen attacked the exhibited works with vituperation and walking-sticks."[36] The weapons might be different, but the feelings were the same: hostility to the new. The only class struggle in art that remains always relevant is the resistance of all classes to artistic innovation of any kind.

Orozco's explanations make it clear that the correlation of mural painting with the Revolutionary movement and of easel painting with the emergence of conservative, middle-class elements after 1940 cannot be accepted without serious reservations and substantial qualifications. Since 1940 a new generation of Mexican painters has continued to develop the mural tradition along modern lines, including technical experimentation with new industrial materials, simultaneously with the growth of easel painting, which at no time disappeared in Mexico. Both Orozco and Siqueiros, as we have seen, gave much importance to easel painting. The most notable easel painter of the present day, Rufino Tamayo, has also painted some excellent murals. The real distinction is not between easel and mural painting, but between what is truly contemporary and therefore international, and what is bound to the past through nationalism, pictorialism, social realism, and similar anachronistic tendencies. In the words of Myers, "With the significant and notable exceptions of Rufino Tamayo and Carlos Mérida, modern abstract expression has left Mexican painting almost completely untouched."[37] Although Tamayo has assimilated Mexican elements in his painting, he has no interest in nationalism or in the political content of art.[38] He has given himself wholeheartedly to the new era of the twentieth century: "All the old molds of art and science have been broken. A new era has been opened with inter-planetary space travel. And if everyone is now looking for a new language, the painter cannot remain behind."[39] With Tamayo, Mexico joined the rest of Latin America in a breakthrough to the twentieth-century world of art.

The most scathing attack on artistic nationalism in Mexico was made by the young artist José Luis Cuevas (b. 1934), whose favored medium is the pen-and-ink drawing, inspired by the macabre visions of death, poverty, and suffering to which he was exposed from early childhood. In his "Recollections of Childhood," Cuevas tells us that in public school he "soon became acquainted with the Mexican trait that I most detest: nationalism. . . . I think I have been an enemy of Mexican nationalism ever since that day."[40] Elsewhere he explained his view of art by saying: "What I want in my country's art are broad highways leading out to the rest of the world, rather than narrow paths connecting one adobe village with another."[41]

Cuevas repudiates abstract art as well as nationalistic art. In the words of Seldon Rodman, Cuevas "is committed to human values by representational but non-propaganda means."[42] During a visit to Mexico in 1962, Rodman found that the new generation of artists "is travelling Cuevas' way." This generation, he says, is "committed to the proposition that abstract formalism is as much a dead end as social realism." Hence the new avant-garde "believes that if it pursues the truth and communicates it with sufficient insight, its power will be capable of changing not merely art but the world."[43]

The particular avant-garde group that advocates this view in Mexico is called Nueva Presencia and it issues an illustrated broadsheet of the same name. The first issue (August 1961) contained a manifesto demanding a re-emphasis on the communicating function of art. "It addressed itself not to a party or a social class but to all men. It decried fashion, academicism of right or left, and 'good taste.' "[44] The manifesto should probably be read in conjunction with the chapter from Orozco's autobiography previously quoted, for whether the artist addresses himself to a party or a class, or "to all men," the problem of communication remains just as problematical as ever.

The changing of the avant-garde really solves nothing. It does, however, point up a characteristic trait of the modern art world (at least that of the Western world): the frequency and rapidity of its changes. Although Rodman found that the younger generation in Mexico was moving in Cuevas' direction, he also found they were moving "so much faster than Cuevas himself that the twenty-eight-year-old maestro is already being referred to in the past tense." This rapid mobility, this proliferation of avant-garde groups with their manifestos and publications which is occurring not only in Mexico but throughout Latin America, is a further indication that artists of the present day are more concerned with change than with continuity, more involved with innovation than with tradition.

Another example, this time from Chile, confirms this widespread desire for change, for renovation through innovation. In Santiago de Chile an architect and a playwright have united to form a cooperative theater group called ICTUS, which also issued its manifesto: "ICTUS was born and will live while it can show, through the theater, that our generation believes in a possibility of change. . . . We live in an epoch of profound transformations. The theater is not a stranger to these changes. . . ."[45] There is an echo here of Tamayo's "the painter cannot be left behind." The more swiftly things move, the greater the danger of being left behind.

If one were to attempt to translate all these various opinions into a declaration applicable to Latin American art as a whole, one might restate them as follows. The younger generation believes in both the necessity and the possibility of change. An effort must be made to participate in the profound transformation of the modern world. Latin America cannot and should not be left behind. Some groups believe that art can change the world, that the problem is mainly one of communication. All agree that as the world changes, so art must change—even when they disagree on what is cause and what effect. Form and expression are more important than thematic content. Abstract and non-figurative art is a necessary conquest of our time, but not necessarily the only road to follow. Some groups are seeking to communicate human values through representational or figurative art.

Tamayo's warning cry, "the painter cannot be left behind," finds a strong echo among the composers of Latin America, particularly those born since 1920. Musical composition in Latin America has consisted largely of following the various trends of European music, from Romanticism to Neo-Classicism, with a considerable time lag (the actual lag differing appreciably from country to country). As long as successive trends did not follow one another with excessive rapidity—that is, up to about the end of World War II—there was little sense of urgency among Latin American composers, apart from those matters affecting their professional status and economic security. But since 1950 musical composition has been in full crisis, chiefly because it has been the last of the arts to catch up with the twentieth century. The rise of what is called *musique concrète* (based on manipulation of recorded sounds, including "noises"), the rapid development of electronic music, the injection of chance and indeterminacy in composition, the exploration of time-space as the basis of musical organization, and the extension of serial techniques to all the parameters of musical composition—to mention only some of the major developments of the last fifteen years or so—have suddenly projected the art of music into the space age with such swiftness that only a handful of persons are really aware of what has happened. Among them are certain of the younger Latin American composers, mostly from Argentina and Chile, who have come to the United States attracted by the experimental work in electronic composition being carried on in New York and Princeton. Electronic laboratories have been established in Buenos Aires and in Santiago de Chile, and before long these centers at least—no doubt others also—will develop their schools of electronic composition.

It was a Mexican composer, Carlos Chávez, who, in the 1930's, wrote a book titled *Toward a New Music: Music and Electricity*, which was one of the first attempts to draw attention to the new technical resources made available to music by twentieth-century technology. Significantly, this book was published, not in Mexico, but in the United States, in an English translation. Mexico in the 1930's was no more ready to accept modern music than it was to accept modern art. As a matter of fact, while Chávez was at work on this forward-looking book he was also writing "music for the masses" in line with the ideology of the Mexican Revolution, such as the "Proletarian Symphony" titled *Llamadas* (1934) for chorus and orchestra, using as a text the same "Corrido de la Revolución" (Ballad of the Revolution) that appears spread out on a banner in one of Diego Rivera's murals. When questioned by his Argentine biographer about why he wrote "proletarian music" during this period, Chávez replied, in effect, that he felt it was his duty to promote the cultural aims of the Mexican Revolution.[46] But this was a brief and passing phase of Chávez's career as a composer, a product of his involvement in Mexican nationalism, which he soon cast aside in favor of international modernism. Today Chávez repudiates musical nationalism and has no interest in "music for the masses." One can say about him what Rodman said about Cuevas: the younger generation is going in his direction—but much faster.[47]

In discussing contemporary developments in Latin American music, one has to bear in mind that there are wide differences from one country to another; not all countries share the same cultural time. While composers in Argentina or Chile long ago adopted twelve-tone methods and are now experimenting with electronic composition, those in Bolivia or Venezuela are still concerned with folkloristic nationalism—the musical equivalent of the *indigenista* movement in painting. All are moving into the second half of the twentieth century, but some move more slowly than others and will arrive later. This rear guard is not opposed to change: it simply falls behind, while the avant-garde pushes onward. The group opposed to change is the "old guard," die-hard defender of the status quo, making its last-ditch stand in the Academies of Art and the Conservatories of Music (where the past is conserved and handed out to each generation).

The symbol of entrenched tradition is the Academy—whatever

the specific form or name that it may take. In Latin America it is usually an official institution, supported by the government. It therefore represents the establishment in the fullest sense of the term. Conservative by definition, it should at least fulfill the responsibility of providing a rigorous professional training, but this is not always the case in Latin America. Within recent years, however, there has been some improvement in this respect, particularly as regards architecture. In music, excellent performers have been produced for a long time, but composers must still obtain their advanced training in Europe or the United States, owing to the scarcity of outstanding teachers of composition. Increasingly the answer to this problem is being found outside rather than within the Academy, through such enterprises as the Composers' Workshop directed by Carlos Chávez in Mexico City and the Latin American Center for Advanced Musical Studies under the direction of Alberto Ginastera in Buenos Aires, which brings distinguished composers as visiting professors each year to teach advanced students selected from all Latin America. Ginastera himself, as a composer, has kept abreast of current trends without becoming experimental. He explains his position by saying, "One foot is firmly placed in the traditional and the other is moving into the future."[48] It is significant that his Center, founded in 1963, is supported partly by the Rockefeller Foundation and partly by the Di Tella Foundation of Argentina. This may indicate that music, insofar as it purports to be a modernizing force in Latin America and not merely a cultural adornment, may receive increasing support from private rather than government sources.

Such pockets of resistance to musical modernism as still exist in Latin America—specifically those resulting from a militant attitude rather than from mere inertia—are often related to political factors; that is to say, they probably indicate a trend toward the far left, if not actual adhesion to the Communist Party.[49] It is well known that artistic modernism of all kinds is anathema to the Communist Party, since it conflicts with the doctrine of social realism and fosters individualism rather than ideological conformity. The leading Brazilian composer since the death of Villa-Lobos, Camargo Guarnieri, published some years ago an "Open Letter" to the musicians of America, in which he violently denounced international modernism, including atonal and twelve-tone music, and strongly defended the nationalist position based on the use of folk music.[50] He definitely represents the old guard, opposed to change and innovation at all costs—even that of being left far behind the rear guard in the aesthetic advance of the twentieth century. Whether his position also indicates a formal adhesion to the doctrine of social realism is unclear. We do know that certain other Brazilian composers who were once adherents of the twelve-tone method have repudiated this modern international trend, and turned toward Soviet Russia in search of a non-aesthetic approach to musical composition that places content above form and in which mass appeal is the main desideratum. The Castro regime has made persistent and apparently rather successful efforts to attract Latin American musicians to Cuba, so that the doctrine of social realism now receives further impetus from that quarter—with what ultimate results it is impossible to predict at the moment. What can be said is that the two leading Cuban composers of our time, Julián Orbón and Aurelio de la Vega (both born in 1925), are living and working outside of Cuba, the former in Mexico, the latter in the United States (actively engaged with twelve-tone and electronic composition). They, at least, have no intention of moving backward.

The Argentine composer and theorist Juan Carlos Paz (b. 1897) has been the most systematic and consistent defender of musical modernism in South America; his views are cogently expressed in a book titled *Introduction to the Music of Our Time,* in which he attacks the national-folkloristic position as incompatible with the very essence of art. Denouncing and repudiating what he terms "the anonymous tutelage of the vernacular," he establishes his aesthetic convictions on the principle that the large city is the focus of all artistic activity, and that this activity, by the very nature of the modern world, must of necessity be international. Together with the sculptor Pablo Curatela Manes (1891–1962), Paz was a leader of the first avant-garde group in Buenos Aires, which identified itself with the most recent currents of European art immediately after World War I—which again emphasizes the role of Buenos Aires as a modernizing center in the artistic development of Latin America. To be sure, the influence of such groups is at first very limited; but they at least prepare the ground for the more general acceptance of contemporary trends at a later date. All artistic movements are initiated by small minorities and in the course of time find a wider public. Familiarity breeds acceptance: the styles of Klee and Léger are now commonplace in commercial art for advertisements, twelve-tone music is used in jazz and in background music for movies. The popularization of electronic music is only a matter of time. To put it another way, the artist anticipates the future. Not all artists do this in the same degree (there are few real innovators); some do not do it at all (they are the adherents of the Academy or the old guard that never changes). In some eras innovation is more necessary than in others: such an era is our own, because accelerated technological development necessarily brings rapid changes. Thus, on the one hand the truly contemporary artist of today reflects the age in which he lives because he thrives on change, innovation, and invention; and on the other, if he is a true innovator (consider Pollock in painting or Varèse in music), he anticipates the future. But the innovator is not only ahead of his time, as the saying goes, but ahead of his time *and place*. In the early decades of this century Juan Carlos Paz and Pablo Curatela Manes, in Buenos Aires, were ahead of their time and place; they would not have been so in Paris. The situation might be described by saying that the modernizing artists of Latin America have been concerned with taking their place in time—with being synchronous instead of anachronistic.

This concern goes far to explain the increasing influence, during recent years, of the United States on Latin American artists. As mentioned above, the younger composers are attracted by the possibility of working in our electronic laboratories (which are now increasing in numbers and spreading across the country), while painters and sculptors find the dynamic quality of New York congenial and stimulating to their present aspirations. An article published in *Americas* in January 1963 contains interviews with some fifteen artists from all over Latin America—Argentina, Bolivia, Colombia, Chile, Venezuela, Guatemala, Nicaragua—who were working in New York at that time. (There were others who could not be interviewed on this occasion.) The Colombian sculptor Edgar Negret said, "The impetus that art has experienced in Latin America during the past few years is astonishing"—and the indications are that a considerable portion of that impetus comes from New York.[51]

The concern with achieving artistic synchronization—and even, in certain cases, the desire to take a long leap ahead in order to make up for lost time—also goes far to explain the tremendous influence of such an artist as Le Corbusier, of whom Oscar Niemeyer is quoted as having said, "He was always the basis of modern Brazilian architecture, the greatest figure of modern architecture."[52] One does not necessarily have to agree with the last statement to understand the enormous appeal in South America of such a book as Le Corbusier's *Towards a New Architecture,* with its array of dazzling dicta, like "Architecture is the masterly, correct, and magnificent play of masses brought together in light." The impact of Le Corbusier's thought was first felt through the periodical publication called *L'Esprit nouveau,* which began to appear in 1919. On the occasion of Le Corbusier's visit to São Paulo in 1929, a member of the legislature of that state made a speech in which he declared: "When the first issue of *L'Esprit nouveau* reached Brazil, we felt the impact of a great event."[53] In that same year—1929— Le Corbusier gave a series of ten lectures in Buenos Aires on problems of city planning and the possibilities of modern architecture. In 1936 he was invited to Rio de Janeiro to work with a team of local architects on plans for the new building to house the Ministry of Education; working with him were two of the leading architects of Brazil, Lucio Costa and Oscar Niemeyer. He also made the preliminary plan for the University City in Rio. In the course of six public lectures he outlined a radical plan for transforming Rio de Janeiro into a city of the future—proposing "a second town of unprecedented form, carried on pilotis 120 feet high with the lower groups of existing buildings radiating from each bay and passing beneath. And, 300 feet up, a level motorway 80 feet wide, linking all the hill tops, and creating order in the plan and townscape of Rio."[54] The plan, of course, was never executed; but it was this kind of bold, imaginative thinking that fired the enthusiasm of Brazilian architects and eventually resulted in the impulse toward the creation of a new and completely modern capital. This culminated in the building of Brasilia (begun in 1957), of which Niemeyer was the chief architect, Lucio Costa the planner.

Reflecting Le Corbusier's influence, Niemeyer wrote of his aims for Brasilia: "I favor an almost limitless freedom of forms, a freedom not slavishly subordinated to technical and functional requirements, but constituting before anything else an invitation to the imagination, suggesting new and lovely forms which surprise and excite with their novelty and creative spirit."[55]

Brasilia represents the new type of national capital, completely contemporary, based on internationally accepted principles of modern design and engineering, but at the same time idiosyncratically related to its environment. It is also a capital that attempts to give tangible form to the triadic relationship of democratic government based on the delineation of the three powers—executive, legislative, and judicial. In Brasilia this concept is expressed through a triangular design, with the Congress Building as its apex. In the words of Stamo Papadaki, "Thus, the mechanics of modern democracy with its safeguards and its promises is presented to the citizens of Brasilia in tangible and finite visual form: the *triangle* of the Three Powers, a shape that is the most stable and self-balanced of all shapes."[56]

On a less idealistic plane, Niemeyer was recently quoted as voicing dissatisfaction with certain social aspects of Brasilia. Speaking of the blocks of apartments, he is quoted as saying: "I designed the apartments, and they told me that all people, rich and poor, would be able to live in them. But now only the rich can live in them. The poor cannot afford them. Twenty miles from Brasilia, people have nothing. They can see the beauty of the city through binoculars."[57] Quite apart from the socio-economic problem involved, one might ask, Could these people, even with binoculars, see the beauty of Brasilia? And is this architectural beauty important to them, or only to the elite that designed and executed Brasilia? Man does not live by symbolism alone. The full meaning of Brasilia will be revealed only through the ecology of Brazil as a whole, for the planners and designers of the city deliberately accepted the challenge of giving to their work a significance beyond that of its aesthetic accomplishments and technical achievements. Speaking of the huge apartment-blocks or *superquadras,* an English commentator wrote: "The social achievement of the *superquadras* is more real than the artistic."[58] But that is precisely what remains to be seen.

On the whole, it can safely be said that architects have been, and continue to be, a strong modernizing force in Latin America. This is not necessarily because they are more advanced—which is not always the case—but rather because their realizations have a public impact lacking in the work of the easel painter or the studio sculptor. The city of Brasilia, the University Cities of Mexico, Bogotá, and Caracas, the office buildings of São Paulo—indeed, the entire complex of housing units, schools, hospitals, stadia, public buildings, and private houses designed by contemporary architects throughout Latin America—exercise a wide and continuous influence not merely by their aesthetic qualities (as in the case of modern abstract painting and non-figurative sculpture) but also, and much more, by their functional relation to the manifold daily needs of society. Conversely, when an architect is not only ahead of his time, but also ahead of his place—i.e., when his environment is unfavorable to the realization of his ideas—his plight is worse than that of the easel painter or the studio sculptor. An architectural drawing or plan can be appreciated only by other architects, whereas there is always a group of connoisseurs that is ready to view new paintings and sculpture, at least in the art galleries of large cities. A case in point is that of the Argentine architect Amancio Williams, who has made some of the boldest and most imaginative designs to be found anywhere in contemporary architecture—particularly the "Concert Hall and Spatial Theater" based on scientific acoustical principles[59]—but who, with minor exceptions, has not found a favorable intellectual or official climate for the execution of his ideas.

In Mexico, the beginnings of a modern architectural movement date from around 1925, with the teaching and the work of José Villagrán García and Juan O'Gorman, who emphasized functionalism based on the assimilation of new techniques. The new School of Construction established in 1932 treated architecture as a branch of engineering, and its graduates were strongly influential in overcoming the decorative tendencies, derived from the Ecole des Beaux Arts of Paris, that still prevailed in Mexico. After 1940 modern architecture in Mexico advanced rapidly in all fields of construction, from private houses to large-scale housing projects. The University City of Mexico, D.F., in which about one hundred architects are said to have participated, represents a masterly reconciliation of functional and national elements, with architectural and decorative factors completely integrated. The project may also be regarded as a successful revival of the ideal of collective effort that was advocated by the artists of the 1920's.

The term "group consciousness" means different things according to the context in which it is applied. Among painters and sculptors the tendency is to form small groups to promote a specific
point of view, generally based on aesthetic considerations, but
sometimes, as in the case of the Espacio group in Peru, also involved
in political issues, especially when such issues happen to be very
hot at the moment. In every country of Latin America there are
such groups, often uniting poets and musicians as well as plastic
artists, with the greatest number concentrated, as might be expected, in Buenos Aires.[60] Although such groups seem to be fewer
in Mexico, those that exist tend to combine aesthetic with ideological concerns in the traditional Mexican manner. Thus, the previously mentioned Mexican group Nueva Presencia stresses "the
communicating function of art" and addresses itself "not to a party
or a social class but to all men." Although its reforming spirit is
similar to that of the Mexican "Revolutionary" artists, its aims are
clearly different, reflecting the universal aspirations of contemporary art. In any case, the leading figures in Mexican art today, such
as Tamayo and Cuevas, are not identified with any group. Cuevas,
in the words of Seldon Rodman, even "shies away from identifying
himself with his own generation." He is a solitary figure, "better
known abroad than at home." The same is true, though in a lesser
degree, of Tamayo, whose professional career has been largely
based on recognition in the United States and Europe. Some of the
leading artists of Latin America, such as the Chilean painter Roberto Matta and the Argentine sculptress Alicia Penalba, live and
work entirely outside of their homelands. Paris and New York are
the two poles of attraction. But some of those who live abroad look
forward to returning to their respective countries; this tendency
will increase as the climate for contemporary art becomes more
favorable in Latin America, and has already become manifest in
such cities as Bogotá, Caracas, Lima, and São Paulo.

During the past twenty years or so, Latin American musicians
have increasingly looked toward the United States for leadership
and support. Most of the leading composers have received grants
and commissions from foundations in the United States; many of
them have studied in this country; they strive to have their works
published and performed here; and those who are interested in
musical education work closely with music educators in the United

States for the purpose of bringing American methods to Latin America. With the cooperation of the Pan American Union and the Inter-American Musical Council, an Inter-American Institute for Music Education was established at Santiago de Chile in 1962. The tendency now is to establish inter-American organizations in the field of music and to promote inter-American projects such as the Inter-American Music Festivals in Washington, D.C., in Caracas, in Montevideo, and in other capitals of the hemisphere. In such matters as copyright protection and performance rights, Latin American musicians look to the successful example of the United States.

The social origins of the artists vary greatly, ranging from the oligarchy to the lower strata of the middle sectors. In general it may be said that the arts offer a means of social and economic advancement to gifted individuals of all classes. In most cases training is free, and government stipends are available for advanced study abroad. The trend has been for an increasing number of individuals from the middle sectors to achieve prominence, prestige, and comfortable economic status through the arts.

Because so much of the artistic activity of Latin America is dependent on the governments, leadership often revolves around access to official positions, such as the directorship of a national conservatory of music, a department of fine arts, or a national symphony orchestra. Thus, in Mexico Carlos Chávez, as director of the National Symphony Orchestra and for a time head of the Department of Fine Arts, held an effective leadership that he could not retain after relinquishing these posts. Again, the great degree of centralization results in a concentration of leadership among the few who hold key positions.

From all of the foregoing, it should be evident that the term artist is not a univocal designation permitting broad generalizations covering a wide range of social, economic, and political attitudes. While it might be possible to generalize, for instance, about the artist as architect, it would be dangerous to venture more than two or three basic generalizations—such as their urban orientation and their bent toward innovation—that could be considered equally applicable to architects and musicians. And, as previously stated, we have insufficient evidence for generalizations about the sociopolitical role of the artist in Latin America.

So far as we can judge, ideological commitments vary considerably among artists, ranging from extreme conservatism to outright Communism, with the majority probably somewhat left of center. Obviously, certain fully documented cases of definite political alignment can be found, notably among the Mexican muralists; Rivera and Siqueiros, for example, publicly proclaimed their Communist views. It is also evident, though statistics are lacking, that a number of artists are pro-Castro. Within Cuba itself, Castro had no difficulty finding a cadre of artists to go along with his regime, including several prominent musicians whose leftist inclinations had long been apparent.

The political views of the Brazilian architect Niemeyer, as reported in a recent interview, may perhaps afford some insight into the general situation: "Depending upon his mood, Niemeyer will tell you that he is a Socialist, a Communist, or that, like his friend Sartre, he is 'a man of the left, who has had fights with the Communists and is his own man.' In 1954 he accepted a trip to Moscow, where he found 'Communist architecture the worst in the world.' ... He theorizes in a flow of often contradictory generalities, having vaguely to do with equality, justice, Marxism and 'any system for the dignity of life.' "[61] Perhaps this is about what one might get from interviewing a random selection of artists in Latin America. A constant factor would probably be the desire for change, the feeling that things cannot continue as they are. There might also be some agreement on the need for social justice, but considerable divergence of opinion on the means of achieving it.

Artists as a class do not favor dictatorship, especially if they believe in the values of modern art, because they know that totalitarianism is opposed to aesthetic freedom and artistic innovation. The typical contemporary artist is an individualist: he strives to achieve a personal style. He also knows that if he achieves such a style, with consequent critical acclaim, he can turn out a product— particularly if he is a painter or a sculptor—that will bring a very high price in the open market of the free world. He can, in short, become a capitalist by the sale of his work. He also knows that the private purchaser—who typically comes from the ranks of the middle sectors—will in the long run prove to be a safer and more stable patron than the government, whose patronage is subject to political fluctuations (as was the fate of the Mexican muralists). Private ownership of art has become a status symbol. This has long been true of the oligarchy in Latin America, but now it may be taken up by the emerging middle sectors. Let us not forget the significant role of the upper middle class in promoting contemporary architecture in Latin America through commissions for private houses. The artists of Latin America may find their largest potential market among other professional urban workers—the successful lawyers, doctors, judges, bureaucrats, businessmen—who may become consumers of contemporary art as have their counterparts in Europe and the United States (where contemporary paintings are even being marketed through chain-store outlets). Ultimately the matter of artistic patronage resolves itself into the question, Who is willing to buy the artist's work? The purveyors of "folk art" have found their answer: the tourist. The creators of "fine art" may continue to rely heavily on government patronage; but eventually they will go into the public market, too—once they are convinced that the market is there.

So-called folk art was once the aesthetic expression of an entire community, which might be very limited geographically and culturally—a village, a district, a region—while fine art in its most advanced and original forms of expression begins as the activity of a small, sophisticated minority of artists and patrons. In both cases there is a small circle to begin with, which becomes wider and wider as the respective products are absorbed by the complex currents of modern society. And there is a borderline area—familiar in every tourist center—where the fine art product almost merges into the folk-popular tradition, to offer the tourist something decorative and visually appealing. The impromptu portraits and facile landscapes peddled by sidewalk artists and souvenir shops are actually a kind of debased popular art, aping the manner if not the substance of the most familiar types of fine art of the past.

One must, furthermore, take into account the immense diffusion of both folk and fine art achieved by prints and other reproductions. All kinds of "handicraft" objects are now mass-produced for the international market, while fine art, though enormously expensive in the original, is reproduced in thousands of books, prints, slides, and films. Eventually even the most revolutionary or advanced art becomes popularized through the mass media, the ultimate evidence of this process being its assimilation by commercial advertising.

The point of all this is that in today's world it makes little sense to think in terms of art for the masses or art for the elites. The truly creative artist, however remote he may appear to be from the social realities and the controversial issues of the moment, however limited his initial appeal may be, introduces new forms, images, and values that in the course of time—and now more rapidly than has ever occurred in the world before—will be diffused and assimilated throughout the whole of society.

5. The Military

Lyle N. McAlister

This chapter examines the role of the military in the dynamics of change in Latin America. The military is defined collectively as the regular armies, navies, and air forces and, occasionally, the gendarmeries of the several national states, since the regional caudillo as military leader and regional and local forces as military organizations have largely disappeared.[1] Although navies and air forces have been significant influences in certain countries, particularly in southern South America, in the main ground forces have been the dominant service, and the collective term "the military" should be construed as referring primarily to them. The armed forces are discussed from three points of view: (1) as organizations performing their primary military functions; (2) as agencies responsible for a wide variety of public services; and (3) as a political group or political groups.

Military Preparedness and "Forjando la Patria"

The constitutionally defined functions of the armed forces are defense of the national territory, support of the constitution and the laws, and maintenance of internal order. To perform these functions armies, navies, and air forces must enlist men, recruit officers, procure and maintain equipment, accumulate and store supplies, build and operate armories, magazines, arsenals, shipyards, and airfields. Occasionally, they may fight a war. The social and economic consequences of these activities may perhaps transcend in importance their purely military results.

Historically the Latin American armed forces have played an important role in developing the nation state as "a concept, an ideal, and an actuality." In 1806 the army of the Viceroyalty of New Spain was concentrated in Jalapa, Córdova, and Orizaba to counter the threat of an English invasion. Here, for the first time, say Mexican historians, Mexicans from all parts of the viceroyalty were brought together in maneuvers and in social intercourse. Through these associations they recognized common interests and became aware of their own strength. A somewhat similar role is attributed to the Argentine forces that defended Buenos Aires against the British invasions of 1806 and 1807. In Mexico and many other parts of Latin America armies won independence, created the new nations, and provided leaders for them. The more responsible military leaders were conditioned to think in terms of *la patria*, and armies regarded themselves as the incarnation of the nation and the guardians of national virtues and traditions. The inculcation of patriotism was an important component of training.

After independence the military continued to be a nation-building force. In the process of raising and training troops, men were removed from parochial environments, and through garrison duty in distant cities or on campaigns were given a glimpse of the extent and character of the nation. They discarded traditional and regional garb for a uniform that epitomized the nation, and in many cases had to learn a national language. In a more direct way they were instructed in citizenship and patriotism. In the course of their military service, they learned that things need not always be dictated by fate or tradition. The course of affairs could be altered by a command, by an act of will. Firm data on the impact of these experiences are lacking, but it seems likely that discharged servicemen were to some degree nationalized, socialized, and politicized; that they found it difficult to readjust to village or tribal routines; that many drifted off to be absorbed in urban proletariats; and that those who returned to their villages became agents of change. It is likely that these processes accelerated in the twentieth century, as military establishments became more professional in character.

The role of the army in social integration is illustrated by a passage from Gregorio López y Fuentes' *El Indio*. An Indian was drafted for military service from his native village. His father heard nothing of him for two years, and decided that he was lost forever. However, one day a merchant of the district, who traveled widely, told him that the boy was alive and serving in the garrison of a distant city. With great hope the father set about accumulating enough money to buy a substitute and arrange for his son's discharge. He scrimped and saved, and finally sold everything he owned. At length he acquired the necessary fee, and commissioned the merchant to negotiate the discharge. The merchant carried out his commission faithfully. Together with the captain of the company, he went to the barracks to talk to the boy. They spoke in Spanish rather than the language of the village. The boy listened without enthusiasm, and replied: "Tell my father that I am grateful for his pains and trouble to bring about my return and that I realize the effort he must have made to get this money together. But I shall not use it, and I am returning it so that he may enjoy it. Tell him that I am contented as a soldier. I have learned to read and write, I wear shoes and other clothing, I hope to be promoted soon, and I would not be happy back there."[2] In short, he was no longer an Indian; he had become a Mexican.

A more recent example is provided by the impact of military service on Bolivians during the Chaco War. Richard Patch writes:

During the war all classes of Bolivians volunteered or were conscripted into the army. For many of the Bolivians who called themselves "whites" or *gente decente,* it was an unparalleled experience to serve in an army with "Indians." The white and *mestizo* officers suddenly found themselves dependent upon the infantry of the once despised *indios.* For the Indians it was an equally strange experience to see unfamiliar areas of their country, to conceive of Bolivia as a nation, and to become the object of propaganda designed to persuade them that they were citizens of a single nation, no longer Indians, a people apart, but *gente,* or "persons," in the same sense as the "whites." . . . The effect of the reiterated slogans, the sudden physical equality of combatants of all classes, the new knowledge of opportunities, all operated to break or weaken those barriers upon which the former system had rested.[3]

The armed forces have played a similar role in education at all levels. Some degree of literacy is desirable for even basic military instruction, and since Latin American armies have been and still are recruited from largely illiterate population groups, the services have been forced to become instruments of primary education. In the Mexican army of the early nineteenth century, military normal schools were established for the training of officers and noncommissioned officers in methods of instruction, and there was some experimentation with Lancastrian educational methods. In the Paraguayan army of Francisco Solano López every noncommissioned officer was theoretically a tutor as well as a disciplinarian. In the mid-twentieth century, this educational function continues. In addition to teaching the three R's, the services must impart to recruits unfamiliar skills such as personal hygiene, sanitation, and first aid—all of which are essential to garrison and field service. Presumably this knowledge is not forgotten after the soldier receives his discharge.

The military has also provided technical training. Rifles and howitzers are machines. Recruits must be taught how to assemble, disassemble, and clean them, and in the course of their instruction they learn the capabilities of machines as well as acquire basic mechanical skills. At a higher level, officers must learn principles of fortification, civil engineering, the mathematics of artillery, logistics, and other technical competences. In the nineteenth century, instruction in these skills was frequently haphazard, and aptitude was only acquired through field experience. Under the impetus of professionalization, however, old military academies were reorganized and new ones established. In a society intellectually oriented toward the arts and the liberal professions, military schools were frequently the only institutions offering systematic instruction in the pure and applied sciences, and today they provide good technical and scientific instruction by Latin American standards. In Mexico, for example, a degree from the Escuela Médica Militar is highly regarded in the medical profession. As military services became modernized, they were forced to broaden their technical education to include such diverse subjects as motor maintenance, radio and telephonic communications, electronics, aviation mechanics, medical technology, and accounting. Moreover, such skills could not be imparted during routine drill periods, but required the establishment of special service schools. Such instruction not only strengthened the armed forces, but contributed to the national pool of trained manpower.

Historically, the Latin American armed forces have provided opportunities to break traditional class or caste barriers. The nineteenth-century success story featured the Indian, Negro, or mixed blood who enlisted or was dragooned into the army, won a commission, and—through ability, ruthlessness, or luck—rose to the rank of general and became president of the Republic. The improvement of status through military service continues, though in a more restrained and institutionalized fashion. The man who enters the armed forces, acquires at least the rudiments of a general and technical education, and rises to the rank of sergeant achieves career status if he remains in the service, or is equipped to move upward if he is discharged. Entrance to military academies is in theory based on merit, and in fact frequently open to individuals of lowly origin, either directly from civilian life or from the ranks. A commission automatically confers middle-group status, and, as in the nineteenth century, opens the door to high military or civilian posts. Military service also offers opportunities to increase income—an important status determinant. Military pay scales in Latin America are generally unimpressive by Western European or North American standards, but they still place company- and field-grade officers in middle income brackets and general officers in upper brackets. Furthermore, alert and ambitious officers can find ways of augmenting military pay. In Mexico, for example, while remaining on the active roll and drawing their regular salaries, air force officers may arrange highly paid crop-dusting assignments, or even more profitable employment with a civil airline. In all the services assignments to the presidential staff, a procurement post, or a developmental agency provide opportunities for valuable contacts and supplementary income. It would be discourteous to elaborate on some of the implications of the last statement.

The nature of their task has induced Latin America's armed forces to support technological progress, industrialization, and economic development in general. A hundred years ago they recognized that effective military action rested on an industrial and economic base. Railroads were needed to move troops, and troops had to be supplied with arms and equipment, produced, ideally, by national, rather than foreign, industry. Army officers in Argentina and Chile led the demand for modern transportation and communications networks, and the railroads of Argentina and Uruguay were initiated and promoted by soldier presidents. General

Antonio Guzmán Blanco, president of Venezuela (1870–89), is alleged to have done more to modernize the country than all other leaders combined during the century following independence. General Justo Rufino Barrios, president of Guatemala (1871–85), was considered the father of technological progress in nineteenth-century Central America. Brazilian army officers who helped overthrow Pedro II justified their action on the grounds that the emperor failed to appreciate the significance of technological progress and industrialization in the modern world. In the twentieth century and particularly since World War I, the younger, technically trained officers have insisted even more strongly on industrial preparedness. In countries such as Brazil and Argentina, which had established the bases for heavy industry, they demanded that the nation produce not only rifles and machine guns, but also tanks and aircraft.

Until the First World War the services of the armed forces in nation-building were incidental to military preparedness. These services, moreover, were not always appreciated. In 1908 a Peruvian oligarch remarked that the army's educational program might prove subversive to the established order. However, in the 1930's, the military services were increasingly encouraged to contribute to national development. The Cárdenas regime in Mexico assigned them a definite role in *forjando la patria,* and after the Bolivian Revolution of 1952 the reconstituted and remodeled army was to provide a school to teach the Indian reading and writing, personal hygiene, agricultural techniques, and his new role as Bolivian citizen. The declared policy of the Venezuelan armed forces is to provide each of the 5,000 conscripts discharged annually with a trade or skill he can practice in civilian life.

Admittedly, the preceding observations leave unanswered many fundamental questions. How many functional literates have the Latin American armed forces (or any one of them) actually produced? How many technicians have they in fact contributed to the national pool, and what have these men actually done with their skills? How many volunteers and conscripts have returned to civilian life with a new image of the nation and of themselves as citizens? How many manufactured goods have in fact been produced as a consequence of the military's interest in industrialization?

Even more fundamental, how do the contributions of the military in these areas compare qualitatively and quantitatively with the work of civilian agencies? Or if the armed forces had not done these things would they have been done at all?

The Public Service Role

Latin American armed forces have assumed or been assigned a wide variety of public service functions. Although these functions belong to the same general class of activities already discussed, they are treated separately because they are not always directly related to primary military missions. Since the early nineteenth century, the armed services have supported geographical institutes, pioneered in surveying and mapping, and conducted linguistic studies among indigenous groups. In Argentina, the army made important contributions to opening the southern pampas and Patagonia, and to frontier colonization. The Brazilian armed forces participated in opening the interior, building communications networks with frontier stations and settlements, establishing agricultural colonies, and protecting the indigenous population. Since the 1930's, the public service role of the armed forces has been in many cases not only explicitly recognized but officially defined. In a message to Congress in July 1956, President Víctor Paz Estenssoro of Bolivia stated: "The New Army, identified with the national destiny and possessing organized human resources, could not be absent from this battle in which the Bolivian people was engaged. It must dedicate part of its energies to productive work, which becomes part of its specific functions."[4]

In implementing this policy the Bolivian army built highways to open the eastern section of the country, and organized a special Colonization Division of four battalions to participate in its settlement. The Peruvian army has assumed major responsibility for opening the trans-Andean frontier and is engaged in the construction of roads and irrigation projects. The Mexican army has participated in reforestation, public health campaigns, the eradication of hoof-and-mouth disease, black-fly control, and disaster relief. In Venezuela, a special service, Las Fuerzas Armadas de Cooperación, was established in 1937 on the same organizational level as the three combat services, and with its own service school. It is designed to perform mixed military and civil functions relating to the conservation of natural resources, petroleum and mineral production, maintenance of jails and penitentiaries, improvement of communications, collection of customs and frontier duties, and provision of rural services.

George Blanksten ventures the opinion that as economic development proceeds and functional differentiation becomes sharper, the military will increasingly confine itself to its professional function.[5] There is little evidence that this is happening. Rather, the public service work of the armed forces appears to be expanding and, as indicated earlier, is being given more explicit definition. Latin American governments favor such employment for various reasons. In some cases the armed forces are the only agencies organized, trained, and equipped for urgent tasks. Moreover, as long as it is necessary to assign substantial budgets to the military, the nation might as well get something for its money. Finally, involvement in service activities may divert military men from political activities, particularly if their assignments take them to regions remote from the centers of political power. The armed services themselves have been willing to cooperate, in part because of a patriotic desire to contribute to national development, in part to create a more favorable public image of themselves. Recent issues of Venezuelan and Peruvian service journals, for example, carry articles that point with pride to the armed forces' contribution to national life and editorially laud their public service. Some officers have undoubtedly thought in terms of a larger role in public affairs and of justifications for a larger slice of the national budget.

One special aspect of the public service function deserves comment: the Civic Action programs recently instituted in a number of countries. The programs involve, first, education of army personnel in civic responsibility, and, second, the cooperative participation of army units in various community development projects —education, health, transportation, communications, agriculture, and the like. They are primarily counterinsurgency or anti-guerrilla devices. Based on the experience of British, American, and Philippine forces operating against Communist irregulars in southeast Asia, they are designed to create a more favorable image of national authority—particularly of the army—in the minds of villagers, who traditionally regard soldiers as predators. It is too early to evaluate the extent of support for such programs, their effectiveness, or how counterinsurgency will be interpreted by governments in power.

In concluding this section it must be asked again how much have the armed forces accomplished both absolutely and in comparison with civilian agencies? Or, if proportionate amounts of military budgets had been transferred to Departments of Education, Industry and Commerce, and Agriculture, would the accomplishments have been greater or less?

The Military as a Political Group

The military as a political group is an ambiguous concept. Armed forces everywhere are to some degree political. Even in countries traditionally governed by civilians, they maneuver politically to promote their point of view on issues related to national security. At the other extreme of action, the overthrow of a legitimate government by military rebellion is difficult to construe as a purely political act. The military as a political group is defined here as the armed forces or parts thereof deliberately participating in governmental processes for purposes transcending legitimate service interests. The focus will be primarily on a middle range of countries in which the military constitutes a competing group or competing groups in a relatively complex political system, rather than those in which it dominates national life or is "apolitical." Some disagreement may arise over which countries lie within this range. For working purposes, they may be taken to be those which in Edwin Lieuwen's typology are classified as transitional: Argentina, Brazil, Peru, Venezuela, Guatemala, and Ecuador. (Cuba, included by Lieuwen, no longer seems to fit.)[6] Observations deal with officer corps, since with limited and countable exceptions, commissioned officers have formed the politically active element of the Latin American armed forces. Some preliminary statements will be made about the sources and methods of officer recruitment and the structure and value systems of officer groups, on the assumption that these factors have some bearing on the behavior of the military.

Historically, Latin American army officers have been recruited by a variety of methods: cadetships in which selected young men receive practical experience and theoretical instruction while assigned to operational units; cadetships in military schools; commissions direct from civil life, often as political patronage; transfer from militia or national guard units; promotion from the ranks; and formalization of commissions assumed by successful caudillos or guerrilla leaders. Since the turn of the century, systems of officer recruitment have tended to become professionalized. The normal source of a commission is through graduation from service academies modeled after those of the United States, Germany, England, or France. Theoretically, admission is on the basis of merit, as determined by competitive examination. Candidates may come directly from civil life or be selected from the ranks.

Historically, the social origins of Latin American officers have been extremely varied. The Wars for Independence were fought by two types of armies: regular and militia units officered in the main by the Creole elite, and irregulars led by men of popular origin. After independence, various patterns developed. In Argentina and Chile, it appears that after political stabilization was achieved, the elite elements that provided civil leadership also staffed the armed forces with officers. In Mexico, however, the aristocracy withdrew from or lost control of the officer corps, except for a number of senior officers who continued to serve. These contrasting patterns of recruitment may have had some bearing on the differing systems of civil-military relations in the two regions in the nineteenth century. In Argentina and Chile, civil and military elites interlocked and shared a commitment to a stable social and political order, while in Mexico a large proportion of officers had no such commitment.

Beginning in the late nineteenth century an increasing number of army officers were recruited from the middle sectors, although navy officers were still drawn from upper-class families. Today, it is generally agreed, army, navy, and air force officers come largely from middle-sector families, and John J. Johnson finds that increasing numbers derive from lower-middle-sector groups and in some countries from the laboring classes.[7] Changing patterns of officer recruitment may be attributed to several circumstances: (1) officership became less attractive to the elite as the aristocratic military values of honor, glory, and individualism were replaced by professional standards of expertise, discipline, and responsibility; (2) at the same time, increasingly professionalized armed forces offered attractive career opportunities to young men of the middle and laboring sectors; (3) in general the new patterns reflected the growing participation of the lower sectors and the declining influence of the traditional elite in many public and private activities; (4) middle-sector governments have tried to create sympathetic military leadership, although such policies are rarely announced publicly. However, at least one deliberate effort to form an officer corps ideologically at one with a nation's political leaders was made recently. Article 6 of the decree establishing the new Bolivian army declared that "military academies must be constituted fundamentally of elements of the middle class, working class, and peasantry, which in addition to the technical training relating to the military art, will be educated to respect and protect the national sovereignty and the aspirations of the people, and to defend the riches of the country against the ambitions of the oligarchy."[8] In implementation of this policy, the military academy was reopened in 1953 and new cadets were selected on the basis of their class background: 20 per cent came from peasant families, 30 per cent from working-class families, and 50 per cent from middle-sector MNR families.

The concept of social origin needs some refinement before it can be used fruitfully to analyze military behavior. The middle sector in Latin America, for example, is so heterogeneous that to say it provides most of the commissioned officers of the armed forces reveals more about where officers do not come from than where they do. Moreover, social origin must be related to other factors such as regional, rural, urban, and possibly ethnic origins. Scattered observations provide a glimpse of the complexity and the challenge of the problem. According to K. H. Silvert, it is generally believed that Argentine army officers are drawn largely from middle-sector families, but a distinction must be made between those from the traditional middle class and those who are the children of immigrants. The latter are reputed to be highly status-conscious, aggressive social climbers, and may have formed the hard core of the Peronist military group. Silvert adds that there is no proof of the last assumption.[9] Robert Potash has stated that the typical Argentine general in recent years has been not only urban, but specifically a big-city product. In 1961, 57 per cent of the generals on the active list had been born in Buenos Aires, whereas in 1956 the percentage was 30, and in 1951 only 12. He observes further that the immigrant factor has been changing rapidly. In 1936, one-third of the army generals were sons of immigrants. In 1951, at the peak of the Perón regime, the proportion had risen to approximately one-half of a considerably larger roster of general officers. By 1961, however, second-generation Argentines constituted only 20 per cent of the generals. Potash adds that "these changes in the profile of the army elite require something more than a middle-sector designation to relate them to changes in political behavior and attitudes."[10] A study of applicants for admission to the Mexican Heróico Colegio Militar in 1955 reveals that out of a total of 445, 174 (39 per cent) were born in the Federal District, and 209 (47 per cent) were resident there at the time of application. Distribution according to family background among 403 applicants on whom data were collected is shown in the following table.[11]

Occupation	Father	Guardian	Total	Per cent
Military men	63	14	77	19.11
Merchants	66	6	72	17.87
Government employees	60	5	65	16.13
Workers	58	1	59	14.64
Agriculturists	28	3	31	7.69
Professors	11	3	14	3.47
Engineers	12	0	12	2.98
Peasants	11	1	12	2.98
Railroaders	12	0	12	2.98
Chauffeurs	11	0	11	2.73
Mechanics	11	0	11	2.73
Doctors	7	1	8	1.98
Accountants	6	1	7	1.73
Lawyers	4	1	5	1.24
Artists	1	1	2	0.50
Others	4	1	5	1.24
	365	38	403	100.00

Upon graduation from military academies officers are normally assigned to troop duty in their service. Promotions in peacetime are controlled by vacancies occurring in higher ranks, and are theoretically based on merit as determined by performance records and/or examinations. Promotions tend to be slow—except for individuals with influence—unless routine procedures are fractured by successful *golpes de estado* or by war. At the rank of major or lieutenant colonel, a separation process takes place. Certain officers with exceptional capacity or influential connections may be posted to advanced service schools, often in the United States or another Latin American country. The *CIMP* (Centro de Instrucción Militar del Perú) enjoys a high reputation for such training. Other officers may be assigned to staff duty as instructors or administrators, or to economic or developmental agencies. After advanced training, the most promising may be reassigned to troop duty as battalion or regimental commanders—frequently in key garrisons or elite units—and tabbed for future advancement to higher staff or command positions. These men comprise a potential military elite who, if they continue to demonstrate ability, maintain connections, and survive political upheavals, will become general officers. The rest, after some advanced training, will continue with troop duty or specialized service within their several arms and branches, generally in provincial garrisons or frontier districts; they will be promoted slowly and retire before they reach the higher echelons of command.

No systematic studies of value systems of Latin American military groups have been published. The following remarks, therefore, are admittedly impressionistic. It seems likely that officers share what might be termed universal military values and attitudes, but that these have been modified by historical and cultural factors peculiar to Latin America. Thus the military everywhere places heavy emphasis on order, hierarchy, and discipline. Without these qualities, military organizations could not function. If, on the eve of battle, men are carrying transistor radios instead of carbines, if the first battalion is occupying the sector assigned to the third, if the ammunition for the assault wave is misplaced somewhere in the rear, operations are likely to go amiss. Order is a result of planning. Where people and equipment are to go, how they are to get there, and how they are to be employed must be thought out carefully in advance. Planning must be implemented by orders passing in a predetermined fashion from higher to lower levels of authority. Moreover, orders must be obeyed at all levels even if logical reasons for deviation appear. To ensure obedience, prescribed punitive measures must be available. Latin American officers unquestionably adhere to these values as ideals. Historically, however, there has been a substantial gap between ideal and practice, perhaps reflecting the conflict between military values and the highly individualistic character of the Hispanic temperament. The gap appears to be closing as professionalism grows.

Closely related to such values are the concepts of service and duty. Officership is something more than a livelihood. It is a calling involving a high sense of mission. "The army," the elder von Moltke once asserted, "is the most outstanding institution in every country, for it alone makes possible the existence of all civic institutions." The soldier's personal and family interests must be subordinated to his duty. He must be prepared to give his time, his energy, and even his life in the service of his country. Again, there have been serious discrepancies between theory and practice in the Latin American armed forces, which, however, are disappearing as military service becomes professionalized.

A key element in military value systems is esprit de corps. As the expression implies, an officer is a member of a corporate body having a transcendental function to perform, which possesses a "glorious" tradition, sets its own professional standards, and through its code of law and system of courts exercises extensive jurisdiction over its members. It stands apart from society as a whole, and is qualitatively different from other social elements. Latin American armies inherited from the Spanish regime a strong corporate tradition which was given judicial sanction in the *fuero militar,* an extensive body of privileges, immunities, and exemptions that made them almost independent of civil control.

The corporate spirit, however, has had an ambivalent history in Latin American officer groups. Not only do the several services have divergent interests and attitudes, but within a given service—particularly the army—the officer corps may be divided. Rivalries and interest conflicts exist among the component arms and branches. On the basis of age, rank, and professional background, Víctor Alba has identified three groups: the *militares de cuartel,* the *militares de escuela,* and the *militares de laboratorio.*[12] The barracks officers are often pre-professionals who owe their rank to political preferment or successful revolutionary activity. They are conservative professionally and politically. Although their number is decreasing through death or retirement, they still dominate the officer corps in many Latin American countries. The school officers are the products of the service academies, and have received advanced professional training in military schools abroad. They are career officers depending on professional competence, rather than influence, for advancement. They constitute the middle-age or middle-rank group. The laboratory officers are the youngest men in the officer corps. They, too, are academy-trained and have had advanced work in the United States rather than Europe. They have the best technical preparation and the most lively intellectual curiosity; they are the least bound by tradition and are inclined to be idealistic. The school and laboratory officers regard the *militares de cuartel* as fuddy-duddies who are blocking progress, and incidentally promotions, while the laboratory officers regard the school officers with some impatience.

Ties and allegiances within officer corps are formed on several other bases. Graduating classes of military academies tend to maintain strong associations throughout their collective careers. Cliques and factions develop from intra-service rivalries and conflicting political and ideological views, and may be formalized in lodges or clubs with specific programs. Such were the GOU (Grupo de Oficiales Unidos) in Argentina, which advocated a program with strong totalitarian and imperialist overtones; RADEPA (Razón de Patria), formed by young Bolivian officers in reaction against the ineptitude of their seniors during the Chaco War and dedicated to national rejuvenation; and the Unión Patriótica Militar, organized by younger Venezuelan officers discontented with rates of pay and promotion, and affecting some secondary concern with social and political reform. In some officer corps there is a sharp division between those who feel that soldiers should confine themselves to professional activities, and those who believe in a military supermission. The Colombian army has divided along liberal-conservative lines, while within the Venezuelan officer corps the *andino* group, based on regional loyalties, has had great influence.[13] Finally, it should be emphasized that divisions along service, age, ideological, and professional lines frequently coincided and, above all, that the entire structure is pervaded by a network of interpersonal relations. Despite internal divisions, however, officers maintain a united front whenever their privileges are threatened. They have lost some ground to liberal governments, but they continue to defend their self-regulatory status.

Closely related to esprit de corps are the concepts of honor and glory. The officer's honor is essentially that of the nobility of the old regime. It does not involve such middle-class virtues as hard work, exact accounting for a trust, equitable dealings, and the like. Rather, it depends on personal and class status, prestige, rank, punctilio, and self-esteem. The concept can be rendered more accurately in Spanish: *pundonor*. Military honor is collective as well as individual; its attributes are possessed by the entire corps. It is also exclusive; it cannot be shared by other groups or persons, nor does it apply to relations with them. The military concept of honor has been highly compatible with Hispanic tradition, and remains a singularly important element in the officer's value system. Glory is closely related to honor. Glory is won by great deeds bravely executed. It adds to the prestige and self-esteem of the officer and the corps. Throughout the nineteenth century, Latin American officers, deeply influenced by the Napoleonic image and the heroic deeds of the Liberators, regarded glory as the "supreme object of ambition."[14] More recently, professionalization and bureaucratization of the armed forces have weakened romantic values, but it is still injudicious to cast aspersions on the honor of the officer, the corps, or the glorious military tradition of the nation.

One of the most essential, but at the same time most troublesome, ingredients in military value systems is loyalty. Military loyalty operates at two levels. The officer swears an oath of allegiance to the constitution or the state; but as the heir of a much older tradition, he is bound by a personal loyalty to his commander and his brotherhood. Within Latin American officer corps the second bond has been reinforced by the highly personalistic structure of Spanish society, and dual allegiances have been a consistent source of tension within the armed forces. Moreover, an oath of allegiance implies the existence of a single institution generally accepted as the repository of national authority. Where competing authorities exist, where there are doubts over what that authority should be or how it should be constituted, or where the legitimacy of de facto authority is questionable, military loyalty is blurred. To whom or to what should the officer be loyal? Situations have been frequent in Latin America in which the legitimacy of public authority has been unclear.

Values and viewpoints acquired in military life inevitably influence officers' opinions of the outside universe. The "military mind" inclines toward a conservative world view. Change disrupts order, or at least requires the creation of a new order. Moreover, a military establishment depends for its form, status, emoluments, and privileges on the social order that gave it existence.[15] Changes in that order are therefore likely to be regarded as a threat. Furthermore, for over a hundred years officers corps were, in the main, recruited from conservative sectors of the population, or found it expedient to align themselves with them, since they controlled wealth, power, and status. By the same token, the military has for the most part deprecated that central value of liberalism, freedom of the individual, which if unrestrained would undermine the military ideal of a properly organized society.

Closely related to these attitudes is an inclination toward authoritarianism. Democratic systems—with their reliance on give-and-take, their tolerance of conflicting opinions, their allowance for the union of public interest and private aggrandizement, and their rejection of excessive efficiency and order—are distasteful to the military mind. Politics (outside the service) is "dissension"; political parties are "factions"; politicians are "scheming" or "corrupt"; the expression of public opinion is "insubordination." The proper way to realize the national destiny is to define objectives precisely, devise careful plans for their attainment, issue orders, supervise their execution, punish deviation, and reward obedience and success. There is abundant evidence that Latin American officers have shared and continue to share these attitudes with their brothers elsewhere. Moreover, it is commonly believed, though never systematically demonstrated, that the Latin American officer has some sort of culturally derived affinity for authoritarian systems.

The direct intervention of the military in politics, commonly and loosely called "militarism," is the most spectacular aspect of their political role, and therefore has received most attention. Yet it resists analysis, for it involves very diverse motivations, forms, and instruments. Historically, military men provided not only military but moral and philosophical leadership during the independence movement in Latin America. After the expulsion of Spain they continued in leadership roles—often as chief executives—and in the first decades of the nineteenth century they were active participants in the struggle to establish basic political philoso-

phies and forms of governmental organization. Throughout much
of Latin America soldiers took up arms to advocate or attack liberalism or conservatism, or to defend or destroy federalism or cen-
tralism.

Toward the end of the century, when basic constitutional forms
had been at least theoretically determined and relative stability
achieved, the military saw their political role as the guardianship
of national institutions, traditions, and virtues. This self-image
followed logically from their conviction that they stood outside of
and above the body politic and body social. They were endowed
with a noble mission and were the repositories of national values.
They had rights and obligations transcending those specifically defined in the constitution and the laws. At the same time, their
image of civilian leadership was frequently one of fecklessness, ineptitude, immorality, and even betrayal. Certain legally defined
functions of the armed forces—the support of the constitution and
the laws and the maintenance of internal order—also bolstered
the image of the armed forces as moral guardians. In theory, the
executive branch determines when the constitutional system has
been subverted or when disorder prevails. But what should the military do when elections have been patently dishonest and the constitutional status of the executive is unclear? Or when the executive behaves in an obviously unconstitutional manner? Or when
civilian administration is so corrupt or inept that constitutional
government, in effect, does not exist?

The military has reserved the right to decide when such situations exist and whether, when, and how to intervene. This right
has been aptly termed the "supermission." Benjamín Constant
Botelho de Magalhães, a Brazilian military intellectual, defined
it in 1889 as "the undeniable right of the armed forces to depose
the legitimate powers . . . when the military feels that its honor
requires that this be done, or judges it necessary and convenient
for the good of the country."[16] Some half a century later, Juan
Domingo Perón enunciated the doctrine that military revolution
was really a constitutional phenomenon. The Argentine army, he
added, was the moral reserve of the nation, and at the time of the
June 4, 1943, disturbances, "virtue had flown to the barracks."[17]
Even officers who profess belief in the political neutrality of the

military have been equivocal. Lieutenant General Carlos Severo Toranzo Montero, a recent commander-in-chief of the Argentine army, while admonishing officers to stay aloof from politics, declared the army "a legitimate force of gravitation in the [nation's] institutional order," and asserted that in the case of national catastrophe, disintegration of normal political processes, or threat of tyranny, the armed forces were the best guarantors of constitutionality.[18] Civilians, moreover, have frequently encouraged the army to perform its guardianship role. Thus the editors of *O Estado de São Paulo*, on October 9, 1955, accused the Brazilian armed forces of "legal fetishism," because "they did not dare cut deeply enough to remove the gangrene which had invaded the national organism."[19]

In the nineteenth and early twentieth centuries, political action by the military was primarily directed toward "maintaining" or "restoring" the "constitution and the laws." More recently Latin America's social revolutions have given the supermission a more dynamic form. As John J. Johnson remarked, whereas in the nineteenth century soldiers "declared for the national will," today they feel compelled "to define the content of that will."[20] The new emphasis was the work of younger officers, Alba's *militares de escuela*, who, because of their social origins, education, and greater intellectual curiosity, were aware of emerging forces and aspirations and frequently sympathized with them. Although some school soldiers were more sympathetic to democratic processes than their elders, or at least thought they were, they were impatient, and asked the same question as their Middle Eastern counterpart, Gamal Abdel Nasser: "If the Army does not do this job, who will?"[21] Moreover, officers who helped overthrow the Medina administration in Venezuela in 1945 and subsequently supported the new regime discovered that democratic government meant relinquishment of their corporate privileges and, indeed, of the supermission itself. This they were not ready for. Social revolution and economic development, therefore, were accepted and endorsed, but were to proceed under military tutelage. Even politically reactionary movements found it expedient to subscribe to the modernized supermission. Colonel Pérez Jiménez promised a continuation of the social and economic programs of Acción Democrática and General Manuel Odría in his inaugural address of July 28, 1950, made a heartwarming profession: "Nothing can interest an essentially democratic government more than to develop an authentic policy of social justice. During my stewardship, as president of the Junta Militar de Gobierno, I have proved my longing to achieve the welfare of working men and women. I know their needs and their suffering and I identify with their sentiments."[22]

The new militarism has displayed other distinctive features. First, rather than being associated with omnipotent military dictators, it generally expresses the sentiment of the military corporation or major sectors of it. Second, unlike the old-style soldier-presidents who left the actual conduct of government to civilian politicians and bureaucrats, the military often participates directly in the departments of government on all levels. Thus, not only the presidency but all or most of the cabinet posts may be held by general or field-grade officers. Soldiers may occupy key positions in economic development agencies, and hold state, provincial, or local office. Finally, military politicians have groped for ideological or programmatic bases for their governments. Thus Perón defined his philosophy as Justicialism; the Pérez Jiménez government spoke of the "National Ideal"; while in Colombia, Rojas Pinilla dabbled with a "People-Army Third Force."

The overall effect of soldiers acting as political men or political groups is extremely difficult to evaluate. Evidence is fragmentary and contradictory, and the problem is heavily value-laden. The eighteenth-century rationalists held a low opinion of armies. They represented violence and destruction, and were incompatible with Progress. Soldiers were the archetypes of wickedness and brute force. As mankind realized its rational potential, the military would wither away. Subsequent generations of historians and social scientists have perpetuated this view. Armies are aberrations; in an erratic and reprehensible fashion they spring from the outer darkness to interfere with normal historical processes. Thus, much of Latin American history has been written in terms of "Progress toward Political Stability" and "Progress toward Democracy," while most of the social science literature in the field is concerned with the extent to which these desirable conditions exist and with the prospects for their complete realization. Within this teleological system, the military is regarded as a primary source of instability and as an "Obstacle to the Achievement of Democracy." Championship of social reform and economic development is regarded as a mere façade, intended to conceal the urge to power historically characteristic of the Latin American armed forces. At best, the new militarists have merely continued programs conceived or initiated by the civilian regime they overthrew. At worst, despite elaborate plans and high-sounding pronouncements, they have deliberately inhibited desirable social and economic change. In no case have they done as well as civilian regimes would have if the soldiers had remained in their barracks. Even if some constructive achievements may be conceded to the military, the price in lost liberties, jailings, beatings, and tortures has been too high.

More sympathetic opinions are available. Modern motivational research has shown that actions of neither soldiers nor civilians can be explained monistically. In the character of officers who became national leaders, such as Simón Bolívar, Bartolomé Mitre, Nicolás Bravo, and more recently, Carlos Ibáñez, there were strong strains of patriotism and idealism. It can be argued, moreover, that old-style military dictators, such as Porfirio Díaz and Juan Vicente Gómez, gave their countries a period of stability that quieted extreme political passions and provided a springboard for economic and social development. With reference to Brazil Alan Manchester wrote: "That the nation has been able to survive the incredibly rapid transition to industrialization without discarding its basic political structure is due in no small part to the army. Under the leadership of the General Staff the army has been the stabilizing factor which has stopped the political pendulum from swinging too far from the center."[23]

The Chilean armed forces performed a somewhat similar role. In 1851 and 1891, they stepped in to arbitrate strife among civilian groups, but after this aim had been achieved they returned to soldiering. Instances can be cited of the military actually championing popular government, although their motives were not entirely disinterested. The Brazilian armed forces dissolved the Vargas regime in 1945; in Venezuela military elements participated in the overthrow of dictatorships in 1945 and 1958; in Argentina they engineered the ouster of Perón.

There is positive, though somewhat scattered, evidence of contributions by the military to social reform and economic development. Chilean officers broke the parliamentary impasse of 1924, and forced the passage of Alessandri's reform program. Subsequently, President-General Ibáñez, supported by the military, provided Chile with a "New Deal," from which the nation appears to have benefited and upon which succeeding civilian administrations built. The Odría government in Peru, Castillo Armas in Guatemala, and Pérez Jiménez in Venezuela conducted some agrarian reform, passed some labor legislation, and built some schools. Whatever may have been his shortcomings, Perón thoroughly and permanently destroyed the traditional power structure in Argentina.

At a theoretical—or perhaps it would be better to say speculative—level, the view of the military as the primary obstacle to political stability and democratic evolution is simplistic. Instability in Latin America has been something more basic than transfers of power among the elite by means of *cuartelazos* and *pronunciamientos*. It has been, rather, the expression of the "profound convulsions of a society which has not yet found its identity and faces great difficulties in shaping its specific character."[24] Democracy, moreover, does not appear spontaneously when obstacles are removed. Instead, the way for it is prepared "by a series of inclinations, feelings, convictions, and habits of thinking in the minds of the people, *long before* its historical realization. . . . When this frame of mind is lacking, democratic institutions cannot grow."[25] In a substantial number of cases, it has been the failure of an incipient democratic system that brought the military into politics. Sometimes civilian leaders have deliberately encouraged or even invited intervention; sometimes political choices have been forced on the military by irreconcilable divisions between civilian factions or the dubious legitimacy of the executive. It can be argued that if regular military forces had been abolished, contending parties and factions would have devised alternative forms of violence to prosecute their interests. Indeed, armed bands in the service of amateur soldiers and civilian caudillos and *caciques,* rather than regular forces, were responsible for much of the disorder of the nineteenth century. To pursue this line of argument a bit further, in the 1930's constabularies in Nicaragua and the Dominican Republic were certainly no less political than armies in neighboring countries. The people's militia that replaced the Cuban regular army can hardly be viewed as a neutral force, and after the Bolivian Revolution of 1952, civilian leaders—while ostensibly reconstituting the army as an apolitical force—saw fit to create worker and party militias for obviously political purposes.

As to the future political role of the military, a variety of opinions exist which can best be summarized in a series of propositions and counterpropositions.

1. *Proposition:* As the Latin American military becomes more professional in outlook, it will by conviction and necessity eschew politics. *Counterproposition:* Historically, professionalism has been no guarantee against militarism. Samuel P. Huntington wrote of the German army, "No other officer corps achieved such high standards of professionalism, and the officer corps of no other major power was in the end so completely prostituted,"[26] while Alfred Vagts states that "one of the consequences of depoliticizing the British officer was his turning to militarism instead, at least potentially so; he became more inclined to place special military interests above general or civilian interests."[27] Recent military interventions in Peru and Argentina have been by two of the most highly professionalized officer corps in Latin America.[28]

2. *Proposition:* Latin American officers will absorb apolitical attitudes through increasing professional contacts with officers from the United States. For example, officers involved in initial resistance to Pérez Jiménez had had assignments in the United States, as did those who first withdrew their support from Rojas Pinilla. *Counterproposition:* In the words of Senator Ernest Gruening, "Most of the Latin American military leaders will continue to react to power struggles in their own countries in accordance with their own estimates of the situation, their own ambitions, their own vested privileges, and their own heritage. Where military professionalism has really taken root in Latin America, the military's new concept of its role has developed from circumstances within the framework of their own institutions, not from the minute and transitory influence encountered in rubbing shoulders with US military people."[29] Three of the four commanders who staged the Peruvian *golpe* of July 1962 had had tours of duty in the United States. One was a graduate of the Command and General Staff School at Fort Leavenworth and another of the Armored School at Fort Knox.

3. *Proposition:* Preoccupation with and pride in public service functions will absorb the time and attention of the military. *Counterproposition:* In the long run such activities are incompatible

with true professionalism and the soldier's sense of high mission. They are not "honorable" in the traditional sense, and they bring no glory.

4. *Proposition:* As enlisted men become better educated and more politically aware, their officers will not find them so easy to manipulate as in the past. *Counterpropositions:* First, they may be less easy to manipulate for reactionary ends, but easier for liberal or radical ones. Second, they may take a notion to become political groups independent of their officers.

5. *Proposition:* Recruitment of officers from middle and lower social strata will produce important changes in military values. More specifically, younger officers will tend to retain the liberal and progressive values of their families. *Counterpropositions:* Military values tend to supersede civilian ones; indeed, many young men become officers in rejection of liberal, middle-class values. In the officer's mind, the ultimate division is not between liberal and conservative but between soldier and civilian.[30] Furthermore, although they may espouse reform, the school and laboratory officers appear to be just as willing as their elders to employ force to achieve their objectives.

6. *Propositions:* The emergence of new, potent, and self-confident interest groups—labor, industrialists, middle sectors, intellectuals, and the like—diminishes the relative political importance of the armed forces. Recent adventures in government have not been gratifying to the military. Hostility from countervailing sources of power has placed them on the defensive; military methods have not proved appropriate for governing complex, dynamic societies; and military ideologists have been at best inept, at worst ludicrous. *Counterpropositions:* First, it is not certain that the military has taken these lessons to heart; second, unresolved conflicts within a complex, dynamic society may demand, at least in the military's mind, interventions to maintain the constitution, the laws, and internal order, and the establishment of caretaker governments until things can be set aright; third, pluralistic societies are no guarantee against militarism. Although they may inhibit unilateral action, they do not preclude alliances between military elements and aggressive, disgruntled, or frustrated civilian groups, or the establishment of a corporate political structure in which the military plays a direct role.

It is tempting to select from fragmentary and conflicting data portents of declining militarism in Latin America, but most evidence indicates that the armed services are still potent forces in the region's political life and will continue to be for an indeterminate future. The social and economic tensions which frustrate democratic civil government are endemic; the armed forces show no indication of renouncing permanently their supermission; and it is likely that ambitious officers will be available to exploit these circumstances. It may be assumed, however, that as Latin American societies become more pluralistic and strong competing interest groups develop, the political action of the military will have to be more circumspect and more sophisticated. The problem for social scientists, therefore, is not whether the military is getting out of politics or how to get it out but how and for what ends it will use the force and influence it unquestionably possesses.

Conclusions

The last observation will serve to introduce some summary conclusions on the role of the military within the broader theme of continuity and change. Historically this has been a dual role. As an interest group, its corporate concerns, its inherent conservatism, and its social allegiances and alliances have inclined to support traditional systems. As an organization performing professional functions, it has contributed, quite often unintentionally, to change in the same systems. Because of the complexity of the processes involved, the lack of data, and the essentially noncomparable character of the two roles, it is impossible to draw a balance between them. It appears, however, that increasingly since the 1930's whatever balance existed has been shifting toward the military as an instrument of change. The armed forces have recognized, accepted, and deliberately extended their functions in nation-building and public service. Politically they have become less conservative. This reorientation appears to reflect the increasing influence of younger officers who are recruited from emerging social sectors, who are better educated and more sophisticated, and who accept the desirability of change. These officers have broadened the supermission of the military to include the obligation and the right to promote modernization through political action. Among them are appreciable numbers who advocate revolutionary action.

6. The Industrialist

W. Paul Strassmann

Industrialists play a singular part in splicing the past to the future.[1] They are in charge of embodying savings in novel structures and mechanisms, of efficiently deploying a growing labor force, and of developing markets that will accept a rising output at a price not less than cost. If these activities are blocked, the odds are that the society will not become modernized or materially prosperous. Entrepreneurship, in this sense, is needed for a better future. But where ability to invest and manage is largely the result of privilege and inequality of opportunity, of family position and property, it symbolizes continuity with the feudal past.

Most of the questions asked about the industrialists of Latin America have centered on these two venerable facets of economic polemics: performance as entrepreneurs and privileges as property owners. Why do some perform better than others? Does the explanation lie in "objective opportunities" provided by the social and economic framework? Or must one look at "subjective" differences in ability and motivation due to the wayward processes of history, now deeply embedded as psychological drags and pulls? Are the industrialists' contributions adequate compared with the tribute to ownership that is entailed? To what extent can public action mitigate functionless diversions of resources and channel investment into more productive outlets?

Tentative answers to these questions have been grouped as follows. The first section of this chapter discusses the extent to which industrialization depends on the availability of talented industrialists compared with general supply and demand conditions. The second reviews alternative explanations of the origin of entrepreneurs in Latin America. The third section examines the goals society assigns to industry as contrasted with those industrialists assign themselves. The fourth and fifth sections try to show how the industrialists translate their goals into policies; and the last is a brief look at the political strategy with which these policies have usually been pursued. These issues have been chosen not because they have been thoroughly explored, but because they merit such exploration.

Determinants of Industrialization

Any account of industrialists centering on social and political life is apt to imply that the growth of industry was due to cultural values and political behavior. But where other factors are also involved, particularly the shifting foreign demand for exports, this rendering may lead to excessive praise or blame for routine performance while obscuring true accomplishments and needless shortcomings. The interesting cases are those in which industry has grown either more or less than can be predicted from ordinary economics.

The viability of an industry in a given place depends on the cost and skills of labor; on the cost of finance, machinery, materials, fuel, auxiliary services; and on markets. Of all these factors, markets are the most important. Where markets are strong enough, technicians, machinery, and supplies can be brought in; and the cost of doing so permits the unprotected underselling of imports, provided that transportation advantages and economies of scale are sufficient. How good markets have to be depends on the production, transportation, and consumption characteristics of each product. Flour, textiles, shoes, soap, beer, cigarettes, and matches develop broad enough markets more quickly than movie cameras and iron lungs. Where geographical markets coincide with national territories (as has been generally true in Latin America), the more numerous and wealthy the inhabitants, the greater the possible variety of manufacturing enterprises. On the basis of numbers alone, Brazil, compared with Central American countries, can be expected to have double the per capita output of manufactured goods.[2] A higher per capita income, of course, reinforces the market advantage of a larger population. Where the higher incomes are themselves due to a relatively large manufacturing sector, one finds the happy circularity of self-sustaining growth or high-level stagnation. But differences in incomes may also be due to fortunate mineral endowment, as in Venezuela, or agricultural superiority, as in Argentina. Where geography favors labor-intensive export crops—sugar, tobacco, cotton—imports of cheap, unskilled labor have led to situations in which dense, impoverished populations hinder the growth of per capita income and markets. The Caribbean lands and northeastern Brazil stand in contrast to Uruguay and Argentina, countries populated by relatively skilled, capital-using, widely dispersed, more productive, and better paid agricultural workers.[3]

By computing regression equations for 38 countries, using cross-sectional data of the shares of sectors in gross national product for the early 1950's, Hollis Chenery has estimated that for a population of 10 million, the share of manufacturing should rise from 12 per cent of output at a per capita income of $100 to 33 per cent at a per capita income of $1,000. Time-series analyses for six Latin American countries appear to verify the cross-section results. Ignoring differences in size, Chenery found that, using a per capita income growth rate of 1.5 per cent annually as a base, "there is no country in which industrial development is either advanced or retarded by much more than twenty years."[4] Value added per capita in industry was very close to "normal" at the relevant per capita income for Argentina, Brazil, Mexico, Guatemala, and Ecuador. It was somewhat above for Bolivia and Peru, and a bit below for Venezuela, Chile, Costa Rica, Colombia, the Dominican Republic, and Honduras.[5] The high positions of Bolivia and Peru are mostly due to the virtual isolation of Andean Indians from the modern economy, but not from per capita income figures. Adding a coefficient for market size would presumably explain the low place of small Caribbean countries. Chile, Colombia, and Venezuela remain as the interesting cases of industrial lag. Chile appears to have been at an impasse since 1952, while Colombia has been catching up in spite of considerable political disorder. Perhaps owing to the high cost of transport in the Andes, Colombia had separate regional markets for most products and offered fewer opportunities for mass production than aggregate population and income figures would imply, a situation that has changed with the growing transport network of recent years.

Further isolation of non-cultural, non-political causes of industrialization with statistical techniques should prove fruitful. They would make it easier to confine cultural and political analyses, less amenable to quantitative probing, to those areas where they are actually significant. After all, to light a lamp where the moon is shining brightly is pure waste.

The Rise of Industrial Entrepreneurs

Who were the entrepreneurs that took advantage of the early tariffs and subsidies (Mexico 1830, Brazil 1844), the export prosperity and railroad expansion of the 1880's, and the isolation from overseas competition by two World Wars and an exchange-exhausting Depression? In general it appears that immigrants took the lead in establishing modern manufacturing before World War I. In some countries they were certainly not the earliest, or even a majority, but rather the most conspicuous and successful entrepreneurs. Few enterprises grew as fast as the Italian Matarazzo complex of Brazil, the German Bunge and Borne industries of Argentina, or the French Compañía Industrial de Orizaba of Mexico. In Brazilian cotton textiles a national group was supplanted by Portuguese importers, who in turn were displaced by the sons of largely non-Iberian Paulistas after 1914.[6] Throughout Latin America, not only Europeans, but also Syrians and Lebanese, called *turcos,* were the organizers of the major factories. Outside of export processing, however, Latin American branches of foreign companies were rare before 1914, not only because markets were small, but also because leading European and American manufacturing enterprises were just beginning to be large enough to think of overseas empires. More industries were started by wealthy merchants going into processing than by foreign peddlers and artisans repeatedly reinvesting the earnings of small shops, but this is largely unexplored historical terrain.[7]

It has never been resolved whether or not foreigners took the entrepreneurial lead mostly because they were better trained, better informed, and lacking other opportunities, or because they carried a different cargo of mental afflictions. Literate native sons are said to have been afflicted with a horror of machine dirt, a compulsion to be genteel, and low "need achievement" conditioned by authoritarian fathers and servile mothers. By contrast, it is said, the immigrants turned their rage at not being aristo-

cratic into marvelous greed. Hybrid theories, in which one group
is afflicted and not the other, also exist. Latin Americans themselves tended to believe before World War I that only natives were
so afflicted. Hirschman reports an "extraordinary orgy of self-deni-
gration, self-laceration, and pessimism," attributed to race, hered-
ity, landholding, and slaveowning.[8] However, Gilberto Freyre
maintains that the sons of old Brazilian families could have managed the industrialization quite well, but that naturally one must
expect sons of immigrants to be "morally inferior . . . men of the
'transition type,' who are willing to do anything to make a fortune
in business or in industry or in politics."[9] Not the culture, but the
fact of migration, whether internal or international, is what makes
a "transition type." Latin culture may be no more a handicap in
Brazil than Anglo-Saxon culture in Jamaica. Indeed, according to
Simon G. Rottenberg:

The Syrians, the Lebanese, and the Chinese . . . are socially marginal
men. They have no roots in Jamaican tradition. They are not plagued by
principles of fair play. They can drive competitors to the wall or make
sharp bargains or seize the advantage of a temporary monopoly and there
is no community whose standards compel them to withdraw from these
tactics. . . . Disrepute does not lead them to some other goal orientation
than that of gain. White and colored entrepreneurs in the same case
would be brought sharply to heel by the threat of social ostracism.[10]

But if entrepreneurship is due to differences in personality,
based on ethnic background and the fact of migration itself, what
happens to it as a result of assimilation? It seems plausible that
efforts to assimilate are greatest among otherwise undistinguished
immigrants, those least able to bear rejection by the natives. If
so, a polarizing effect may occur. Successful entrepreneurs (especially those entering society near the top) retain their pragmatic,
materialistic zeal in defiance of possible native disapproval, and
therefore flourish. Less effective ones have to salve disappointment
with a little assimilation, further impairing business flexibility and
success, which again heightens the wish to melt into the new society. The really transitional types would be the half-assimilated,
moderately unsuccessful entrepreneurs. Tomás Roberto Fillol implies that something like this has happened in Argentina.[11] On the
other hand, in many cases a little assimilation may improve business prospects, and entrepreneurial success may be seen as provid-

ing the wherewithal for quicker social acceptance. Bernard Siegel reports that Japanese and Syrian businessmen in Brazil assured themselves of clients by sponsoring scores of godchildren and otherwise participating in *compadresco*.[12] Moreover, the second generation of immigrants may require even more success than the first to stay entrepreneurial but unassimilated. Much remains to be learned about the relation between entrepreneurship and assimilation.

The rise of native stock entrepreneurs is more intriguing and in the long run perhaps more significant than that of immigrants and their descendants. Outstanding are the Antioqueños of Western Colombia and the Regiomontanos of Monterrey, Mexico. Both groups have founded clusters of thriving industries; both are known for thrift, finesse, and energy; and both are extremely paternalistic, pious, and politically conservative. To many of their fellow countrymen, Antioqueño and Regiomontano business acumen appears so pronounced that only an ethnic explanation will do. But claims that both groups are really of Jewish descent have been almost entirely disproven, and the early presence of Basques in Antioquia does not appear a sufficient explanation of entrepreneurial success.[13]

Some well-worn explanations hold that self-reliance and energy were forged by centuries of struggle with sparse resources in isolated regions, lands so poor that Spaniards themselves had to pitch in with manual labor. Everett E. Hagen, however, suggests that Antioqueño poverty forged character, not directly, but in response to denial of status by more fortunate Bogotanos, Caleños, and Popayanos. Feeling unfairly despised, the Antioqueño, when given a chance, restlessly sought to prove his worth through economic activity, and to refute thereby the opinion of his disparagers.[14] If Hagen's argument is tenable, a psychological study of Regiomontanos would show that imagined slights from Mexico City or increasing awareness of the prosperity across the border bred similar creative tensions. Further tests of these theories might include studies of communities that should have responded to similar shortages and disappointments elsewhere in Latin America but failed to do so. For the Pozuzo colony of Bavarians in central Peru, for example, did the severity of the challenge more than offset possible cultural advantages?[15]

In neither Antioquia nor Monterrey can we be sure that economic expansion would not have occurred at the same rate without any previous sharpening of personality. After all, in the late nineteenth century, land good for expanded coffee cultivation was more amenable to settlement from Medellín and surroundings than from most other Colombian population centers. Monterrey not only had favorable railroad connections early and tax-exempting governors, but its strategic location for handling Confederate trade and its access to natural gas twenty years ahead of other large Mexican cities were mostly fortuitous advantages. Such luck, as Hirschman has noted, is easily transmuted into morality tales that later generations believe and live up to.[16] Henry G. Aubrey has gone further and traced even the entrepreneurship of immigrants to occupation and opportunity rather than culture and emotion. Not only is entry into trade more accessible to the immigrants than landowning, government service, and so forth, but their experience and contacts abroad give them a relative advantage. Their activity as large traders, peddlers, or artisans provides information, widens horizons, reduces uncertainty, and otherwise leads to early recognition of industrial opportunities.[17] In areas neglected by nineteenth-century immigration, such as northern Mexico or Antioquia, native groups had to become the traders and mechanics. As industrial opportunities arose there, these groups learned to exploit them, and ultimately they established a base from which to expand operations to the rest of the country and abroad.

The rise of state intervention in economic affairs after 1930 produced a new group of industrialists in some countries. These were men who prospered from controls, tariffs, public credit facilities, and government contracts. Originally their chief resource was influence on official decision-making. In Mexico, for example, they had connections with the Revolutionary party.[18] The distinctions between the old and new groups have faded as wealth made the children of the new group eligible for credit and shrewd marriages, and as the old group discerned the uses of government connections. In Mexico, however, the new group was allowed to organize its own chamber in 1942, the Cámara Nacional de la Industria de Transformación, and this organization, described later, continues to advance policies independently of the older Confederación de Cámaras Industriales.

New manufacturing firms are now less likely to be founded by traders and artisans in countries well along the road toward industrialization. In new, locally owned firms in Mexico and Puerto Rico, artisans undertaking manufacture appear to expand steadily but slowly because of limited capital. Former importers and other traders begin with more capital but little or no production experience. Their firms are more likely to run into cost and quality troubles requiring drastic reorganization or change of ownership. The largest and most successful proportion of new firms are the offspring of older manufacturing enterprises, and indeed are usually, but not always, managed by the young relatives of old manufacturers: sons, nephews, and especially sons-in-law. With manufacturing activities now large enough to provide for their own expansion, the traits of industrialists may not again show the discontinuity of an influx of immigrants or some other new group.

As industrial families proliferate, so do enterprises. Family firms may change legal form through incorporation to secure tax advantages and legal continuity without actual loosening of control.[19] Stock may even be sold to the general public if there is no other way of financing expansion, but not to the point of jeopardizing family domination. Few stocks are traded daily. Indeed, the Rio de Janeiro exchange can handle its volume of stocks in half an hour a day, while several hours are devoted to trading foreign exchange and public bonds. Many new firms are formally separate from a parent concern for legal reasons, but the essential unity of the family enterprises remains unimpaired. The Latin American industrialist values an enterprise mainly insofar as it is a contribution to family interests, not as an achievement in itself. His first loyalty is to the family, for he has been brought up to expect continuity and stability only in his family. A typical result of this family-centered outlook is reluctance to merge with other enterprises even when the separate units are much too small for optimum efficiency. Speaking of Puerto Rican sugar producers, Thomas C. Cochran writes,

The barrier to mergers, a process that seemed so inevitable in the United States, appears to have been the same kind of unyielding individualism and family pride that had prevented combination among importers. Not only did the sugar producers fail to coalesce into five or six big companies, they did little to promote joint action on industry-wide problems. The Association of Sugar Producers of Puerto Rico, formed in 1909, had carried on "practically no collective activities on a permanent basis."[20]

But such family-centeredness has been typical of early industrialization everywhere, and is still common in France, Belgium, and Italy.[21] Its ill effects on the structure of industry are probably less than those on the internal structure of the firm. It not only limits the upward mobility and incentives of non-family personnel, but also restricts the downward flow of information and the delegation of authority—both necessary for optimum efficiency in modern, large-scale enterprises. Instead, the tensions associated with the culture traits of *dignidad* and *machismo* (that withdrawn but potentially aggressive pride and suspicious hostility) are preserved in a setting in which they have no place.[22]

It appears, nevertheless, that, as in countries outside Latin America, restrictive family control has weakened in many large enterprises. Control has loosened because opportunities would otherwise have turned into unmanageable problems; because middle-management groups have exerted organized pressure; because knowledge of modern management practices abroad has been increasing; and finally, because the efficiency and morale of certain foreign subsidiaries and public enterprises have been observed. Reorganization typically begins with a family member returning from study abroad, with the retaining of a foreign consulting firm, or with the hiring of a foreign manager, usually someone with a reputation established in operating a subsidiary. With this path to higher positions, higher income, and consequently investment opportunities, men with limited family connections may join the class of industrialists. In those countries in which many industrialists are themselves of recent origin, perhaps mestizos without aristocratic claims, this further increase in social mobility should dampen class conflict.[23]

Goals, Social and Private

Are the goals of Latin American countries, as viewed by intellectuals, politicians, and bureaucrats, consistent with the private goals of industrialists? The public is said to yearn for higher output, employment, stability, equality, as well as social welfare in the form of schools, hospitals, sanitation, public housing, and social security. Conceivably these may reinforce each other, so that more of any makes possible more of all. Unfortunately the conditions necessary for such a happy confluence are usually absent. Building one more factory can mean one less hospital. The factory itself may allow greater stability but less income growth than an export-oriented mine. A deliberately labor-intensive factory employing many workers may not yield the highest possible return, and might therefore reduce the growth of capital, output, and employment itself. Minimum-wage legislation and progressive taxation may reduce inequality with similar effects. Gaining a little here can mean sacrificing a bit there. All these dilemmas have been frequently noted by writers on economic development.

In the inter-war period, the dissident urban groups could see little conflict of goals. Given the presumably rich resources, any honest government independent of foreigners and landed oligarchs could assure both prosperity and justice. Instability was caused by overemphasis on exports. Poverty, unemployment, and inequality were similarly due to neglect of the domestic economy by privileged export and landed interests. Everything fit together. Paradoxically, though, the solution to poverty among rich resources lay in shifting attention *away* from resource-oriented economic activities. It lay in encouraging neither mining nor agriculture, but manufacturing. This mercantilist, state-protected industrialization program was not originated by established manufacturers or intended for their special benefit. Their gains were a mere by-product. What counted was that the manufacture of import-substitutes should employ surplus workers, raise living standards, free the country from international cycles and adverse price trends, and weaken the political power of agriculture through proliferation of non-agricultural workers.

Some writers, among them Víctor Raúl Haya de la Torre, recognized that natural resources needed capital for development and that raising it abroad could involve a lower cost than raising it domestically. But the subsequent benefits would be higher if its inflow and allocation were controlled by the state; and this, indeed, is the policy of both national and international development banks today.[24]

Other writers expressed the view, still current among Marxists, that foreign investment leaves a country poorer because both resources and profits leave the national territory, with profits soon exceeding the original investment. Exploitation of labor means no gain there. Foreign entry into manufacturing reduces growth because its threat to domestic industry inhibits native enterprise and saving. A recent version adds that even foreign technical assistance means a net loss.[25]

It is interesting that some of these early views have been revived in Venezuela, which postponed tackling many economic problems because of oil prosperity and dictatorship. Domingo Alberto Rangel writes that factories are needed to create a solid proletariat, but that the state cannot do this as well as the "bourgeoisie." Given protection, this group will readily turn toward industry, inevitably become anti-foreign, and even support agrarian reform. The industrialist is bound to support "the democratic experiment" because he knows that if he does not, his immovable investment will "suffer reprisals through the irate revenge of the masses."[26]

But things turned out differently, and ideology had to be modified.[27] In the post-Korean decade the public goals of output growth, stability, employment, welfare, and greater equality remained unchanged, but they were no longer presumed so interlocked that a pattern of precedence was unthinkable. In some revised doctrines of industrialization, therefore, welfare and equality measures could temporarily be reduced to levels of political expediency. The neglected sectors—agriculture, utilities, and various exports—could be granted a larger role, which, varying with the degree of radicalism, implied concessions, reforms, controls, or expropriation. Though industrialists were not inclined to agree, others thought progress had perhaps been disappointing because protection had been "empirical" rather than planned or "programmed." Even rancor at the terms of foreign assistance was soothed by rediscovery of the inertness of natural resources and population without physical and human capital, again within limits of political expediency. Interest in the Latin American Common Market showed that autarchy in general could be seen as more confining than invigorating.

But how do the social goals for industry compare with the aims of the individual industrialist? On the basis of his study of the Puerto Rican business elite and a survey of the literature, Thomas C. Cochran has pictured Latin American entrepreneurs as being

(1) more interested in inner worth and justification by standards of personal feeling than they are in the opinion of peer groups;

(2) disinclined to sacrifice personal authority to group decisions;

(3) disliking impersonal as opposed to personal arrangements, and generally preferring family relations to those with outsiders;

(4) inclined to prefer social prestige to money; and

(5) somewhat aloof from and disinterested in science and technology.[28]

In coping with their business problems and opportunities Latin American industrialists, like those elsewhere, above all seek to avoid risks. Expanding fortunes is secondary to and tied in closely with establishing or maintaining family prestige. The wish to build an exemplary industrial empire is weak by comparison, and still less discernible is identification with social progress, technological advance, democracy, capitalism, and other global abstractions.

The sensitivity of Latin American (and all other) industrialists to actual and imaginary risks is well-known. Fear influences the amount, direction, and variability of investment. It makes Latin American capital seep abroad in spite of higher domestic returns, and diverts much of the remainder to commerce and construction.[29] Paint a slogan on a wall, or let distant bearded men send a few thousand hostile pamphlets, and blueprints tend to vanish.[30]

Is there reason for Latin American industrialists to be even more cautious than those of developed countries? Without a doubt, yes. In many cases the chance of loss is actually higher, and what amounts to almost the same thing, uncertainty may be greater because lack of information makes opportunities harder to evaluate. The availability of power, transport facilities, repair shops, adequate materials, skilled workers, foreign exchange, experienced advisers, relevant statistics, and impartial public administration are mostly taken for granted in developed countries, but raise questions without answers in much of Latin America.[31] To avoid using labor of doubtful skill, some factories use more automatic equipment than capital-labor cost ratios would suggest. In Mexico the writer found American branch plants making greater use of second-hand equipment than Mexican plants, mainly because they had better knowledge of where to buy and how to repair—in other words, lower cost without greater uncertainty. But most frightening in Latin America appears the unpredictability of the tax assessor, the labor-court judge, the foreign exchange allocator, the representative of the power or water authority, and a variety of official inspectors. When not corrupt, these are seen as behaving "with an unshakable indifference, like an occupation army in a defeated country."[32] Moreover, a given financial loss can be viewed as a disaster of varying magnitude. Where bankruptcy might disgrace one's family, managers will be more cautious than where it is regarded impersonally as expedient corporate strategy.

But it is also possible that fears are due to imaginary uncertainties, caused by a mentality that suspects malice and rivalry where there is only routine and reciprocal fear. This may be the familiar, self-protective pattern of *dignidad* and *vergüenza*, the ritual pride and suspicion of Spanish nobility, transferred to economic affairs. From it flows the attitude that "secrecy is the soul of business." Reluctance to communicate obviously means less information and greater uncertainty all around. But what good is exchange of information where others are expected to use it at one's expense? This skepticism about the possibility of widespread growth's benefiting all characterizes economic transitions. While ancient collaborative patterns erode with the unsettling of society, combative values are often reinforced. This atmosphere may be conducive to unscrupulous scheming among a few entrepreneurs, but among the vast majority it leads to extreme caution in undertaking novel projects, and therefore exposing oneself to the possible treachery of suppliers, distributors, creditors, subordinates, and government officials.[33] Sharks, businessmen recall, are dangerous only to those who go swimming. No action will be forthcoming unless expected profits can accommodate a large risk premium.

Differences in the technological decisions of Mexican and Puerto Rican entrepreneurs compared with those of managers of foreign subsidiaries, which I surveyed during 1960–61, lend themselves to a game-theory explanation. If all the alternatives may be drastically reduced to two categories, one could correspond to a strategy of operation that assumes society or the environment is malevolent whenever possible, and another could hold that the universe is neutral. Losses will be smaller or gains larger if the assumption on which the chosen strategy depends proves correct, other things being equal. Differences among foreign and national enterprises in ways of attracting capital, handling labor relations, arranging technical flexibility, channeling information internally and externally (and even willingness to respond to impertinent interview questions) are all consistent with an interpretation that the native en-

trepreneurs view society as probably malevolent and that the foreigners would have stayed home if they agreed. Moreover, any loss
"out in the bush" can easily be rationalized without loss of reputation among peer groups back home. It so happens that managers
of new foreign subsidiaries seemed far more optimistic about their
surroundings than cynical "old hands" managing branches dating
back to the 1920's. But looking at the record of the Mexican government in ignoring monopoly, discouraging labor militancy, al-
lowing generous tax exemptions, and letting profits grow to a
steadily larger share of national income, who can doubt that it is
vigorously benevolent toward manufacturing? An even stronger
case could be made for the Commonwealth of Puerto Rico. Yet
it would be easy to overemphasize the relative boldness of American export capital. Economic Development Administration officials in San Juan estimate that reluctance to venture abroad is
such that it can be overcome only by a prospective quadrupling
of the after-tax rate of profits.

The other goals of industrialists do not require as much elaboration. Making and expanding fortunes means maximizing access to
capital, labor, materials, technical expertise, public service, foreign
exchange, and markets, at minimum expense. The drive to enhance family standing rather than corporate prestige has already
been discussed. Transition to a corporate form of organization is
pressed by the complexity of a modern economy, but for decades
corporations will not command the loyalty that uncles and cousins
do. As the Aztecs found the idea of territorial domain too abstract,
most Latin American industrialists have yet to think of business
organization as anything other than a facet of the kinship structure. Cochran reports an estimate that "it takes mainland training and five or ten years of experience to make entrepreneurs
with relatively strong, traditional Puerto Rican culture into effective operators in a business world of hierarchical organizations,
cooperative teamwork, and abstract systems of control."[34]

In the numerous instances in which pride in building an exemplary industrial empire has caught on, priority again has gone to
the less abstract accomplishment first, without close reckoning of
maximum profits. Owning the most modern equipment will have
more appeal than efficiently rearranging what is on hand, but even
layout and flow changes come before serious efforts to build an effi-

cient organization, "the most precious of all entrepreneurial skills."[35] No doubt these attitudes can be partly attributed to the difficulty of tacking toward small or intangible cost reductions when the strong gale of inflation demands attention, when domestic and foreign competition have been conspired out of the picture, and when government subsidy is not expected to fail in time of crisis. I visited a manufacturer who tried to duplicate his Peruvian operation in Puerto Rico, and found that rigid economies necessitated by competition from the mainland were not only essential, but possible.

Least significant as an influence on the industrialist's short- and long-run decisions, because most abstract, are hopes for the society at large. He likes to own a modern enterprise, perhaps, but he does not see himself as a herald of "technological advance." Technology is developed by scientists in laboratories of other countries. Nor is the industrialist's dedication to social welfare likely to exceed paternalistic concern for his own employees and fear of general unrest. Latin American industrialists are seldom dogmatic advocates of capitalism, because they usually have but a raw notion of its rationale. The general portrait of a rising middle class suggested by Kerr and his associates applies: "They do not advance on the wings of a rigid ideology; rather they tend to be pragmatic. They favor a structure of economic and political rules which best permits them to pursue their gains. . . . They seek to impose their will piecemeal, and their assault is carried out through concentration on specific issues."[36]

Family and fortune are thus of infinitely greater concern than the ideological "big picture." If industry looks safe from disruption by violence or decree, industrialists will come to terms with centralists, federalists, Masons, Jesuits, landowners, soldiers, agrarian reformers, or any other group that will shield their operations.

Do Latin American industrialists with their diverse origins and family-oriented mentality ever see themselves as a distinct group and work together accordingly? To some extent they do. Membership in chambers of industry, specialized and general, regional and national, is customary and even compulsory in most countries with substantial industry. These chambers provide the formal channels for exchanging information about proposed legislation or dealing with unions and other groups. A unique organization in Brazil is the Serviço Social da Indústria, through which industrialists collectively carry out a nationwide program of paternalism.[37] And, to be sure, there are a number of political parties that reflect business interests.

But even though industrialists may show fervor against the "demagogic" demands of labor and "red" government, they will not confuse the oratory at the industrialists' club with the problems of sales, purchases, finance, and production that command attention back at the office.[38] Owners and top executives see few alternatives to the survival of the enterprise they serve—or rather, the enterprise that serves their family. A worker who loses his job in the course of political turmoil can usually get another if the movement fails and he survives, and perhaps a far better one if it succeeds. But unless expropriation is imminent, an industrialist has little incentive to neglect or disrupt business operations for the sake of politics. If his business goes bankrupt, he cannot easily get another. The risk of dedication to politics or other group activities (as distinct from shrewdly cultivated official contacts) is therefore relatively high; but since this is understood by the group, expectations of peers are lower in proportion. As a power structure, industry is a loose federation of intensely self-interested clans. It is more sensible to use but a part of one's fortune to get others, especially poor relations and subordinates, to pledge *their* lives and sacred honor. Needless to say, where poverty is widespread but some fortunes very large, small fractions discreetly allocated can be effective.

There are certainly men who aspire to represent the industrial groups politically and sometimes, like Jorge Alessandri of Chile, reach the President's chair. But often these are regarded as ambitious nobodies or distinguished eccentrics, tainted by politics. Industrialists are not likely to succumb to *personalismo* because in terms of erudition and general worth, they will consider themselves the equal or superior of any politician. However, an industrial family may contribute to all major political parties, or, alternatively, a firm will have one or more senior men in each party that stands a chance to influence national economic policy.

Managers of public manufacturing enterprises may be bureaucrats, not industrialists, and therefore beyond the scope of this chapter. Yet in Latin America, public firms mill grain, pack meat, assemble cars, refine steel and petroleum, and make cement, chemicals, paper, and other commodities. One cannot visit these enterprises or follow their performance in the press and see them as happy alternatives to private industrialization. The short-run political goals of government take precedence over long-run economic considerations in painfully obvious ways. Top management provides the ideal spot for discarding eminent politicians and their friends. Publicity is as important as sales in initiating output. Indeed, if increasing sales infringe on the welfare of, say, organized small-scale producers, output must be cut. Prices and wages are set to minimize political repercussions.[39] If low-interest government funds can be secured on productivity grounds, fine, but if the enterprise needs the money to spare the government the embarrassment of another failure, that is fine too. Some managers of state enterprises are undoubtedly dedicated to efficient and profitable operations. These men are horrified at seeing their earnings turned over to politicians. Accordingly, regardless of the general scarcity of capital, they will put every available centavo into new equipment, some of it unnecessary by any severe standard.

The Public Policies of Industrialists

The policies advocated by the private industrialists arise from their dread of uncertainty and a longing to extend their resources and markets at minimal cost. On issues not directly touching these concerns—constitutional questions, education, land reform, foreign policy—they may be found taking a variety of positions. This is the politically negotiable area. Often, however, some indirect tie-in will be sensed, usually the possibility of higher taxes. Land reform, if not ushered in gingerly, might seem a threat to private property in general. The possible disruption of food production might cause menacing social unrest, and force the state to divert to agriculture the finance and public works that industry hoped for.[40]

Where industrialists are notably devout, as are the Antioqueños and Regiomontanos, they may become involved in church-state conflicts. The prolonged dispute in Monterrey over the introduction of progressive educational methods and the compulsory use of government-selected texts in private schools has been led by prominent industrialists.[41] But when the industrialists themselves sponsor educational institutions like the University of the Andes of

Bogotá or the Technological Institute of Monterrey, the aim is to produce engineers and accountants, not pious conservatives. Faculty members may find it unwise to advance strong views about income inequality or checking population growth; but they would find encouraging student political activity, right- or left-wing, even less judicious. On these grounds, as much as the endemic over-supply of attorneys, the industrialists have avoided adding that combustible academic ingredient, a law school.

With respect to economic policy specifically, industrialists are not shy about agreeing that economic progress means industrialization. Compared with the proposals of intellectuals and bureaucrats, their program naturally shows less evidence of a theoretical base. If their self-interest cannot logically be shown to always deserve preference over that of other groups, the industrialists' spokesman has to choose between sounding consistently logical and consistently self-interested. The resulting priority for self-interest is especially evident in programs of industrial groups that exclude foreign enterprises and are not closely linked to general financial and commercial groups. The greater the homogeneity, the less the need to enlist reasoning to unravel conflicts of interest within a group.

These unkind statements can be illustrated with the program of the Mexican "new group," the Cámara Nacional de la Industria de Transformación. Praise for agriculture, labor, government economic action, social welfare, and the rights of the consumer is scattered throughout the publications of this organization; but when it comes to cases, none of these are to be promoted at the expense of industrial profits. Thus, in 1953, its Second Congress concluded that agriculture should be promoted, but that the state should intervene to keep agricultural prices low to industry and industrial workers, and that exports should not be allowed as long as domestic sales could be made at these low prices. Imports of food and raw materials, the Congress found, serve many useful purposes from price control to conservation; but manufacturing would be discouraged by competing imports, with ill effects on investment and employment. The government and foreigners, however, should not participate in expanding manufacturing employment, except "in a supplementary and marginal way," and without the tax exemptions granted to Mexican private firms. Export taxes on manufactured goods, but not raw materials, should be abolished. There was fear that state enterprises, foreign suppliers, and Mexican commercial groups might raise prices monopolistically, but no demand for implementation of article 28 of the Constitution of 1917 to eliminate monopoly wherever it might be, including national private manufacturing. Nor was there fear that the volume of credit extended to industry might be an inflationary pressure. On the contrary, the banking system had channeled all too little credit toward industry (but too much toward commerce and agriculture), and that at excessive interest rates. In the absence of voluntary banking reform, the Congress recommended legislation to make banks lend more to industry and at low interest rates. Toward labor the tone was less aggressive; but regretfully, the true inflationary danger was seen in wages rising faster than productivity.[42] All possibilities were covered.

The older group of industrialists in Mexico, represented by the Confederación de Cámaras Industriales, includes more enterprises with foreign participation and close connections with banks. Perforce, its spokesmen feel that "elimination of foreign or national competition represents an economic cost, and, therefore, is not a progressive but a retrogressive measure, making not for abundance but scarcity."[43] This group treats private banks with less hostility. One thoughtful recommendation was that Alliance for Progress funds should be handled by private banks.[44]

The industrialists' pursuit of their immediate self-interest appears generally as straightforward as the Mexican examples cited, though it varies with economic conditions. During the depressed 1930's, Brazilian manufacturers sought and obtained outright prohibition of machine imports wherever production was "considered excessive."[45] Throughout the postwar period, the Chilean business classes, "though voicing platitudinous denunciations of the evils of inflation, resisted attempts to impose credit restrictions or to close loopholes against tax evasion."[46]

Industry and Labor

Preserving the status quo with his labor force usually comes first on the industrialist's policy agenda. The industrialist does not enjoy the persistence of misery among his own or other workers, or the great differentials in living standards. If labor's share of a growing national income rises because skilled occupations are expanding faster than unskilled, he will not be alarmed. What harrows his soul and freezes his plans, to repeat once more, is uncertainty. Curtailment of credit or foreign exchange, increased taxes, or vigorous competition, while irritating, are yet somehow distant and impersonal. The enemy is outside the shop. But trouble with labor, which usually represents only 5 to 15 per cent of costs, can disrupt operations at any time through strikes or sabotage, and when over, leaves the air poisoned with resentment. Even an acceptable change in the status quo initiated by labor shows that the status quo is changeable, and may lead to excessive requests, and thence to disagreement and loss of harmony. To forestall this trend is the objective of paternalism.

Among highly religious and tradition-minded industrialists, particularly those of Spanish American or Brazilian stock, paternalism fulfills a deeply conditioned sense of obligation. But would any industrialist be surprised to learn that industrial tranquility has a pecuniary as well as a spiritual value? In extreme cases the firm supplies not only hospitalization, free transport to work, company stores, recreational facilities, low-cost housing, and social counseling, but also chapels, schools, and dormitories for single women, at times under the supervision of Catholic sisters. In the absence of detailed financial reports, one cannot say whether paternalism yields employers any benefits in addition to tranquility. The possibility of keeping operations secret and under their own control, excluding government inspectors and minimizing reports, may itself be regarded as an advantage. Fragmentary replies in interviews at 51 Mexican plants suggest that combined wages and fringe benefits were no higher in paternalistic than other enterprises, and lower compared with foreign subsidiaries. But insofar as the differential means exploitation in the economic rather than moral sense, because of monopsony and immobility, it must be balanced against the protection afforded the worker from landlords, merchants, moneylenders, and other potential exploiters. His lower pay may go further. For workers new to city life and used to rural paternalism, these practices of employers have often been regarded as helpful. I will not attempt to put a price tag on the elaborate spy systems and the danger of blacklisting for entire families that, whether legal or not, often afflict the employee of a paternalistic enterprise.

If in spite of all these arrangements the workers' sense of identification with the interests of the enterprise fades, the employer, not the worker, will probably want to eliminate paternalism. The employer's economic advantage, after all, lies in organizing production, not a cluster of welfare services. The inability of paternalism to guarantee employer domination of labor relations has led to its diminution in Chile, and may partly account for the unique, employer-financed and controlled, nationwide paternalism of Brazil.[47]

But the decline of paternalism has not generally meant a substantial increase in labor's power to bargain for itself. Such power leads to the pursuit of equity (on which minds never meet), which negates a poor society's priority for growth and creates the turbulence and uncertainty that smothers the candle of entrepreneurial daring. The 1951 report of the International Bank mission to Cuba implies that things had reached that point around 1950. Strikes were being called for comparatively trivial reasons; job tenure and seniority requirements were extreme; increased benefits were to be accompanied by shorter hours at lower productivity; and mechanization was staved off from tire-building to candy-wrapping and noodle-twisting.[48] To avert comparable labor problems, the Mexican Revolutionary party gave up much of its version of the class struggle after 1940.[49] By 1950 a large part of the labor movement itself had been brought into line, especially when Fidel Velázquez abandoned his former radicalism and gained official support for control of the Confederacíon de Trabajadores de México.[50]

Except perhaps in Chile and Uruguay, the decline of paternalism has strengthened the state's hand more than labor's, and has led to the state's holding the balance of power in labor-management disputes. This development has been to the short-run disadvantage of workers, because government and industry in Latin America tend to agree in their emphasis on tranquility and on minimizing consumer expenditures for the sake of capital accumulation and growth. In Brazil and Argentina, government still acts through the systems of labor courts established by Vargas and Perón. In Mexico union leadership is subject to government pressure, since the labor movement forms part of the structure of the official party and the personal ambitions of the leaders are apt to be primarily political. An industrialist dealing with a nationally affiliated union must therefore have a strategy toward labor that is, in large part, political.

The Political Strategy of Industry

Given the personal goals of industrialists and the policies needed for their implementation, the political strategy of industry follows readily from the general pattern of economic and social development, with but a minimum of deflection for personal and regional eccentricity. A small number of obvious factors seem to determine whether industrialists can and will make concessions that permit alliances with landowners, bankers, bureaucrats, labor, or the military. Is the industrial center the national capital? Is it located in a principal agricultural region? Are the industrialists ethnically identical with any other groups? How far has the political system progressed toward the enfranchisement of all groups?

Industrialists will cooperate with urban middle-class groups and even labor while a caudillo rules in league with a landed aristocracy, especially one that is ethnically and geographically separate from the industrial and commercial center. To obtain a voice in public affairs and remove unpredictable abuses and the toll of corruption, industrialists will let these allies seek a free press, the secret ballot, separation of church and state, and other "nineteenth-century liberties." The allies, depending on the industrialists for funds, will postpone a general scrutiny of property rights.

Once in power, someone in the alliance inevitably sees a chance of promoting his ambitions through demands for further social and economic reforms. A left wing forms. If this wing gains control, the industrialists are likely to shift their allegiance to the landlords, who will chivalrously modify their views on secularism and industrial protection. Where there are social ties and geographical proximity, the shift will be especially easy. A solid property front has usually been strong enough to gain military support and to remove a menacingly active left wing from office. Exceptions have occurred only in Mexico, Bolivia, and Cuba, where the left wing mobilized agricultural workers, among others, and subdued the military. Perhaps learning from this history and its own previous loss of power in 1948, the Betancourt government of Venezuela pressed landowners a bit harder after 1958, but took a more moderate view of private industry.[51] In Argentina, a split between agricultural and industrial property partly enabled Perón to introduce his brand of radicalism. He also made it a point to mobilize rural workers.

A middle-class group in power that subdues its left wing, or loses it, may retain industrial support. Such governments, catering to all except Bourbons and Marxists, are not likely to generate consistent policies. Each group will receive support for its most vital apparent interest but will be squeezed indirectly, particularly through inflation. While the economic pie is expanding, all may go well, but an export crisis and its repercussions can set the stage for reform. A Jânio Quadros, advocating honesty, high taxes, tight credit, and wage freezes, seasoned with international self-assertion, may have a short interlude in power. But each interest group usually sees itself as making the bulk of the sacrifices while other groups generate the bulk of hypocrisy. All policy-making may then be encumbered, as each checks the others through the bit of government machinery available to it. Strife rises, and the society reaches an impasse. The far left gains strength.

At this point the industrialist welcomes the military junta. Controls and absurd public works may result, but these are well worth the end of disorder and uncertainty. If elections are promised early enough, the industrialists may even support whatever "national unity" party the leader of the junta organizes in his own behalf. They will withdraw support only when uncertainty reappears, when corruption does not go their way, when repression mounts and too many students are shot, and when the Church protests reprisals against dissident priests. After the general strike sends the strong man to Madrid, the industrialists will support the new "united democratic coalition," hoping everyone else in it will now be ready to make the sacrifices needed for stable industrialization.

Ownership of an industrial enterprise does not compel hostility toward social welfare. Schools, hospitals, and better housing are not inconsistent with industrial expansion in the way land redistribution is with large estates. On the contrary, they are apt to be complementary. Land approximates being a fixed resource that can be either equitably or inequitably distributed. Industry, however, is a resource that can be vastly expanded, and here the interests of owners and society at large coincide. Helping the mechanism that raises productivity and accumulates capital eventually means raising the output available for social welfare. But even industrialists who keep grumbling that welfare is carried on at their expense (through taxes) will not incite curtailment as long as profits grow. They protest tampering with any system that is currently working smoothly for themselves.

Uruguay, Puerto Rico, and Mexico can be cited as examples of acquiescence by Latin American industrialists in government economic intervention and vigorous social-welfare measures. In spite of restrictions on themselves and expensive welfare programs, Uruguayan industrialists kept supporting the Colorado party for decades after the accession to power in 1903 of José Batlle y Ordóñez. Industrialists were benefiting from its policies; political turmoil was quelled; and until 1958 it did not seem likely that the Colorados would lose office.[52] With their emphasis on land reform, the Puerto Rican Populares of Luis Muñoz Marín were in many ways more radical in 1940 than the Colorados of Uruguay. Local property owners were terrified, and desperately opposed the programs of Muñoz and Governor Tugwell.[53] Yet today the native industrialists are not complaining about their share of welfare costs. On the contrary, their goal of making Puerto Rico the fifty-first American state means a strong chance of higher taxes, collected relentlessly. They accept this chance as the price of banishing the fear of being left alone in the perilous Caribbean. Mexican industrialists today similarly proclaim themselves adherents of revolutionary land reform and social progress. Employers of more than a half dozen workers are excluded from the official party, yet numerous industrialists contribute to Revolutionary party expenses more or less voluntarily. Several have participated in the government. Others, particularly in Monterrey, support the Party of National Action, which oscillates between loyal opposition and intransigence, but even these industrialists would oppose nothing as much as a real uprising with a possibility of violence.[54] On the contrary, their approach is a paternalistic "me-too." As one spokesman claimed proudly:

In Monterrey, the entrepreneurs with their progressive vision of the problems and their solution, have reached objectives that surpass, and by far, those cited by the State as examples of proud and glorious deeds. . . .
    The Regiomontano worker possesses requirements of social well-being surpassing the standards of the State because the Regiomontano entrepreneurs, with Christian concern for human problems, maintain the best clinics, subsidize excellent systems of food distribution, finance housing— slightly more than four thousand units in Monterrey—maintain healthy recreation for the family. . . .

The Regiomontano entrepreneur has imagination, push, and a dynamism—someone called it kinetic—for carrying forward the great task of production. He travels hurriedly in a Cadillac and only needs paved roads because his goal is to produce more and at lower cost, maintaining the standards of quality demanded by the consumer, obtaining reinvestable profits, and he asks only those guarantees he needs to open new sources of employment.[55]

In conclusion one might recall that a few generations ago British, American, and Scandinavian industrialists behaved in about the same way as Latin American industrialists today. Family firms, nepotism, paternalism, repression of labor, bribing of public officials, empires of fraud, panic before sizable reforms and sanctimonious acquiescence afterward have been characteristic of most pioneering industrialists, however creative, in all economic history. In setting the political scene, therefore, other groups will do much to hasten or delay the ripening of entrepreneurship from wary parochialism toward somewhat more open and scientific procedures.

7. The Urban Worker

Frank Bonilla

Of the many manifestations of change in Latin America few seem so consistent and relentless as the concentration of a growing population in urban centers, and more specifically in the largest cities. The typical Argentinean, Chilean, Uruguayan, Venezuelan, and Cuban is now a town or city dweller. Mexico and Colombia are about to become primarily urban nations. The projected growth rates for urban populations between 1960 and 1975 are three times those for rural populations; for the South American countries these rates are 67 and 22 per cent respectively; for Mexico and Central America, 85 and 26 per cent. Latin America will be predominantly urban by 1970.[1]

While the five most urbanized countries rank among the top six in per capita income, prosperity is not an exact reflection of the degree of urbanization. Uruguay, with 81 per cent of its population city dwellers, is third in per capita income. Venezuela, which is at present about 65 per cent urban, has a per capita income that is the highest in Latin America, and nearly three times that of Chile, which is equally urbanized.[2] Recent growth in national product has been slow or nil in such urban countries as Argentina, Chile, and Uruguay, while substantial expansion has marked the economies of nations such as Brazil, Nicaragua, and Ecuador, all with primarily rural populations.[3]

These commonplace observations merit repetition here because of the persistent tendency to equate urban growth with economic expansion, industrialization, and other vaguely "modernizing" forces.[4] Yet in Latin America, the tide of urbanization (or at least the growth of urban agglomerations) seems to flow inexorably, irrespective of advances in the economy. While the locus of industrial advance has been the city, and industrialization and urbanization may indeed be related, Latin American city dwellers have only marginal involvement in industry. In most of the more advanced countries in the region, between 10 and 15 per cent of the labor force is engaged in industry.[5] An even smaller proportion work in industrial enterprises that can be considered modern in size, organization, or technology. The industrially skilled constitute a growing but still small fragment of the work force. To assess the role of urban workers in current social change, some peculiarities of the Latin American city and the labor force it harbors must be noted.

The facile dualism that makes the city representative of everything modern and progressive in transitional societies and attributes the total burden of backwardness to rural areas must be discarded. Every major city in Latin America is an amalgam of old and new; the rapacity of some modern urban types at least equals that of feudalistic landowners. The urban laborers, for their part, are hardly a skilled elite in the vanguard of national development. The typical urban worker is but a step above his rural counterpart —poorly schooled, ill-housed, granted a survival wage by governmental fiat, cozened by politicians, weakly organized when not regimented. His leaders are absorbed in tactical and ideological struggles beyond his comprehension.

Still, the impetus for certain kinds of change in this century has always originated in the cities. The recent efforts at mass organization of rural workers look to the city for leadership. The long struggle for redistribution of the national income, political power, and the social appurtenances that go with wealth and influence has the city as a backdrop and the urban laborer as a leading actor. But the charting of this many-sided fight has until now touched largely surface aspects of urban social change. The complex ways in which the city and the worker act upon each other to protect and perpetuate traditional values as well as to accommodate new values and institutional forms have yet to be adequately analyzed.

The City, the Worker, and Social Change

Sociologists have advanced relatively little in defining a city beyond the observation that it is a large concentration of people in

a circumscribed space.[6] Nevertheless, substantial theorizing and research have been done on such concepts as city functions (the city
as temple, citadel, market, production center, political and administrative headquarters), patterns and processes of city growth, the
characteristics of urban occupations, urban social organization,
and the pathologies of city life. In Latin America, however, writing about the city has been left largely to the Sunday supplement panegyrists, tourist pamphleteers, and nostalgic literary elder
statesmen. While smaller, more compact communities have been
intensively analyzed, few attempts to go beyond the census data
on the big cities have yet been completed.[7]

Latin America has some 24 cities with a half million or more
inhabitants. (The United States has 21 cities of this size, according
to the 1960 census.) A dozen of these are or have been national
capitals—the traditional nerve centers of politics, commerce, and
culture. Largely in the few decades since World War I a productive industrial apparatus has slowly interpenetrated the consump-
tion-oriented bureaucracy and trade that still dominate all but one
or two of these cities. The periodic plaints about the hypertrophy
of the major cities stem not only from the grave lag in such urban
services as water, power, sewage disposal, housing, and transport,
but also from a sense of the irrationality of growth that far exceeds
the creation of new jobs, and that in any case adds chiefly un-
assimilable elements to the labor force.

This imbalance, in which manpower expands most rapidly precisely on the unskilled levels that the urban economy is accommo-
dating with increasing difficulty, means more than that large numbers of people are without work. It is related as well to the persistent small-town, almost rural atmosphere of large areas within
the Latin American metropolis. The city grows irrationally because life in the rural areas is intolerable; the faster the city grows,
the less urban it becomes. Not only are large areas within the cities
indistinguishable from small towns, but almost every major city is
ringed by encampments of recent arrivals from the country.[8]

Thus the concentration of people in cities, especially within the
last fifteen years, has far outpaced industrialization, and continues
to swell the ranks of the marginally employed and increase the
pressure to create jobs in government and other services. The city
harbors and preserves a variety of traditional social elements: not

only the constantly renewed influx of rural migrants, but also the still dominant old, middle-class elements, small businessmen and shopkeepers, professionals, commercial and governmental white-collar workers. The cities, as already noted, are in some ways as tradition-bound as any rural fief. Furthermore, the tenacity of old social patterns is tied not only to the city's past, but to the very process by which it is growing.

Recent estimates of the number of people in upper- and middle-status occupations show that at best, i.e. in Argentina and Uruguay, they amount to only about 30 per cent of the work force. In a few other countries that have experienced economic surges in the past or are experiencing them now, the proportion ranges from around 15 per cent, in Brazil and Mexico, to 22 per cent in Chile and Cuba. Since total employment in industrial enterprises of five or more workers hits a peak of 13 per cent of the economically active in Argentina and Uruguay and in other countries is generally 7 per cent or less,[9] and since most of those industrially employed are doubtless laborers and skilled workers, the percentage of middle and upper class employed in industry can only be minuscule. This helps explain why the industrial and urban revolution in Latin America remains a surface phenomenon, leaving the underlying structure of attitudes and values pretty well intact. Though the political challenge to traditionally dominant elites has been mounted in the cities and led by elements from the so-called urban middle sectors, neither the expansion of the cities nor the growth of these middle sectors necessarily implies value changes concomitant with social and political development.

Conventional assumptions about the social dynamism inevitably accompanying urban industrial growth also bear re-examination with regard to Latin America. There is unquestionably a great deal of movement socially, but it is not clear what this movement has meant for the society as a whole or the individuals caught up in it. The most intensive study of social mobility in a Latin American city (São Paulo) concludes: "First, industrial development did not produce a dissolution of class barriers as had been anticipated. Second, the greater access to the educational system did not produce an increase in social mobility." These findings are especially significant because they refer to a city whose pace of industrialization, in both scale and intensity, is probably unmatched anywhere in the West. Clearly, São Paulo has added millions to its population in the last few decades and continues monthly to incorporate thousands of new workers, now chiefly rural migrants, into the industrial sphere. But Bertram Hutchinson could find no evidence of an acceleration in the rate of upward social movement since the turn of the century.[10] There were, to be sure, important changes in the *kinds* of occupations that people moving up socially were entering, and concurrently, important shifts in the proportions occupying certain occupational strata. But actual *rates* of movement from one stratum to another remained fairly constant over the period studied, with self-recruitment most characteristic of the highest and lowest strata.

Furthermore, the standard findings regarding the personality characteristics of socially mobile individuals and the impact of mobility on personality may be seriously incomplete. It may turn out that insofar as mobility is oriented toward occupations or social groups whose status and style are importantly rooted in traditional values (which remains true of most middle- and upper-status occupations in urban Latin America), mobility, far from impelling change, serves to reinforce tradition.[11]

Yet despite evidence of direct and subtle survivals of older values and forms of social organization, the urban experience seems to have a decisive impact on people. Romanticizing about the persistent yearning for a "return to the land" and the wholesome moral consistency and affective solidarity of rural life notwithstanding, the mass exodus to the cities continues. It does not seem too great a task to make confirmed city people out of rural migrants, but the reverse seems almost impossible. This is in part linked to what may be the most crucial difference between city and country in Latin America: the city is literate. It monopolizes all higher education, and provides for the rural areas a poor and incomplete version of its own deficient primary school programs. The city arms the worker in a way as yet unknown to his rural counterpart. The city worker may in many cases be as liable to economic exploitation and political manipulation as the worker on the land, but he is increasingly literate and there is strong pressure to educate him further. Most change that has occurred in the cities reflects a multi-faceted competition for the basic determinants of social position and power—education, money, and political influence. Willingness to concede new educational opportunities to workers far exceeds the disposition to grant them a greater share of the national product or political power.

On one level, substantial changes seem to have occurred in the last half century in the overall distribution of social position in Latin America. The middle sectors, for example, have grown greatly in numbers. Yet one cannot escape the feeling that in some fundamental way, nothing has changed. The gains of some middle- and most working-class groups have been superficial, slow, and precarious. Moreover, objective reapportionments of education, money, and political influence do not appear to have precipitated real changes in the values that affect the acquisition and use of these resources. That is to say, the histories of social movements, and even the biographies of radical leaders, generally chronicle the progressive diversion, muffling, or accommodation of protest, and the ultimate revelation of its human agents as not basically different from those they had opposed. Most social history and biography in Latin America consequently concludes on a note of frustration. The impact on the society at large of changes in power has generally been diffuse and tenuous. The task of redefining areas and sources of value change that can bring rationality and efficiency as well as broader loyalties to bear on the use of economic resources, political power, and the cultural capital of Latin American societies is only beginning.

Education is of central concern here for many reasons. It has always been presumed a powerful instrument for social change. It has flourished almost exclusively in the city. Today education is a passionately desired social asset in short supply, and more clearly than ever a vital element in future development. Yet despite the general commitment to the expansion and diffusion of educational opportunities, the schools still largely reflect existing social rigidities rather than the dynamics of directed change. In the major cities, the basic goal of universal literacy is close to realization for the youngest generation. As the pressures mount for a rational expansion and qualitative improvement of education, the basic issue to be settled will be who shall control educational policy. Beyond this, the question becomes how much of what kind of education will be programmed for whom.

The middle-class monopoly over secondary and university education—not only effective in public education, but increasing in proliferating private, mainly religiously sponsored institutions—will be confronted with a double challenge from the working class. The first demand will be for the improvement and extension of primary education to prepare more than a select handful for the secondary level. The second demand will be for the allocation of resources to good, free, public secondary schools and universities and an end to public subsidy of private schools. These pressures are not likely to alter the quality of education initially. On the contrary, the working-class drive for more education is likely to imitate the content and style already established by the middle sectors rather than affirm new values. At any rate, in studying the impact of city life on workers, it may be more fruitful for the present to think of the city as a school (including more than the formal educational apparatus) than as a factory.

The city not only opens the door to literacy, but also admits the worker to a new world of consumption. The city's hold over consumption in Latin America is almost as complete as its monopoly of learning, and though the worker's share in this consumption may remain marginal, the desire for it is an explicit goal of migration to the city. Moreover, the urban experience itself tends to stimulate consumption demands further. Cries of alarm that the unchecked growth of cities and an imprudent expansion of education are outpacing economic growth and employment opportunities flow largely from the view of the city as a voracious consumer of goods and services and awakener of insatiable appetites. A principal feature of the grave imbalances in income distribution in Latin America, of course, is the sharp difference in per capita income between urban and rural areas. The per capita income in Brazil's almost entirely urban Guanabara state, for example, is ten times that of chiefly rural Piauí. The minimum salary, which tends to become the prevailing wage for the mass of unskilled urban manpower, was in 1960 about $50 a month in the capital of Guanabara state (Rio de Janeiro) and $18 in Teresina, the capital of Piauí.[12] Yet these minimum wages remain subsistence wages; gains in real income for workers have been meager, insecure, and won at great cost. The capitalization of new ventures and plant expansion through high profits, along with the abundance of unskilled labor, have combined to keep wages low, despite the partial political effectiveness of the workers' demands for a living wage. In the chronic inflationary situations characteristic of Latin America, wage scales advance along with the cost of living, but rarely lead prices for any significant period of time. Consumption patterns of working-class families do not sustain the proposition that much inflationary pressure stems from their demands for consumer goods besides the basic essentials.[13]

The weight of new consumption demands from workers in the city probably falls most heavily on government services. The maintenance of depressed wage scales increases dependence on government for a wide variety of wholly or partially subsidized services. Substantial areas in every city still await "urbanization"—the construction of permanent housing and streets, the provision of a water supply, power, sewerage, basic transport, health services, and police protection. Consequently, the workers' consumption demands are felt less as individual economic pressures in the market place than as the political objectives of a class. This is not to discount the impact of such things as advertising (the expenditures for which very likely outrun those for education in many cities), or the mere propinquity of highly publicized consumption opportunities from which the worker is barred. The point is, rather, that notwithstanding reports of sybaritic living in city slums, city life remains for the mass a life of poverty and accentuated deprivation.

The third and perhaps most important redistribution in the city has been in the realm of political power. This shift of power, or at least of certain types of political control, from a small circle of land-based oligarchs to a broad and shifting alliance of urban-based middle-sector and working-class groups has been well documented for most countries. Labor's role in this long and sometimes savage struggle has had less attention, but its main outline is well established.[14] The Marxist-oriented literature on the theme tends to push the history of the conflict as far back in time as possible, pointing to early insurrections and flashes of rebellion as part of a continuing class struggle. It attempts to identify and glorify those leaders of authentically proletarian or worker origins, and to stress those gains won through heroic activism and resistance.[15] The present power of the shaky alliances of middle- and working-class groups rests largely on their dominance at the polls at a time when

the vote is less and less manipulable and resistance to the flagrant
disregard of electoral decisions is deepening. Still, the worker cannot realistically look to the patient exercise of the franchise as his
chief weapon. The capacity to bring production to a halt, to para-
lyze city services (especially transport), and to unleash public disorder remains the ultimate base of labor's power. Such extreme
measures will be adopted so long as more moderate procedures
seem to leave the present structure of privilege unshaken.

Actually, despite periodic waves of unrest, sabotage, rioting,
and insurrection, the characteristic mark of Latin American labor
has been not its militancy, but its passivity in the face of great
deprivation and long-standing abuses. Radicalism and political
activism among workers is a by-product of city life, but is by no
means characteristic of all or even most workers in the city. Still,
unlike the drive for better wages and consumption standards or
for more education that impels the worker cityward, the perceived
need, opportunity, and taste for politics are city-born. With few
and largely quite recent exceptions, labor organization has been
city-bred and city-bound.

Ironically, the political skills, organizational strength, and access to power that rural migrants have acquired in the city have
never generated urban pressure for rural reform. The recent ar-
rival seems shortly no more concerned over what he left behind
than the veteran city dwellers, who have always been comfortably
oblivious to the distress of rural Latin Americans. Until recently,
the indifference of organized labor to problems of agrarian reform
matched that of any sector of urban society. In part that indifference has been a realistic acceptance of the limited capabilities of
union organization. The task of organizing rural workers, even
when seen simply in terms of the availability of money and men,
is staggering. To some extent the concessions granted workers in
the city have been based implicitly on the maintenance of the
status quo outside the limits of the cities. When one adds to this
the sure knowledge that in most countries every serious attack on
the sacred preserves of landowners has been met with uncompro-
mising repression, it is not hard to understand why it is only recently that organized labor has joined the chorus calling for the
social emancipation of rural workers.

The labor unions are now competing for leadership of the

groups of rural wage workers, tenants, and small landholders beginning to stir throughout Latin America. As the rural electorate
grows and voters free themselves from traditional controls, urban
interest in the rural worker has been awakened. The flight of rural
people into the cities has finally forced rural problems into the
national consciousness, provoking a counter-invasion of rural areas
by city-based reformers. But, for the moment, union action in this
sphere is largely limited to verbal pronouncements. Rural reform
has become one more resolution in the standard package that labor
conferences dutifully vote. Despite their stale rhetoric, such reso-
lutions, covering as they do practically all facets of international
and national politics, are often the outcome of hard contention
among leading factions at national and international meetings.
The mass of workers, organized or not, is far removed from such
concerns. The labor union is at once extravagantly political, its
leadership pursuing ideological refinements bordering on the bi-
zarre, and politically inert in its rank and file.[16]

More subtly, the city politicizes by virtue of the government's
physical and psychological presence, which is only feebly felt in
rural areas of Latin America. This is especially true of the government's impact on labor, which within the city is extensively and
fairly effectively regulated, and in the country remains largely beyond the reach of such controls. Labor conditions are more extensively and effectively regulated than any other aspect of business
in Latin America.[17] It is often alleged that government fiat, rather
than union action, accounts for labor's major gains. Business
sources routinely complain about the burden of "uneconomic"
fringe benefits, which in some cases amount to as much as 50 or
60 per cent of wages. But whatever the real impact on the national economy of elaborate social legislation, genuine benefits
to needy workers are generally recognized to be well below the
statutory definitions—and extremely selective in the bargain. The
military and the police, government employees, certain professional and white-collar workers, skilled operatives in selected industries—these are, in practice, the main beneficiaries of existing
laws affecting wage-earning and salaried workers. In Latin America, as elsewhere, the most needy seem to benefit least from the welfare state.[18] For the city worker, the state nevertheless becomes the
ostensible champion and guarantor of new gains. The gradual con-

solidation of state power and development of political loyalties focused on state and nation has been a primarily urban process. The nation has taken shape as an organic entity primarily within the cities; for the rural worker, migration to the city brings the first encounter with the national community.

The city then has meant four major changes for the worker. It has incorporated him, albeit marginally, into the nation's main consumption centers. It has opened the way to literacy and gradually more extended education. It has provided him the conditions and instruments for a defensive class organization, the labor union. And it has alerted him to the existence of a central mechanism of political power that can be made responsive to his needs.

The city, of course, serves not only the worker, but all who live within its confines in closely analogous ways. We must therefore try to define and locate the urban worker, with whom this essay is primarily concerned. Reliable detailed data about the occupational distribution of the wage-earning work force in cities are scarce, and rarely directly comparable from one city to another. But some useful generalizations can be ventured on the basis of what we know.[19] Only a small fraction of the work force is in industry, and of those in industry only a small proportion have industrial skills or work in plants that can be regarded as "modern" in size, technology, or management. The small proprietary enterprise, family firm, and partnership remain dominant, not only in numbers, but in the proportion of the work force they absorb and the total value of their production.[20] The average wage earner is unskilled, and only marginally or insecurely employed in menial services or unspecialized tasks in construction and manufacturing. The high proportion of "self-employed" persons to some extent merely masks unemployment, and the dissipation of considerable entrepreneurial talent and drive in a ferocious and often degrading competition to stay alive. Legally fixed low wage scales, the abundant labor supply, and inflation that is chronic when not acute create a treadmill on which the worker must constantly struggle for no more than a subsistence wage. Sharp differentials in wage scales and bargaining power between skilled and unskilled workers, and between blue-collar and white-collar (including technical and lower management) occupations, serve to block effective working-class solidarity. The existence not only of separate unions, but also of wholly separate machinery for dealing with the different labor categories within certain firms and governments is a further barrier to labor unity.

Except for modest industrial apprenticeship programs and vocational schooling in a few countries, training for skilled occupations remains almost entirely in the hands of management—that is, it takes place on the job. In the larger firms, particularly those with international operations, screening of personnel by intelligence and personality tests is increasingly commonplace, even for unskilled jobs. The actual effectiveness of such personnel-selection techniques in ensuring production efficiency and company harmony is by no means certain. Little is known about how such tests are actually used. Nevertheless, these and other features of the "rationalization" of recruitment for industrial work may have some disquieting human and political implications, particularly in the Latin American setting. The conventionally recognized dangers of such methods, for example, take on a special character when they are applied on a labor pool that by and large (1) is in desperate need of work or intensely desires a particular kind of job; (2) is only recently removed from a work milieu in which strong authority and dependency prevail; (3) is poorly educated and unfamiliar with testing processes; and (4) is only beginning to see the potential efficacy of worker organization independent of management.

Beyond these aspects of the recruitment process, problems of turnover and absenteeism seem to be clearly more a function of the existing structure of employment than of any cultural hangover or built-in incapacity to adjust to the demands of urban or industrial employment. Commitment and productivity prevail where working conditions support them. At the unskilled level, the constant floating from job to job in search of quite small advantages largely reflects the insecurity of most jobs and the inadequacy of wages. At the higher levels, where skills are at a premium, the element of competition among employers for the limited pool of already experienced workers also contributes to labor turnover.

Thus the law, the prescriptions of social status, and the degree and security of commitment to industrial work sharply differentiate categories of workers. But the workers themselves are in fact likely to be jumbled together residentially and socially. The term "urban wage earner," even restricted to non-supervisory laborers

with or without specialization or specific skills, covers a quite heterogeneous group. This population not only is diverse in composition and occupation, but also shares many of the social characteristics of some non-worker groups. In place of work and residence,
income, education, social origins, political associations, and union
activity there is considerable overlap with groups who cannot be
classed as laborers. Thus, while it has been possible to discriminate
part of the meaning of urban life for workers and especially for
the new arrivals from the countryside, the far more complex task
of tracing the impact of this experience on specific sectors of the
urban labor force is more than can be attempted here.

Working in the opposite direction, that is, in describing the impact on the city of the workers' presence, and particularly of the
worker as an organized force, similar limitations must be acknowl-
edged. By and large, it is not possible to isolate or pinpoint sources
of action and their effects—to say, for example, that a particular
union or occupational sector touched off a given process. While a
fair amount is known about the impact of labor groups as organized collectivities, the underlying effects of the urban work experience, including union membership, on basic attitudes and values
are only beginning to be explored.

The Labor Union

The growth of organized labor as a political and economic force
has been a central feature of political change in Latin America for
the last fifty years. Labor organization has not escaped or entirely
transcended the political ailments of these countries. Trade unionism has been beset by factionalism, driven to unnecessary crises by
extremists, and splintered by ideological hair-splitting over the
true mission of labor organization. Labor unions have been the
prey of irresponsible and self-seeking leaders as well as the tools
of stronger political forces that have not hesitated to sacrifice the
interests and even the lives of workers to achieve their own objectives. Yet few substantial rearrangements of political power have
occurred without the support of workers. Labor organization may
not have achieved a great deal in modernizing Latin American
politics, but it has transmitted democratic values even where imperfectly practiced. The readiness of the union to attack injustice
and resist political oppression has forced a degree of moderation

on other political forces. Labor leaders, whatever their defects, have shown courage, self-sacrifice, political acumen, humanity, and social conscience that measure very favorably against the qualities of leadership in other social sectors.

There are no hard data on the number of organized workers in Latin America. In 1955 the total was put by one source at about twelve and a half million.[21] A current estimate by the regional ICFTU office, Organización Regional Interamericana de Trabajadores (ORIT), fixes its affiliated strength at approximately twelve million. Of this number, some two and a half million represent groups linked to international trade secretariats who may or may not be also directly affiliated with ORIT and therefore may have been counted twice. According to ORIT, the equivalent of about 1 per cent of its own affiliation (some 120,000 outside Cuba) now belong to the rival Confederación de Trabajadores de América Latina (CTAL), which is the Latin American arm of the Communist World Federation of Trade Unions. Efforts to replace CTAL with a new and invigorated Marxist central organization were apparently foundering during 1962.[22] Another 60,000 or so workers belong to a third confederation of Christian trade unionists, Confederación Latino Americana de Sindicatos Cristianos (CLASC). The Peronist international labor organization, Agrupación de Trabajadores Latino Americanos Sindicalizados (ATLAS), has passed out of existence, though ORIT still claims only about 240,000 of Argentina's three to four million organized workers.[23] To these numbers must be added about a million and a half organized workers in Cuba, as well as another four to five million who belong to independent unions without international ties.

Taken together these figures come to about twenty million, which indicates a sharp gain over the 1955 figures quoted earlier. However, country-by-country comparisons based on these numbers and cross checks with additional data from US Labor Bureau studies show sometimes inconsistent gains and losses, as well as no difference at all in reported membership over the past few years for individual countries. It follows, therefore, that the totals cited must be used with considerable reserve.

Though it is not possible confidently to establish just how large the labor movement is, or the fraction of the labor force now organized, and it is even less possible to ascertain how many of the organized are genuinely involved in union activity, there seems little doubt that generally the labor movement is expanding in numbers and influence. Ongoing structural changes, including the continued growth of cities and the universal efforts toward industrial expansion, in themselves favor growth in the labor movement. The legalization of the right to organize, along with legal mechanisms that make the process of organization almost automatic, also seems likely to encourage growth in union membership —despite the inhibitions on independent union action that government regulation and support often mean.

The central problem appears not to be whether labor organization will continue to grow, but how it will attack some of the dilemmas it faces everywhere. These dilemmas have to do fundamentally with the autonomy of the labor movement and its effectiveness in defending workers' interests, at a time when planning under state guidance (that is, a drift toward total politicization) is becoming increasingly important. In more immediate terms, the issue turns on the relations of labor organization to government, to political parties, and to management, whether private or politically centered.

Latin America now provides practically every possible variant in these relations. Communist Cuba has absorbed the labor movement into the apparatus of government and the revolutionary party. The revolutionary government of Bolivia in a sense rules jointly with a semi-militarized, militant labor organization. Brazil and Mexico have large and highly developed labor movements, which are beginning to show signs of restiveness and independence after long years of tight bureaucratic and legal controls. In Argentina, Chile, Colombia, and Venezuela, the labor movements, though subject in varying degrees to government controls and police repression, are primarily undermined by deep and bitter rivalry among political parties, which are fighting to win the loyalties of workers and to use labor organization to advance party causes.

In the view of perhaps most of the non-Communist, "free" trade unions outside Cuba, the Cuban worker has passed into a regime of forced labor; the right to work has become the obligation to work, with forced cuts in pay, losses in benefits, loss of the right to strike, and forced contributions in money and military services in the bargain.[24] From a Marxist, revolutionary viewpoint, of course, the disciplining of labor and the workers' focusing on increasing productivity rather than consumption is entirely logical during a period of presumed working-class ascendancy. At this juncture, the point is not to question the Cuban worker's acceptance of such a role, but to note that the present dilemma of labor organization throughout Latin America flows in part from the unions' being pushed toward a socialist stance on economic development before any real socialization of other elements of the economy. That is, the union is under strong pressure almost everywhere to participate "responsibly" in economic development, however haphazardly programmed, and to collaborate with the various austerity measures periodically introduced to curb inflation and other monetary imbalances. Since "responsible" participation here generally means the acceptance of wage freezes, the abdication of the right to strike, the deferment of grievances in the interests of productivity, and a keying down of open manifestations of independent union power, the collaboration demanded seems premature or at least extremely one-sided under present conditions. Moreover, unified labor action along these lines requires a degree of control over internal dissidence that is hardly compatible with the strengthening of democratic practices within labor organizations.

The desire of many union leaders to play a positive role in the task of national development and to keep the unions from appearing as a viciously disruptive element is tempered by the repeated failure of governments, owing to either incapacity or lack of good faith, to live up to their pacts with labor. The persistence in law and government of the operational principle that business must be persuaded or enticed to compliance, but labor can be forced, has also blocked such collaboration. The dogged militancy of Communists and allied groups in the labor movement also hampers or adds risks to the open espousal of more moderate positions. Nevertheless, the impulse is there, born in part from genuine growth in the sense of national identification and responsibility among some labor leaders, in part from the growing acceptance of restraint, since utopia is clearly not around the corner anywhere, and in part from sheer political fatigue and disillusion. The recent drive for labor education, especially leader training, reflects a desire among some labor elder statesmen to rise above or bypass politics and move into a phase of leadership by labor "technicians," whose decisions would be accepted as the judgments of specialists, not requiring the political certification of approval and support from the rank and file.

Thus, desires and dissatisfactions within the labor movement, as well as changes in the milieu in which labor acts, impel it in new directions—toward professionalization of leadership, genuine autonomy, political unity on a base broader than commitment to specific parties, and technical preparation for more effective collective bargaining. But these are long-term aspirations. More immediately, the weight of past as well as present tensions absorbs and exhausts the union in more conventional tasks and political byplay. The union acts against the going system but is nevertheless part of it. As alternative conditions emerge for promoting the kinds of social change the labor movement has always fought for, a substantial sector of labor seems disposed to work within a framework of democratic, rationally paced reform. Whether that is in itself a rational or feasible option remains to be seen.

Almost all recent national or hemispheric pronouncements on proposed reforms and programs of economic and social development make obeisance to the principle of a labor union voice in planning and in the execution of such plans. When referring to programs in which United States financing, and therefore policy guidance, is decisive, these pronouncements have a special poignancy. For it is in Latin American labor circles that the US has in the past encountered the most determined opposition, the most widespread skepticism of the motives of aid and reform programs, and the greatest practical difficulties in establishing a reasonable basis for dialogue and effective collaboration. Yet as soon as the US ranged itself with those who believe that fundamental reforms to genuinely transform Latin America are indispensable, it had to seek a firm base of popular support for a policy unpalatable to many of its long-time Latin American allies in business, diplomacy, and international welfare. Thus union support became essential, in part to bring pressure on governments to adopt concrete reforms without which continued aid would remain a palliative. Successful mustering of labor backing would also demonstrate that mass political loyalties could be mobilized around a program of democratic reform, provided it were quasi-revolutionary in scale and intensity. The opportunity to extend labor power and influence into this new sphere cannot be lightly cast aside. Responsible labor leaders may have some reservations about the motivations or chances of success of the many plans being formulated, but they cannot abdicate responsibility for getting reasonable labor and social-cost calculations into economic plans.

In point of fact, both the capacity of national governments or their agencies to plan and the capacity of the labor movement to contribute to such planning remain untried. Even in such rare cases as Colombia, which responded quickly with a ten-year plan for development under the Alliance for Progress and passed an agrarian reform law that was widely hailed as a model, subsequent progress has been disheartening. A Colombian official has pointed to the existence of two oligarchies who are in conflict on the issue of planned reform—one based on political power, the other on professional and intellectual capacity.[25] Labor is within neither of these oligarchies. Neither in Colombia nor elsewhere in Latin America have unions been represented on national planning bodies. The main drive behind programs of planned change lies with a small elite of professionals and technicians who, except in a few nations, have a much more solid base abroad than in their own countries. The political standing of such planning groups is generally precarious. The professionals and technicians who guide them, whether well-disposed toward labor or not, shy away from the multiple problems that genuine labor participation would imply. They are anxious to keep their functions "nonpolitical," fearful of labor radicalism, inclined to doubt that labor leaders are intellectually equipped for dispassionate and rational planning. Unfortunately, all these reservations have some foundation, though they do not justify the exclusion of labor from such councils.

Internationally, there were initial breakthroughs in 1962. ORIT made formal representations in a number of United Nations agencies, before the Inter-American Development Bank, and before the Inter-American Economic and Social Council ministerial meeting in Mexico City. In October 1962 ORIT on its own initiative called a meeting of the many agencies involved in social and economic planning in Latin America to discuss labor's role. Earlier in the year, ORIT had formally established a Department of Economic and Social Affairs with a small full-time staff. ORIT affiliates are being urged to press for representation in national planning agencies and delegations to international planning bodies.

At the same time, unions are beginning to formulate their own social projects (housing, cooperatives, savings and loan associations) and to seek international financing for them. The first Alliance for Progress loan granted to a labor organization (a $400,000 Agency for International Development loan for housing construction in Honduras) has, however, been labeled by an academically sponsored United States journal as a reward for anti-Communist zeal to a company-controlled union.[26]

Labor's ability to deal with these new complexities and to consolidate gains in organizational strength and union power within both the plant and the polity at large doubtless depends on the training of new leadership. Various efforts in this direction are under way, both at the national level and through ORIT and the newly created American Institute for Free Labor Development in Washington. By late 1962, some seventy-five labor leaders had completed a two-month course broadly covering the history and functions of the labor movement, with special emphasis on techniques of collective bargaining and organizing campaigns at the ORIT-operated Inter-American Institute for Higher Labor Studies (Instituto Interamericano de Altos Estudios Sindicales). Similar efforts were being undertaken by several international trade secretariats with headquarters in Latin America.

US labor leaders associated with these endeavors are no doubt moved by a sincere desire both to shape United States foreign policy and to help make that policy effective by strengthening non-Communist trade unionism. The increasing personnel that will be drawn into these activities by the intensified United States commitment in the area will probably have considerably less experience with and sensitivity to Latin American needs. The question also arises whether United States unionism has shown itself capable of effectively dealing with the kinds of issues Latin American labor organization now faces, and whether the skills and experience that US labor can offer its Latin American colleagues are what they most need at this point. At least one recent diagnosis paints the contemporary situation of US labor as one of arrested growth, stalemate, and lassitude.[27] Notable weaknesses in the United States labor movement, according to that diagnosis, are its failure to formulate and champion any moving message of social reform and its willingness to let management and government make the decisions on economic development. Since US labor has been least successful in organizing precisely those groups whose social situation is most closely analogous to that of most Latin American workers (i.e., the unskilled, uneducated, ethnic minorities, inhabitants of the most economically depressed regions), one may reasonably wonder how efficacious its organizational techniques will prove in an even more refractory setting.

These doubts arise partly because United States labor and its apologists present abroad a selective portrayal of its past and present situation. Thus United States labor is made to appear innocent of collectivism in ideology or practice from its beginnings, as operating freely in a basically classless society with little opposition from an enlightened management, carefully abjuring overcommitment to parties or political factions, and led by a democratically selected, proficient, and responsible leadership.[28]

The combined effect of this model and some of the internal impulses that have been described may be a premature technification and depoliticization of labor organization in Latin America. The gains of the worker in the city have been primarily political, and won with political skills and action; nothing in the present situation suggests that the need for politically able leadership has diminished. Successful economic planning may smooth the way for new kinds of political accommodation and for some degree of rationalization of political life, but it will not make politics obsolete.

In short, politics may frequently appear to have served labor poorly, but this is because commitment to politics has for the mass of workers been halfhearted, poorly directed, and limited to alternatives not of their own making. The city emancipates and modernizes slowly and selectively. Only a small fraction of the labor force is caught up in the dynamic sectors of the economy and is creating and responding to new political norms and loyalties. In view of the harshness of long-standing inequities, labor protest can be regarded as sporadic and feeble. The city opens the way for the worker to certain limited forms and degrees of economic, political, and intellectual liberation; at the same time the city accommodates, sustains, and feeds on a subculture of poverty that is not far removed from the rural or small-town models. That subculture of poverty is not a mere encumbrance that will be readily dislodged, ejected, or remolded, but an integral part of the social landscape of the city as now constituted.

8. The University Student

K. H. Silvert

The profundity of change and the immense differences among coexisting groups in Latin America, both inside and outside the university, are what make of most political disagreements an intense and sometimes total clash. Rural Latin America is occupied by persons living in hunting and fishing cultures, in stable isolated agricultural towns, and in fiefs; there is also the small rural aristocracy professing the religious universalism of the medieval upper class. Urban Latin America, by and large, is inhabited both by traditionalists who respect hierarchy, oppose change, and judge all social action by religious precept, and by very different persons of modern temperament and relativistic ideas who are willing to accept some compromise on social issues and are ideologically committed to at least a limited secularism.[1]

University students represent many but not all of these social segments. They are recruited overwhelmingly from urban centers. They are not by definition a modernizing element; indeed, they may form part of broader social groups whose strength powerfully inhibits development. But whatever the students' basic value commitment, they are in a world of disagreement more profound than explicitly ideological division. Two ways of life, two ways of thought, oppose each other in the Latin American city, and the accommodations tenuously lacing them can be only temporary, an adjustment forced by the need to maintain the mechanics of urban and quasi-national life. In the absence of a single national community to which all citizens unequivocally belong, Latin Americans are split into qualitatively different kinds of loyalty patterns. Villagers are concerned first with family and tribe, traditionalists with family and church and friendship commitments, and modernizers with building the impersonal mechanisms of national, industrial society. Given this situation, no single set of criteria of legitimacy can provide the consensus from which flows the power necessary for stable public institutions. The Latin American university student must make a relatively conscious choice from among a set of worlds, for he cannot merely fit himself into an already established and coherent community embracing all his peers.

Mediterranean traditionalism can coexist for relatively long periods with some degree of modern social and economic organization. Indeed, all of Latin America's more economically developed states offer persistent demonstration that the payment of the privileges of the old for the benefits of the new can be deferred for quite a while. But the price of this indulgence is a weak institutional structure, unable to guarantee either continuity or predictability and thus inhibitive of contained and ordered change. The power that Latin American student groups have demonstrated since the first decades of this century is, then, in inverse relation to the strength of governments and the efficacy of the university administrations themselves. The relative influence of organized student movements must be heightened by the essential fragility of societies in transition toward modern nationhood.

Class and the Nature of Student Power

Weak social institutions make more salient the power of any organized group, whether composed of students, military officers, or clergy. The nastily sharp class distinctions of all Latin America also serve to protect rebels against the established order if they enjoy the power of high social status. The Latin American university traditionally has served to certify the elite position of the sons of the upper class. Access to higher education is still so restricted for the general population that one might reasonably conclude that the student selection process in most Latin American countries still effectively excludes the economically underprivileged. The educational pyramid narrows so abruptly that such a conclusion is inescapable. As recently as 1950, for example, 49 per cent of the population over 15 years of age in Latin America had no primary schooling at all or had failed to complete the first year; 44 per cent had more than a year of primary education, but only

8 per cent had completed it. Six per cent had some secondary school training, and 2 per cent had graduated; only 1 per cent of the population over 15 had attended an institution of higher learning.[2] This steep decline in school attendance was expressed graphically in the Mexican ten-year educational plan submitted to President Adolfo López Mateos on October 27, 1959:

According to recent information (1956), of every thousand children who manage to put their feet on the first rung of primary school [on the same base, 460 more never get even that far], only one reaches the last grade of the professional school. . . . During the course of the first six grades . . . no fewer than 866 are left on the road. Only 59 get to the threshold of secondary education; but of these, 32 drop out during the three scholastic grades of secondary, pre-vocational, and special education, who added to the previous ones give us the figure of 973. Only nine arrive at the *bachillerato,* vocational education, and the professional cycle of primary normal instruction, of whom three drop out in the two or three grades involved . . . , with whom the total of desertion rises to 994. And, finally, only six get to higher education, but of these five drop out. . . . In summary, through the course of the sixteen grades that comprise a complete educational scale, 999 abandon their studies and only one finishes. . . . [To this we must add] the alarming circumstance that 471 abandon school . . . in the first grade.[3]

The survey adduces reasons for non-attendance and abandonment that are a direct function of class position: it estimates that at the time the report was prepared, 600,000 children then of school age had never attended school, and that an additional 366,000 had abandoned school for economic reasons, while 175,000 were out of school because of illness. Because the Mexican data are certainly not atypical,[4] we may reasonably conclude that despite important differences in primary- and secondary-school attendance between, for example, Haiti at one extreme and Argentina at the other, higher education as such remains the privilege of the few. The favored, moreover, come largely from families in the middle and upper-middle occupational categories in the national capitals; a somewhat smaller group comes from the same occupational levels in smaller cities; and a still smaller element is from the homes of higher-level workers and artisans, almost invariably from the capital. Numerous studies confirm the generality of this pattern, despite a few variant situations, mostly in provincial areas. For example:

The group that receives higher education is naturally very much smaller than the "middle sectors," but in all the Central American countries it is observed that the majority of university students—as well as secondary school students—come from those urban middle sectors comprised of professionals, businessmen, and white-collar employees; and an important minority from artisan or worker groups.[5]

A 1961 survey of the law students in the University of Panama[6] showed that about a third of the sample had fathers in the ranks of skilled, semi-skilled, or unskilled labor. It is worth adding here that only in Argentina, Chile, Cuba, and Panama, of all the Latin American republics, is the modal point of the educated population among those who have completed from four to six years of primary education. To put it another way, it is only in these four countries that there is a sufficiently broad base of persons with primary education to provide some social heterogeneity to the student body passing through secondary education into the university—a fact that goes far toward explaining the relatively high percentage of persons of lower occupational origins in the Panamanian law school.

There should be no presumption, however, that the Latin American university in general serves as an important group-mobility channel for lower-class persons. Students from working-class families rarely attend the most prestigious faculties or complete the full course of study. Further, it is probable that students with "worker" fathers have a life style characteristic of the lower-middle classes. The situation at the University of Chile accurately reflects the general state of affairs:

The University's 13,000 students constitute no more than 1.5 per cent of the young people between 17 and 25 years of age in Chile, and the sons of working-class families have little hope of reaching any of the major professional schools. But this is not because of anything inherent in the University itself but rather is a reflection of general economic conditions and the desperate poverty of Chile's rural and urban masses. . . . The University remains a stronghold of Chile's middle class, many of whom themselves are hard pressed by need and are able to stay in the University only with great sacrifice.[7]

Student leadership also reflects this class influence. The only large-scale empirical study of student leaders in Latin America, an inquiry into the Chilean Student Federation (FECH), unequivo-

cally establishes the middle-level occupational origins of those student leaders since 1920.[8] The relatively large number of leaders
coming to the capital from provincial cities, however, suggests that
we should look to physical mobility as a probably significant element in the more general social picture.

The well-advertised interest of some Latin American university
students in practical politics is a direct consequence of the introduction of new middle elements into full social participation in
the more developed countries after the turn of the century. The
symbol of their emergence is the Córdoba Reform of 1918, a declaration of academic independence and political intent. Wherever
stimulated by the Argentine initiative, the Reformists adopted a
populist tone reflecting the identification of newly integrating
groups with all alienated elements, in a pattern not unlike the
all-embracing national spirit of the French bourgeoisie in their
own revolutionary day. The Reform created an elaborated body
of doctrine that has been in constant use throughout Latin America ever since.

The traditional elitist social function of the university was by
no means in direct contradiction with the thoughts of the newly
mobile, who had assumed the responsibility of assisting their less
fortunate fellows. The politics of the situation, however, were violently wrenched. Instead of producing only leaders of stasis, the
university also began to create leaders of change. Within their
academic environment the two elements mingled in fashions quite
like those of the new strata developing in society as a whole. Rightists, forced into activism to maintain their positions, fomented the
importation of new ideologies of conservatism from Europe, partially accounting for the Nazi and Falangist strains in the politics
of Chile, Brazil, Argentina, and many other countries in the 1930's
and 1940's, and still in full bloom in Argentina. Meanwhile, leftists
seized on the traditions of elitism to justify a tutelary stance in
anticipation of the reality of the victory of populist democracy.

Eduardo Frei, leader of the Christian Democrats in Chile and
a leading exponent of "government by technician" in Latin America, provides this contemporary expression of the university as an
agency for training elites:

The University cannot isolate itself from this historical process [of mod-
ernization]; and in its fashion it can be a decisive factor in its orientation.

Is it prepared for it, or does youth follow one set of paths, the University others, without giving them any reply? Is it only a machine to produce professionals who, on leaving the University, feel themselves frustrated . . . ?

. . . The University is a social force and a great moral reserve. . . .

It is now time for the University to provide ideas and cadres of responsible men capable of recognizing and stating the truth in an objective manner, and capable of elaborating and utilizing formulas that do not rest on intuition or on ambition disguised as "ability." . . .

The University can provide the governing elites for this decisive historical crossroads, giving them a vision of the world and of our own America.[9]

The conscious acceptance of direct social responsibility by the new university students is an implicit identification of themselves as actual or aspirant members of an expanding elite. If there is some negative correlation between group size and elitist attitudes, then the exclusiveness of higher education in Latin America would seem to contribute importantly to the psychology of leadership. In the mid-1950's there were in all Latin America only about 350,000 registered students in institutions of higher learning, both state and private.[10] Of this number, 40 per cent were registered in Argentine institutions, and almost half of them matriculated in one university—the National University of Buenos Aires. And once again it should be recalled that the drop-out rate is extremely high, so that very few of even these small numbers will ever be graduated.[11]

There is some disagreement about these figures, for criteria concerning which institutions and which students should be considered of university level vary widely among countries and experts.[12] Some estimates, for example, exclude schools of fine arts and theology, and other schools dedicated solely to the humanities. The student count is also a problem, for in many countries the central national university has some administrative responsibility for the college preparatory work in the secondary school system, and sometimes the universities either run the entire system or maintain one or more prestigious secondary schools. In any event, the highest enrollment figures given do not exceed 550,000 for 1960,[13] still a very small figure when compared with that for the United States (four million students in higher education on approximately the same population base), and of course made even smaller by the high drop-out rate. On a percentage basis, the above figure is very small, especially when viewed against the large urban populations of many Latin American countries. Yet in absolute numbers it is large enough to cover a broad social spectrum including significant middle elements and some marginal upper-lower ones. Relative smallness and objective largeness justify ideologies of planned development, reinforcing the students' view of the university as a training center for the future holders of the power they expect at least partially to create for themselves.

The Student in the Large State University

Available information is much too sparse to permit a detailed discussion of differences between students in private and religious institutions and those in the state-operated universities. With few exceptions the only student organizations that historically have had important roles in political life are those of the major national universities in the capital cities. However, where regional universities do experience student convulsion, they, too, are almost always within the state system. The State University of São Paulo, for example, has been consistently involved in national politics, and contributed not a few martyrs to the anti-Vargas cause during the early days of his experiment in authoritarian populism. Other cases could be cited of significant student activities in the regional public universities of Argentina, Chile, Peru, and Mexico, but even so, their effect on national life is usually indirect. This generalization holds true even though it was the regional university of Córdoba that played host to the delegates who promulgated the Reform of 1918. The ideal of the academic republic promulgated on that occasion had more profound ideological effect outside Argentina than within it. Nevertheless, even there the influences of the Reform were felt more strongly in other parts of the national university system than in Córdoba. As one Argentine authority summarized the results of the Reform in his country: "In truth there was no such reform, for the structure of the university, substantively as well as legally, was maintained. There were, on the other hand, statutory reforms, all tending toward seeing that the universities acquire a more flexible and efficacious rhythm of life."[14]

The same author points out that within twenty years the na-

tional university system doubled in size, while administrative reform promoted a fresh academic spirit of freedom and innovation.
The point here being made is that only the politics of national
integration and development have stirred significant student action in this century. This ideological commitment behind student
action explains why it is that both secular and religious private
institutions are of little importance in general student movements,
and why only major national issues have served to arouse students
of the regional universities.

Of all Latin America's universities, the University of Buenos
Aires is by far the largest, having something over 70,000 students.
This number comprised about one-fifth the total university enrollment in Latin America less than a decade ago, and is still probably
no less than 15 per cent of the total.[15] This institution particularly
merits discussion here not only because of its mammoth size, but
also because the Student Federation of the University of Buenos
Aires (FUBA) has long been politically active as well as formally
participant in the administration of the university. Many of the
generalizations hurried travelers make about Latin American universities and students are in reality but extensions of impressions
of the famous case of the University of Buenos Aires.

Exactly 58,684 students were tallied in the census of October
1958 of the University of Buenos Aires, from which the following statistical profile is derived. (The number now is estimated
at more than 70,000.) Seventy-five per cent of the student body
was male, although the ratio varied widely from school to school
within the university. In Philosophy and Letters, which embraces
the education program, the sex ratio was reversed, while only two
per cent of the engineering students were female. Ninety per cent
of the students were below 30 years of age, the modal age being 20
years for the university as a whole, 21 in Engineering, 22 in Medicine, and 19 in Philosophy and Letters. These figures are not significantly different from those for any large United States university, and cast some doubt on how many "professional students"
there actually are in at least this Latin American university. Nine-
ty-one per cent of the students held Argentine citizenship, four
per cent were from other Latin American countries, and the rest
were resident non-citizens. Seventy per cent of the students were
born in Greater Buenos Aires and 13 per cent in the surrounding

provinces. Only 2.2 per cent were born in towns of less than 2,000 population. The secondary school record of the students makes the urban nature of the student body even more apparent, for 80 per cent completed high school in Buenos Aires. Seventy-five per cent attended public secondary schools, while only 11 per cent were graduated from secondary parochial schools; the remainder were from secular private schools. As a group, then, the students were of normal university age, urban origin, and secular training.

Over 85 per cent of the students were single; 90 per cent had no children, and only 3 per cent had two or more children. Ninety per cent of them lived in a family situation, with either parents or a spouse. Thirty per cent were supported entirely by the family, a figure rising to 52 per cent in Medicine and 58 per cent in Dentistry. There were also 514 members of the armed forces registered. Only .6 per cent of the student body were employed in blue-collar occupations!

Twenty-seven per cent of the students' fathers and 33 per cent of their paternal grandfathers had been or were in employer positions; 10 per cent of the fathers and 5 per cent of the grandfathers had been or were professional. But only 5.4 per cent of the fathers and 8.3 per cent of the grandfathers had been or were of the laboring group.

Few of these students will ever receive their degrees. Approximately 30 per cent were in the first year of study at the time of the census, though this figure varied considerably by faculty. In Law, the freshmen were 49 per cent of the total. With 58,684 enrolled students, the university granted only 3,324 degrees in 1958.[16] Normally the proportion of degrees awarded to freshmen registered is about 15 per cent. Drop-out rates for recent years vary from as much as 80 per cent in Architecture to 64 per cent in Law and 44 per cent in Medicine.

In terms of party affiliation and attitudes toward the university, the students seem close to the Argentine national norm. A poll taken in 1957 in the Faculty of Letters (often considered quite leftist) indicated that over 50 per cent of the students clustered about the center; 7 per cent said they were Communist, 8 per cent chose one or another of the conservative parties, and 22 per cent did not reply. Only 1 per cent avowed themselves Peronists.[17] This student body has consistently returned reformist (center and left) student delegates to office, but only Exact Sciences has in recent years elected frankly Marxist student officers. Indeed, in the last two student elections the choice in the majority of faculties has fallen to the center and the right, and the reformist left and center-left have been forced to support moderate candidates in order to retain some power in the university administration. In short, the University of Buenos Aires reflects all the political schisms of the upper and middle groups in Argentina. It is hardly surprising that Peronism, a lower-class political movement, finds few supporters in this haven of the middle- and upper-class Argentine.

Although the usual majority grouping of students calls itself reformist, in deference to the Córdoba Reform, splits for electoral purposes are common, and there is even striking evidence that some of the basic academic tenets of the Reform are now being rejected by the Buenos Aires students. Democratization of the university and its establishment as a kind of autonomous academic republic governed by students as well as faculty remain the goal of most students and professors. But apparently there is much backsliding from some of the pedagogical precepts implicit in these ideals.[18] Only 1 per cent of the student body receives scholarship assistance, for example, and certainly the scramble for grades and academic advantage in Buenos Aires is as heated as in many United States universities. On the crucial question of whether the university should have entrance examinations (strongly opposed by orthodox reformists), fully 70 per cent of the students supported some kind of entrance examination or qualifying year of studies. Significantly, in the most "popular" or socially least prestigious school, Economic Sciences, 47 per cent opposed any entrance requirement beyond the requisite secondary schooling.

FUBA has been politically restrained for the past several years, because of the general political instability of the country and the consequent threat of military intervention to force the government to oust the elected university administration and appoint a new rector and deans. The last major political student action of a public nature was a massive demonstration in 1958 against permitting Catholic universities to confer legally valid degrees. FUBA lost, and Argentina now has three more or less regularly functioning clerical universities, two in Buenos Aires and one in Córdoba. Otherwise, the fairly close collaboration between majority faculty and student groups has thus far prevented major incidents and saved the university from intervention.

There is logic and relevance to the drift by reformists into a more professional attitude toward the university and into politics of coalition and limited compromise, activist but not narrowly fanatical. A recent survey conducted among freshmen, seniors, and graduates of the Faculties of Economic Sciences, Medicine, and Exact Sciences shows unmistakably that there is a strong correlation between those students taking a modern view of society (and who also are likely to be reformists), and those accenting the vocational and technical aspects of learning.[19]

Taken as a whole, about a third of each sample [from Medicine] favored education for good citizenship and the building of a national spirit [the view of the old aristocracy as well as of the Reformists of 1918, although with a changed ideological substance], while the remainder favored a more vocational and generally cultural orientation. The figures as taken by mobility . . . indicate that with fair consistency the upwardly mobile tend to respect more highly the practical and vocational functions of education, as do those who rank highly on the national identification scale [the measure of modernism]. Low scorers on the national identification scale are consistently above average in their desire for the formation of good citizens and the national spirit.[20]

These correlations held constant through the Faculties of Economic Sciences and Exact Sciences as well. It is only reasonable that technological change, the necessity for a high degree of specialization, and emphasis on economic development should lead modernizing Argentines to insist upon improvement of vocational training at the university level, even if at the apparent expense of some cherished notions of the "popular university." This attitude explains a seeming contradiction in the literature concerning Latin American student movements. John P. Harrison, for example, states in an article on the "political university" that "while all of the aims of the reform movement mentioned above touch directly upon the university as an institution, it is readily apparent that none of them is concerned with curriculum revision or in improving the professional training of the student." Several pages later the author points out, however, that reformism and curricular improvements are not necessarily mutually exclusive. "There has been, if anything, even less interest in reforming university curricula and professional training to meet mid-twentieth-century needs in those universities that closed their doors to the reform movement than in those where it found fertile ground."[21]

Several interim conclusions would seem justified at this point: first, that the Reformists of 1918 inherited the elitist notion of the university from their predecessors; second, that because of their class origins and general changes in the political environment, they imbued their assumption of an elite role with a populist and nationalist ideology vastly different from the ideals of their traditionalist predecessors; and third, that with the passage of time the traditionalists have continued to conceive the university's role as that of forming citizens in the Greek sense, while the reformists have begun to value the quality of education as indirectly contributory, through broader social processes, to nation-building. In an important sense, then, the innovating student is approaching the prevailing view of academicians in developed lands, while still continuing to place a greater weight on the immediate applicability of learning. This view was given strong expression by Risieri Frondizi, brother of ex-President Arturo Frondizi and rector of the University of Buenos Aires from 1957 to 1962:

The Argentine university has wasted much of its energies in the search for ingenious solutions to administrative questions, without becoming aware that the problems of the university are of a pedagogical nature. . . . [It seems not to] matter that the university does no research, that one turns one's back on the needs of the country, that there are no professors fit to teach many courses, that the students still keep on repeating by rote the worn-out notes of past years . . . that there is no university life. . . . The university . . . should not be at the orders of a governor —or of a political party or an ideology—but rather ready to serve society, the people, who maintain it: not to give it what this or that person demands through his political spokesman, but what it [the society] needs for its progress, enrichment, and material and spiritual elevation.[22]

Student Power and Political Activism

The ascription of great political influence to student organizations implies that these organizations are surrogates for other interested social groups. It also suggests that if young persons can gain sufficient influence to change, on occasion, the course of national political life, then, as already noted, other power centers must be in such disarray as to elevate the relative power of any organized group. This argument has often been advanced to explain the prominence of the military's role in Latin American politics; it holds as well for student groups.

The following propositions may serve to explain relative student political strength in a more specific and functional sense:

1. All Latin American countries, with the possible exception of Cuba, are still in a pre-national state. Government is thus by definition weak; it can count on little anticipatory adjustment to law and thus, by the same token, has few means for the unequivocal imposition of regulation and sanction.

2. Instability and disorganization are characteristic not only of governments, but also of all interest and occupational associations. But because not all fall into disarray—or the same degree thereof —at the same time, the significance of and the relative power generated by the very fact of group organization vary from time to time and place to place.

3. The very explicitly defined class divisions, reinforced by tradition and custom, promise the university student an elevated chance of success in life. He comes from a middle- or upper-class family; he is acquiring the social certification of achievement and status. Even though he may be disappointed and fall into the "intellectual proletariat," his life chances are still very high, and he is realistic so to consider them. The following views expressed in the previously cited study of Panamanian law students imply that at least some students use politics to bolster their already high chances of attainment:

Their [the Nationalists'] expectation of success is high, and they seem to have a stronger motivation toward achievement than do the Moderates— radical nationalism may thus have been embraced because the success of the movement would mean the expansion of socio-economic opportunities, and because the Nationalists have projected their drive for achievement onto the nation as a whole.[23]

4. Traditional as well as modern persons place great stress upon the need for adequate leadership in Latin America; the university is viewed as a necessary element in the training of leaders, and within the university, the faculty of law continues to produce the greatest number of political figures. As we might expect, during the Aramburu government in Argentina (1955–58) 95 per cent of all high policy-making government officials were graduated from either a university or a military academy, and this figure rose to

100 per cent in 1960. Even during the quasi-populist Perón regime (1945–55), about 85 per cent of the policy-makers had higher degrees. Over half the persons at this level in 1960 were lawyers, and even during the Aramburu military interregnum, the career officers outnumbered the lawyers by only 14 to 12 in the top positions.[24]

5. Youth is a relative concept to a certain extent. The exclusiveness of the university, coupled with strong family and class identification, makes of students apprentice professionals from the moment they matriculate. Thus the word *universitario* denotes anyone connected with the university, whether student, teaching assistant, professor, or graduate. The Latin American student is, then, not considered so callow as his North American counterpart, and may be trusted with public power at an early age. For example, eight years after a revolution in which law students had played an important role, the Congress of Guatemala was still composed of deputies half of whom were 35 or below. Only six of 54 deputies were over 50 years of age.

6. The strong desire for development on the part of major urban groups in Latin America has created a demand for a new socioeconomic ideology. The university is the natural site for the *pensador* and for the diffusion of his ideas.

7. The needs of Latin America's new industries have already impelled curricular revision and expansion in many Latin American universities in such fields as business administration and the sciences. But at least as important have been the effects of governmental commitments to partially planned procedures of economic growth, which are now given formal approval as an announced requirement of the Alliance for Progress, but which have been a long-standing administrative practice in such countries as Uruguay, Costa Rica, Mexico, and Chile. Economic planning has naturally force-fed the growth of faculties and departments of economics, but has also been felt in engineering, sociology, and public administration. Increased demand for technicians has fortified the power of the universities in these areas and has at the same time increased the student's certainty of success. The invitation to early manipulation of public power is quite explicit.

8. These circumstances, taken in sum and added to the social propinquity of the university situation, provide the conditions for the creation of student organizations that parallel the national

parties. Wherever students have been studied for their politics, only a minority (albeit usually a large one) of students are found to "belong" to national parties in any positive sense. Student leaders, however, usually have some party coloration if not a firm identification, and factions within universities have at least a tenuous identification with national parties.

To say that the student organization is "captive" or riddled with political factions is not to say that it is a passive instrument of more powerful and experienced politicians. The FECH [the Student Federation of the University of Chile] is really in the hands of students with strong political convictions, who have a firm sense of dedication and allegiance to their parties. The University political groups enjoy considerable independence within the broad framework of basic party policy and organization. They are able to influence party decisions through their dominance of youth sections and by allying themselves with sympathetic elements in the party hierarchy. They ordinarily experience no conflict between their loyalty to party and their responsibilities to fellow students because they believe their parties offer the only acceptable solutions to the problems of youth and the nation.[25]

9. Latin America has always been a hearty consumer of European ideas and practices, and the university has long played a vital part in the process of importation, adaptation, and propagation. The present search for ideology, technique, and science has broadened the university's role in the mimetic process. Even though this imitation means that "much research is accomplished by waiting for the mail," as several Latin American university administrators have sarcastically put it, the postman brings ideas that increase the power of the university establishment.

The nine above propositions suggest the basic reasons for the inherent institutional strength of Latin America's universities in relation to other social groupings. Not all students, however, attempt to use institutional power for public ends, nor do all activist students agree on how best to use it. Attitudes toward the proper use of power vary widely.

In the study of Argentine students already cited we find, for example, that medical students engage in little overt political activity. Well over half of them report that they argue politics with friends and acquaintances, but only 6 per cent of the freshmen and 8 per cent of the seniors attest to any party activity, and only 20 per cent of the former and 15 per cent of the latter attended a student association meeting in the six months prior to the interview.[26] Only 17 per cent of the practicing physicians reported attending a professional association meeting during the same period. Students in the Faculty of Exact Sciences take a much more active part in student organizations than those in Medicine, but levels of participation and involvement in politics are not much higher. A strong sense of school identification and the familiarities fostered by small enrollments help to explain this higher level of student-oriented political activity.

The most surprising findings of all relating to political activity concern the numbers of students who participated in some sort of street rally or demonstration during the six months prior to the interview. For the three groups in Sciences (freshmen, seniors, and graduates), the percentages were 39, 11, and 12 respectively; for Medicine 16, 15, and 10; and for Economics 14 per cent among freshmen and 18 among graduates. The time period covered was one of quite intensive national political activity, and an affirmative answer may have meant only that the respondent listened to political speeches in a public plaza.

The study appears to show that few students participate extensively in both university and public political activities, that normally at least half in all the groups examined are passive, and that between one-quarter and one-third of the students constitute an "immediately available public," ready to be tapped for special occasions. This potential for action is paralleled in the community at large. It is estimated, for example, that at least 250,000 persons in Buenos Aires demonstrated in favor of religious higher education in 1958, with another 300,000 appearing later to oppose it. That half a million persons in a city of approximately seven million demonstrated on the church-state issue, in a period of only normal political tension, indicates the large reservoirs of readiness to respond to the leadership of university students and professors of Catholic as well as secularist persuasion.

The Effectiveness of Student Political Action
To this point we have sought to describe the nature of student political activity and to link student power with social organization and the institutional nature of the university.

Unless the unique historical development of each country is taken into account, however, attempts to categorize the range and effectiveness of student participation in politics may appear simplistic. For example, the location of the national university in Nicaragua outside Managua, the capital city, certainly has something to do with the relatively little one hears of Nicaraguan students. The much more important case of Brazil is strongly conditioned by the very late start that country had in higher education, which only came with the inauguration of several professional schools in the nineteenth century.[27] The Reform was already two years old when the Brazilian government decided to merge existing schools of medicine, engineering, and law to form the nucleus of the University of Rio de Janeiro. In 1937 the University of Brazil finally emerged, a combination of the University of Rio de Janeiro and an embryonic Federal Technical University, and by 1959 Brazil had twenty universities plus some private institutes. This delayed development clearly affected the growth of a student political tradition.

Still, it should be possible to derive a set of categories sufficiently flexible to give realistic play to each unique case, yet precise enough to be meaningful. We know that students have been important in recent political events in Cuba, Colombia, Venezuela, and Guatemala—in all of which they have participated in the overthrow of dictatorial regimes. In the same countries, the students subsequently lost whatever decisive power they may have had. Probably the most realistic appraisal is that the students were in no case the decisive element in the overthrow, but rather participants in a broad national movement involving the military, the clergy, businessmen, industrialists, and labor groups. The ouster of Perón is a case in point. The intellectual community, including the students, provided the rationale for action, but the physical power to overthrow constituted authorities lay elsewhere. The effectiveness and the potential results of student action may be judged broadly according to the following scheme:

Situations of Stable Traditional Societies. In very rudimentary, almost bi-class social structures, necessarily governed under crude dictatorial forms, students normally play a very limited role in innovation and political activity. This was the situation in the colonial era, and present-day Nicaragua, Haiti, and Paraguay fall into this category.

Situations of Beginning Modernization and Disarray. As the city begins to grow, as an industrially oriented middle class emerges, and as the politics of change begin to operate, students assume a most important role in the importation and adaptation of ideology, in the organization of power as well as ideas, and in government itself. Factionalism is one of the earliest signs of modern pluralism. El Salvador, Guatemala, Ecuador, Peru, the Dominican Republic, and Panama are currently in this state. Here, more than in any other social milieu, the student, representative of aspirant elites, finds a situation sufficiently simple for him to exercise relatively great power over political events.

More Mature Situations of Temporary Resolution. When the social structure is relatively complex, politics turbulent, and at least interim political decisions made with the immediate future in mind, student groups are usually very active, but limited in their role by other established interests. In such situations, student activity can still be of great importance in defining issues and in precipitating incidents or even full-scale revolts. But usually the university as an institution begins to turn inward, preparing to meet the demand for professionalism that always arises in times of rapid economic and political development. Colombia, Venezuela, and Bolivia, for varying historical reasons, all fall into this category.

Situations of Institutional Complexity and Relative Strength. Where the student finds himself in a plural interest structure and complex class system, his relative power becomes even more limited. The Mexican experience is a useful case in point. For some time the Mexican student has had little organized voice in national affairs. The bus strikes of 1958, which broke a peace that had lasted almost a generation, had little significance. Only the Technical University—the "poor man's University of Mexico"—has given the authorities much difficulty, and then only on matters having principally to do with the school's internal administration. The strength of the Mexican government, the ideological weight of the Revolution and the institutional expression of this ideology by the state, the single governing party, and the intellectual community all combine to strip from the students much of their political reason for being. To take another example, active as the Cuban students were against the Batista regime, they are now contained by the ideological as well as military strength of Castro's modern dictatorship. Even amidst Argentina's present institutional disarray, the massiveness of Buenos Aires, the strength of the competing interest structure, and the complication of motivations and values impede pointed and effective student action in public affairs. In these situations the students may and usually do have much influence over university policy and affairs, but their role in national politics must of necessity be one dependent on other, more primary, definitions of interest. Brazil, Mexico, Argentina, Uruguay, Costa Rica, Chile, and Cuba are all within this category.

Ideological orientation, too, will vary with the kind of developmental problem the country faces and with the particular student body involved. Ideologies of nationalism are felt but weakly, if at all, by the public at large in the least developed countries of Latin America. But the intellectual and modernizing student caught in the midst of the disorder of rapid change may indeed become impregnated with nationalistic views. Only certain students and student groups, however, will embrace exclusivism, impersonalism, anti-imperialism, and other of the more extremist views implied by nationalist ideologies. Students in Catholic and other private universities tend toward conservatism; i.e., they are opposed to the nationalism, secularism, and impersonalism of modern society. They may be anti-American as well, hostile to both capitalism and Protestantism as Latin conservatism traditionally has been. The state universities, leading in the modernization of the traditional academic disciplines along with a growing dedication to the physical sciences and empiricism, attract the innovators—and thus the nationalists—in much greater measure than such schools as the Catholic University of Chile or the Javeriana (Jesuit University) in Colombia. This political array is common to some degree throughout Latin America, describing students as much as other politicized groups. The nationalistic student of the state university draws more attention to himself than any other non-party group of ideologists, since he is also the innovator, the modernizer, the politically concerned, and likely to be pursuing studies closely involved with the developmental process. This constellation of attitudes and practices accompanies modernization everywhere, for wherever economic and social development has occurred, the nation-state has been its political vehicle.

Social Change and the Student

A complex mythology of the Latin American student has grown
up in the United States, in large measure a result of the excited
findings of observers scurrying to make up for irrevocably lost time.
We hear that the Latin American student is a radical, uninterested
in study, the pawn of professional agitators, the persecutor of his
professors, and the bane of responsible university administrators.
Some students are all these things. Others are serious and question-
ing young people working well and serenely in rapidly improving
faculties and departments. Still others are apathetic playboys, or
yearners after the glories of National Socialism, or social climbers
thirsting to become oligarchs, or desiccated youths who aspire to
no more than the routine life of the bookkeeper. Probably the majority of students in the state universities are more secularist than
not, more nationalist than not, more middle-class than not, more
center and left-of-center than not, and more worried about individual fortune than the fate of the state. They form the reservoir
of modern men and women upon whom the nation can draw for its
development, susceptible to national leadership and willing to
take the risks demanded when societies break from one world of
thought and action into another.

The Latin American university student is the child of his parents. To assume that the student is but a hot-eyed revolutionary
is to presume that somehow registering in a university is sufficient
to cut family ties, break class and other group identifications, and
produce a special kind of creature divorced from his society. The
intellectual community can be "ahead" of society as a whole, but
it must have identifications with some sectors of the community,
and can pull along only those people susceptible to its particular
suggestions or prodding. To single out the Latin American student
for special disdain is to forget that it is truly debatable whether
he is more irresponsible, rapacious, corrupt, and foolish than his
elders on the farm, in the government, in the bank, or in the trade
union. Indeed, there is some reason for advancing the thesis that
the student is at least temporarily a better citizen than his elders.

The simple fact of youth also crucially distinguishes the Latin
American student from his parents. He still remains free to believe
in and to attempt to apply the long-held ideals of the old liberal
aristocracy—those desires for freedom, dignity, growth and progress so often honored in the breach since Independence. With

whatever ideological superficiality, misplaced enthusiasm, and youthful conviction of ultimate right, the reformists have preserved and modernized these ideals, and often have displayed a courage and selflessness in their defense that merit admiration rather than contempt or condescension.

Over and above nationalistic feeling and the commitments to party, there exists a set of canons governing and inspiring student action. In Chile these are not often articulated but they are recognized as going back to the very beginnings of the student federation. . . . They include the courage to hold and defend a point of view on fundamental issues, a readiness for self-sacrifice, loyalty in friendship, love of country, hatred and distrust of the military, a sentimental identification with the working classes, and solidarity with the youth of other Latin American countries. Students have been a force of progress within the university; their dedication to democratic ideals, their readiness to protest injustice, and their resistance to political repression have helped keep Chile politically moderate.[28]

The university is a propitious place for demonstrating the relationship between freedom and development. For long the reformist and neo-reformist students have instinctively linked the two in their hatred for authoritarianism on the one hand and their search for modernization on the other. If they have been tempted to adopt ideologies that the Western world rejects as totalitarian, it may well be that they have been offered no other seemingly viable alternative, have heard no objective and authoritative voices reaffirm the convictions of 1918, and have seen corruption and dictatorship blessed with international respectability. To leave the university and to grow up means to accept measures of conduct in contradiction with those avowed social ideals the student has been taught in civics texts, the speeches of his leaders, and the writing of the *próceres* (Founding Fathers). Rarely indeed is the gulf between ideal and real behavior so broad as it is in Latin America. But a major reason for hope lies precisely in the insistent presence of those concepts of free inquiry whose routine application must be a part of the modern university if it is to accomplish its pedagogical and research functions. There will always be tension between Academia and the public so long as the bold pursuit of ideas is hampered by cultures that fetter minds with archaic measures of hierarchy and demand ultimate commitment to unchanging standards of the good.

9. Latin America & Japan Compared

R. P. Dore

The outsider, it is quite clear, does not see most of the game, but he may see different parts of it, and it is the hope that he might which provides the sole justification for this paper. It is in two sections; the first touches on differences in the situations, advantages, and constraints of foreign scholars studying Latin America compared with those studying Asia, more particularly Japan. The second and main part attempts some comparisons between the recent histories of the two areas. A more accurate title might have been "Random Thoughts on Latin America by a Student of Japan," or even "Reflections on Japan prompted by the first impact on a state of pristine innocence of a few facts of Latin American life."

It is not easy to generalize meaningfully about differences in the approaches of American social scientists to the two areas; there is approximately the same diversity in assumptions and preoccupations and theoretical frameworks. One meets the same fashionable metaphors of thrusts and drives and mixes and inputs; there is the same evidence of terminological confusion, the same fondness for those protean words like "modernization," "development," "nationalism," which can mean all things to all men and consequently nothing precise to anyone; and in conference discussions there are the same occasional bouts of linguistic self-consciousness when the confusion becomes plain and attempts are made at definition (though I have never heard Asian scholars reach such an advanced stage of terminological agnosticism that they questioned the proper use of words like "writer" and "peasant"). In these respects the differences seem greater between different disciplines than between students of different areas. Economists more often know what they are talking about than do other social scientists, because more of their terms are clearly related to quantitative measures. The economist can define economic growth in terms of an increase in per capita income at constant prices, and discussion can proceed with a clear idea of the issues at stake. Sociologists and political scientists are much less certain of the connotations of social or political "development," and they can even sometimes be heard arguing in fruitlessly essentialist terms about what such words might *really* mean. Nor are there signs of a consensus gradually emerging; the only cure for free-enterprise humpty-dumptyism would seem to be the appearance of a caudillo, who would legislate the meanings of words by arbitrary fiat.

There are, however, some differences between the students of the two areas largely determined by the nature of the areas studied. In the first place, students of Asia tend to be more narrowly specialized in a single country. There are a few who take Southeast Asia as their oyster, some who bestraddle China and Japan, but most confine their research to only one society. By contrast, one hears of Latin Americanists, but not of Bolivianists or Peruvianists, and although the papers in this volume often draw heavily on personal experience in only one or two Latin American countries, the assignment to generalize is at least accepted as desirable and feasible.

The advantages of such a global, or at least semi-hemispherical, approach are not immediately obvious. It is not easy for any one man to know enough about so many different societies, and the attempt to be comprehensive may lead to a diffusion of energy, to the quick survey of formal structure rather than the detailed analysis of process. The attempt to arrive at *descriptive* generalizations seems in any case to be of dubious value. The predicate of any sentence beginning, say, "Students in Latin America . . ." is likely to be so general, so vague, and so hedged about with qualifications as to be neither informative nor useful.

On the other hand, Latin America does provide excellent opportunities for the kind of comparative sociology that seeks to arrive at generalizations about *causal* connections of the type: "X is likely to lead to Y, other things being equal." Obviously, one has a better chance of arriving at such generalizations with fair confidence if other things *are* as equal as possible. It is in this respect that Latin

America offers a promising field. Its societies do have so many
points of similarity that an examination of their differences might
yield new information about the way those differences are interrelated. Thus, Latin America is an excellent place to study, say,
the relation between levels of literacy and the political role of
labor unions; between the size of the professional middle class and
the strength of liberal democratic parties; between the real extent
of racial or cultural differences and the political or social importance attached to such differences; between the types of land tenure and the political involvement of peasants; and so on. Economists have used such methods in a purely statistical way, for instance in seeking a correlation between inflation and the rate of
economic growth. But there is still not enough systematic collection of data to enable sociologists or political scientists to use the
same technique effectively.

A second difference between students of Latin America and students of Japan is, I think, that the latter are better informed. This
is not a sign of any particular virtue of their own. It derives in part
from the fact that Japan has had a strong central government for
the last century, dominated by a bureaucracy that saw no part of
life as falling outside its purview and sometimes displayed a veri-
table mania for recording and tabulating every piece of information it could lay hands on. Second, it derives from the development of Japanese scholarship. There was a time when Westerners
led the field in the academic study of Japan. The first professor of
Japanese philology at Tokyo in the 1890's was, in fact, an English-
man. At the beginning of this century Western students of Japanese history were still more acutely critical of their sources, less
easily content with mere chronicling, and more sophisticated in
their analysis of motive than their Confucian-trained Japanese
counterparts. In the newer social science fields Western superiority persisted (partly thanks to the handicaps imposed by Japanese militarism) until much more recently. There is, for instance,
no prewar Japanese village study with quite the breadth and sophistication of J. F. Embree's *Japanese Village*.[1]

The situation today is very different. The Japanese themselves
have acquired the same attitudes toward research, the same canons
of evidence, and the same comparative knowledge of other societies
as their Western colleagues, and Japan has become rich enough to

maintain a very large number of professional scholars in all the social science fields. This means that the Western student of Japanese history now has a vast body of secondary Japanese sources to draw on; that the Western anthropologist making a village study in Japan will waste his time unless he first works through the substantial production of Japanese rural sociologists.

The similarity of styles and standards makes more painfully obvious the one major disadvantage under which the foreigner labors —the fact that he rarely starts to learn Japanese young enough to acquire a native fluency in the language. I know of no Western historian who can handle Japanese historical documents with anything like the speed and accuracy of his professional Japanese colleagues. Consequently the Western scholar is perhaps best employed as a synthesizer for Western audiences of the results of Japanese scholarship, though his synthesis may in itself make original contributions to the subject, inasmuch as his position outside the tangled web of personal relations in the Japanese academic world enables him to challenge accepted shibboleths and suggest new lines of enquiry more easily than those inside can.

This is not altogether a popular role, however, and relations between Japanese and foreign scholars are not wholly free from strain. The linguistic handicaps of the foreign scholar combine with a long tradition of cultural isolation to convince many Japanese that foreigners can never "really understand" Japan. They may therefore be reluctant to take the writings of foreign scholars very seriously. This tendency to deprecate their work may further be exacerbated by a more specific *anti-yanquismo* of various kinds —either political, as in the Japanese Marxist's scorn for the naïve bourgeois interpretations of the American historian; or personal, as may happen when ill-paid Japanese scholars are induced by the lure of better research facilities, extra income, or the opportunity for foreign travel to become involved in American research projects and accept the direction of American scholars whose scholarship they respect less than their financial resources.

My impressions of how this compares with the situation in the Latin American field are uncertain, but it seems safe to assert that much less reliable information about Latin American societies is available from their own governmental sources and that the development of the social sciences in Latin American universities has been quantitatively much inferior to that in recent Japan. Given, further, that Spanish and Portuguese pose lesser obstacles for the English speaker, it follows that there remain greater opportunities for foreign scholars to do useful fundamental research in the Latin American field. Second, the initial gap between native and foreign scholarly approaches and critical standards was undoubtedly smaller in the case of Latin America. The Mediterranean academic style may be different from the Anglo-Saxon, but still these are differences within the European cultural tradition, all elements of which have been constantly interacting over the whole course of their development. As such they are of lesser magnitude than the gulf between the Chinese and the European traditions, which developed for millennia in mutual isolation. It would seem easier, therefore, for Latin American and North American scholars to work together in easy collaboration, but it is not altogether clear that this is the case. In the first place, the smaller initial gap between the predominantly philosophical and normative bias of Latin American academicism and the more pragmatic and scientific bias of its North American counterpart may prove even more difficult to bridge, partly because subtler differences of style and orientation are not always consciously appreciated and allowed for, partly because in the Japanese case the gap was closed entirely by the Japanese themselves. It was *their* historians and social scientists who abandoned their own intellectual heritage and consciously assimilated Western—predominantly German, British, and American—academic traditions. Latin Americans are not disposed to make the same kind of capitulation; they are more likely to look on their intellectual heritage as a cause for pride rather than self-disciplinary correction. And it is perhaps harder for two parties to meet in the middle of a stream than for one to leap over it. The other irritants noted in the Japanese case are also relevant. The American scholar cannot escape the consequences of his greater affluence, or of the political and economic involvement of his country in Latin American affairs.

This closer political involvement suggests a third difference between North American studies of Latin America and of Japan. It could be argued that by a process either of selective recruitment or of acculturation the students of an area tend to take on the characteristics of the people of that area. Thus, students of Japan tend to be industrious, circumspect, and serious-minded, members of a harmonious integrated group; while the students of Latin America are personalists, irresponsible, disorganized, ideological, and preoccupied with demonstrating their *machismo*. This would be a gross exaggeration, but it does seem that Latin American studies give rise to sharper divisions of opinion, for the very good reason that Latin America has very serious problems of poverty, political oppression, and economic stagnation, the competing solutions for which evoke strong political emotions. Should labor unions be encouraged to play a leading political role? Should there be land reform? Should the state play a predominant part in industrial development? Can the military be a benign source of national leadership? North American students of North American politics may celebrate, with Daniel Bell, *The End of Ideology,* but the political battles that enlivened the ideological thirties have real contemporary relevance to modern Latin America. By contrast, Japan, economically very much a going concern, politically relatively stable, has fewer social problems that do not seem to be on the way to gradual solution. Consequently there is today (though this was not the case fifteen years ago) a lesser tendency for American students of modern Japan to "point with pride" or "view with alarm," to look on Japan as a society about which something should be done.

If this means that Latin America is a more exciting field in which to work, it also means that it is potentially a more painful one, for Latin America, besides having problems of Latin American welfare, is also a sensitive area in the cold war. The American student of the region cannot be indifferent to the fact that the majority of his countrymen are chiefly concerned with how Latin America can be kept free from Communist influence, friendly to the United States, and hospitable to its businessmen. This may place him in an uncomfortable dilemma. The more he studies his area, the more time he spends there and the more friends he makes, the more he is likely to define his problems less in terms of what would be good for the United States or for the West and more in terms of what would be good for Bolivians and Mexicans and Paraguayans. In the days when it was Britain rather than the United States that considered itself the bearer of "the white man's burden," British colonial administrators spoke with rather ambiguous distaste of the dangers of "going native." Should the American student of Latin America in fact go psychologically native, and should he decide, as he well might about some Latin American countries, that a left-wing revolution (at the expense of American political influence and American business interests) offers the best hope of social improvement, he is liable to be suspected of treasonable Communist sympathies. In the Asian field the experience of students of China stands as a case in point. In the aftermath of Congressional inquiries into the Communist take-over of 1949, those who had shown a sympathetic understanding of the Communists' social aims, or even a realistic assessment of their political and military chances, found themselves suspected of disloyalty. The shock this created has set back the American study of modern China a good many years and threatens to restrict it to the narrow confines of Pekinology, the apolitical study of China that avoids the expression of controversial evaluation and aims only to predict the next moves of the opponents in the international game. It does not seem that the Cuban revolution has yet had the same consequences for the field of Latin American studies, but it is to be hoped that Cuba, too, has not become a dangerous minefield that will in future be avoided by all except accredited Havanologists.

Students of Japan are lucky in being free of this particular kind of pressure, for Japan is not obviously a problem area in cold war terms. The policy relevance of Japan is now primarily as a shining example of forced-pace modernization, and the fashionable question to ask is: "How did the Japanese manage to pull it off?" And this, perhaps with the addendum "while Latin American countries did not," provides a useful starting point for a comparison of the two areas. In the mid-nineteenth century both Japan and Latin America were underdeveloped areas; they were predominantly rural, lacking all but the rudimentary beginnings of a modern industry or transport system, lacking a rationalized bureaucracy or judiciary, lacking even, as cellular societies knit together by authoritarian personal bonds, a coherent society-wide polity. In both areas there were individuals who preached the need for a drive to modernity, to emulate the industrial and political systems of the Western powers and equal, if possible, their economic and military strength. In Japan that drive was successful in terms of values that most of us share today—successful, that is, in achieving a highly developed industrial potential; a level of living already approximating that of the original industrial countries, and a rapidly rising level of living at that; a high level of universal education; an impartial system of justice; a relatively impartial bureaucracy; and a political system that imposes minimal restraints on the freedom of expression, permits wide popular participation, and appears to have a good chance of proving stable. By contrast no single Latin American country could be described in quite such terms, although Latin America started with a more favorable endowment of natural resources in proportion to population and with a much more long-standing acquaintance with the intellectual traditions that had produced modern Western industrialism and the variety of modern Western political forms.

I have said that the value implications of the word "success" in this context are such as are today generally shared in the West, but one ought perhaps to pause at this point to recall something of the cost of Japan's "success," the cost that in the thirties or forties would have made a Western observer reluctant to apply the word "success" to any aspect of Japan's transformation. And one has to remember that the cost of Japan's foreign wars in human lives and resources was not incidental to Japan's development but an integral part of it. Aggressive nationalism and an expansionist foreign policy helped maintain internal unity, which enabled the state to mobilize resources for industrial development and even conditioned the disciplined acceptance of recent postwar reforms. Military objectives dictated a great deal of the investment in heavy industry; the expansion of technical education for military purposes before and during the war was a precondition for the industrial growth since; and so on. On the debit side of any balance-sheet assessment of their last century of history, one would have to set against the propensity of Latin Americans for oppressing and killing each other the cost of Japan's development in terms not only of the hardship of her own people but also of the lives and property of Chinese and Filipinos, Russians, Koreans, and Americans.

The present concern, however, is not with such overall appraisals but with the attempt to account for differences, and although war may be a partial explanation of how Japan achieved her present status, a lot more needs to be said if one is to explain why.

In the first place Japan enjoyed a number of advantages at the beginning of her transformation that offset her disadvantages in terms of natural resources and the alienness of the Western culture from which industrialism had sprung. Her very density of population, perhaps, was one such advantage. It meant that Japan was already a much more closely "governed" country, one that had, in Salvador de Madariaga's phrase, much greater "strength of being." Her peasant agriculture was already quite productive and, moreover, operated in a framework of village-wide cooperation that required responsible behavior and some "public spirit" from a sizable proportion of the population.[2] The mass of the people was, indeed, by no means wholly sunk in misery and ignorance, as witness that other major advantage of nineteenth-century Japan, the relatively wide spread of education. It is probable that the literacy rate in Japan in the mid-nineteenth century was at least as high as in Chile, and higher than in any other Latin American country.[3] The schools for the masses were mostly small private establishments supported by parents; the governmental authorities gave only moral encouragement, but at least they did not actively discourage. In the version of Confucianism that dominated Tokugawa Japan, man was not the repository of original sin but a being capable of infinite improvement. The more he improved himself, however humble his status, the better society became, and the most important method of self-improvement was learning to read the moral classics of ancient China, or at least the summary versions of their message written in simple Japanese. The masses, in short, had minds, not simply souls, to be saved.[4] It was this tradition, catalyzed by the discovery of northern European educational systems, that prompted the new central government in the early 1870's to institute compulsory education as one of its first acts of reform, and the existence of numerous private schools and of a widespread popular demand for education ensured that the decree was eventually translated into reality. By the end of the century practically every Japanese child was going to school for at least four years.[5] The contrast between this Confucian tradition and those versions of the Catholic tradition still surviving in parts of Latin America that make the Bible a forbidden book needs no elaboration.

The attempt to build a system of universal education well before

industrialization got under way suggests another important difference between Japan and Latin America. The sense of responsibility which the leaders of Meiji Japan felt for the mass of the Japanese peasantry, and the importance they attached to the peasant,
argue a sense of common Japaneseness far deeper than any sense
of common nationality binding, say, the *porteño* lawyer to the
gauchos of the uplands, or even the rural *hacendado* to his *colonos*. There are, of course, many obvious reasons why this sense of
a nationality which embraced *all* the population should have been
stronger in Japan than in Latin America: the absence of internal
racial divisions and of anything comparable to the cultural and
linguistic gulf that, conceptually at least, divides the Indian from
the mestizo and the mestizo from the creole; the absence of the
immigration that made nationalism when it came in Latin America often an internally divisive rather than a unifying factor (witness the legislation in Uruguay and Argentina reserving employment opportunities to the native-born); the geographical isolation
of Japan; the powerful initial stimulus given nationalism in the
nineteenth century by the very real threat of direct military colonization. Japan's nationalism was, in Rostow's terms, largely a re-
active nationalism, and as such sharper and stronger in proportion
to the dramatic suddenness and clarity of the threat it reacted
against. In Latin America, in the shelter of the Monroe Doctrine,
there was only the more elusive threat of economic domination, or
frontier wars, to provide anything like the same kind of stimulus.

Most important of all, perhaps, is the fact that Japan was not
only culturally homogeneous but also culturally distinct from the
outside world. The boundaries of Japanese culture and of the Japanese nation-state were coterminous. It is a familiar observation
that there is little in, say, the Chilean cultural tradition to distinguish it from the Argentinean. The Venezuelan writer defines himself only partially as a Venezuelan; he is also a Latin American,
and beyond that he belongs to European, or at least to Western,
culture. Presumably the groups distinguished in Fred Ellison's paper as the narrow nationalists, the *fidelistas,* and the cosmopolitan-
universalists exemplify precisely different emphases among these
three circles of identification. But the Japanese was not at the
center of widening circles of loyalty and cultural identity; he dwelt
in a cultural island. Only with China did he feel any sense of cul-

tural kinship; and this was a tenuous bond, much weaker, probably, than the bond betwen a Portuguese-speaking Brazilian and
a Spanish-speaking Argentinean. And beyond that there was the
West—to be approached in books only through the blur of a foreign language or through often barbarous translations; to be approached in personal intercourse only with the accompaniment
of awkwardness and confusion in the cues of etiquette.[6] Even when
the Japanese overcame those barriers, the ideas and values he
absorbed came to him with the label "Western culture" firmly
attached.

Even today the tendency of the Japanese to analyze their modern culture into its indigenous and Western components has survived the de facto coalescence of these cultural streams. Thus, for
instance, the annual exhibition of the official Japanese Academy is
still divided into a section of Japanese and a section of "Western"
painting (though the Japaneseness of the cubist, tachiste, and abstract productions in the Japanese section is not always immediately apparent). Universities do not have history departments, but
departments of Japanese, of Chinese, and of "Western" history.
Houses have rooms and "Western rooms." Clothes are *kimono* or
"Western clothes." Umbrellas are paper and bamboo affairs or
else cloth and metal "Western umbrellas." And so on. Biscuits,
beds, ink, and toothpaste are all marketed under brand names
whose peculiar phonology and often romanized script proclaim
their foreign origin, though they have long since become a familiar
part of Japanese material culture. Translators of Western academic works do not normally even attempt a style that would make
the translation indistinguishable from an original Japanese work.
Like Germans speaking guttural English with displaced verbs in a
Hollywood film, foreign writings are expected to sound alien.

In this way the everyday experience of the Japanese, and especially the educational experience of the Japanese intellectual, has
constantly served to remind him of his Japaneseness, even when,
or rather more particularly when, he was absorbing or using elements of Western culture. Such an enhanced sense of the separateness of Japanese culture could hardly have failed to reinforce his
sense of membership in the Japanese nation and his commitment
to the goals of the Japanese state.

The contrast with the cosmopolitanism of urban and intellectual Latin America is very marked and had, I would suggest, important political and economic consequences. The isolation of Japan set rigid boundaries to the possibilities of political opposition. The absence of easy opportunities for tolerable exile was a powerful teacher of the virtues of compromise. The Argentinean newspaper editor in danger of arrest or assassination could slip across the river to Montevideo and still find himself at home, amid familiar sounds and faces and familiar books, easily able to find friends and a new job. (Nowadays, perhaps, he would arrange a refuge in one of the mushrooming international organizations beforehand.) But to all but a tiny fraction of Japanese only one place has ever been home. In the repression of the thirties only a small handful of the most totally alienated group, the Communists, felt a sufficiently stronger attachment to the international Communist movement than to the Japanese nation to choose exile.

The sense of cultural separateness meant, second, that Japanese nationalism was not just an occasionally useful political weapon to channel frustrations into harmless xenophobia, but a real motivating force among Japanese political leaders and intellectuals, with roots in history and contemporary culture strong enough and broad enough for these leaders to make of it a coherent ideology, which could be diffused through the schools and through the conscript army to the whole Japanese nation.[7] The petty traders in the nineteenth century who started National Advancement Laundries and National Benefit Match Factories may well have had a personal as well as national profit in mind.[8] The great entrepreneurs of the nineteenth century may not have been so overwhelmingly inspired by patriotic motives as they often claimed to be—most of them died uncommonly rich men. But if only as a marginal element, patriotism, it seems, did enter into their calculations. The real desire to see Japan develop economically and expand militarily did on occasion prompt a willingness to sacrifice sectional interests for the sake of overriding national interests, to accept taxation or protective tariffs that might seriously inflate their costs. One may contrast the remark in W. Paul Strassmann's paper that the least important influence on Latin American businessmen's decisions is their hopes for the society at large with the experience of an American student of Japanese industry in the early fifties. He was told by employers, when he asked them why they quite obviously employed more workers than they needed, that apart from their paternalistic duty they felt it was their proper contribution to solving the national problem of overpopulation.[9] There is rather more in this, one suspects, than a mere difference in national styles of hypocrisy. The same sense of the national interest was also important in conditioning the readiness of bureaucrats and generals to keep their salary scales within fiscally feasible proportions, and to temper their inclinations to nepotism by some effort to see the state served with reasonable efficiency.

There is another aspect of the sense of separateness and of the sharpened awareness of the alien nature of Western importations that is relevant to economic development. Modern technology came to Latin America piecemeal and simply as technology. It came to Japan as part of a package deal with the whole of Western civilization. It has been rather neatly said, and with some truth, that the greatest innovation is the idea of innovation itself. If enough people can be induced to make enough new departures from traditional habits with what seem to them beneficial consequences, they may finally acquire the disposition to regard novelty in itself as desirable; and when this happens the psychological preconditions for technological take-off are fulfilled. In Japan in the 1870's and 1880's the tempo and impact of innovation were extremely great. Moreover, all the new things that invaded Japan came bearing the same label of newness and foreignness; wearing a stovepipe hat, eating beef, forming a joint-stock company, using soap instead of friction, running committees by formal rules, planting new strains of wheat, consuming tobacco wrapped in paper rather than in a pipe, reading the Bible, adopting double-entry bookkeeping, sitting on chairs, were all part of the new, Western, and, in the cant-phrase of the time, "civilized and enlightened" way of life.[10] Because they all came together, the acceptance of one element of the package helped to create the psychological predisposition for acceptance of other elements. The farmer who had taken to cigarettes and soap would look more favorably on a new plow that came from the same certified source. In Latin America, which had no period of seclusion followed by a sudden opening of the floodgates and which had always been, albeit on the periphery, a part of Western culture, there was no such supporting reinforcement of the predisposition to accept technological innovation. What is suggested here, of course, is a variant of the psychological aspects of the "big push" theory of economic development. The addition of cultural and ideological elements to technological ones can spur the snowballing propensity to innovate.

Nationalism, of course, is a two-edged weapon. It can provide those anxious for change with a charter for innovation (innovation in the national interest) and with a powerful argument for cajoling the recalcitrant. It can also provide those anxious to preserve the status quo with a charter for resisting change (protecting the national essence). The innovators may be attacked as traitors to all that is sacred in the national life.

The intellectual and even the political history of modern Japan can plausibly be interpreted as an oscillation between the dominance of these two types of nationalism, with first the innovators and then the traditionalists dominating the ideological airspace.[11] The enthusiasm for all things Western that characterized the fifteen years after 1870 gave place to a traditionalist reaction by 1890. Twenty-five years and three wars later came the so-called liberal twenties, when again the West was the model for progress and progress was again in fashion. The reaction of the fanatically "nativist" thirties was followed in the late forties by a widespread and genuine enthusiasm for the Occupation's message of democracy, business efficiency, and the American Way of Life.

But the common metaphor of the swinging pendulum is less apt than that of the zigzag forward movement. At each change of direction accommodations were reached between the traditionalists and the innovators that allowed the strengthening, or the preservative embalming, of elements of the national tradition which hardly impeded and even sometimes helped the process of economic growth. In the "largely irrelevant but no impediment" category, one might include the preservation of elements of Japanese material culture. Japanese dress and domestic architecture, Japanese food and wine, government grants for the protection of ancient shrines and temples, the vigorous continuation of Japanese arts and crafts such as flower arrangement and the tea ceremony, all helped to reassure the conservative Japanese that in some respects at least Japan was still Japan. Perhaps only the Mexicans in Latin America have anything like a symbolic base for this kind of assured sense of national self-identity.

In the field of social relations the role of the preserved traditional elements was more subtle. They were modified and mobilized, not simply preserved.[12] The Emperor, restored to nominal power in 1868, legitimized the new innovating government and offered a personal focus of loyalty that helped to make the new nationalism intelligible to the mass of the people. Without the sanctioning authority of the Imperial tradition, further fortified by the mystique of a reconstructed Shinto religion,[13] nineteenth-century governments might never have had the strength and stability to impose high taxation and otherwise mobilize resources for state-sponsored economic development.[14] Other traditional elements were similarly utilized. The old samurai code of Bushido, refurbished and idealized, provided an integrating ideology for the armed forces.[15] The Confucian ethic of personal relations was reformulated as the "fine virtues and noble customs of the Japanese family system"—the uniquely *Japanese* family system. It was explicitly taught in primary school ethics courses,[16] and reinforced by incorporation in the juridical system by the Civil Code of 1897.[17] The Confucian ethic served to preserve an image of society as properly hierarchical and based on personal loyalties, and thus to strengthen authoritarian tendencies in general, enhance the docility of the labor force, and check the erosion of the government's traditionally sanctioned authority. It also rationalized family aggrandizement as a proper and laudable motive for entrepreneurial activity. It provided a rationale for, and thereby made a more consciously planned policy out of, the new impersonal and bureaucratized paternalism of the large corporations—the so-called enterprise-family ideal—which developed in the twenties.

It can be quite justly argued that this conscious reincorporation of traditional elements in Japan not only satisfied the sentiments of the traditionalists, but also aided at least the economic development of the country. It can equally be argued that it impeded political and social change toward a more liberal and egalitarian structure. But again one can make out a case for saying that this, too, was in the long run beneficial. The authoritarian exploitation of tradition postponed the establishment of liberal democracy until industrialization and the development of education had sufficiently transformed the social base to give democratic institutions a good chance of stability. Latin America, by contrast, abounds with examples of what, if one was not hesitant about assuming a necessary and proper sequence of historical stages exemplified in European history, one would call premature political development: the establishment, under pressure of ideas originating outside the national boundaries, of political institutions that assume a degree of sophistication on the part of voters, a sense of responsibility in the exercise of power and the practice of opposition, and a minimum degree of consensus about national goals, which simply do not exist and which the new institutions themselves cannot succeed in creating before they are perverted beyond redemption.

Similarly, welfare-state ideologies, originally the product of an advanced stage of capitalism, have combined with traditions of the paternalistic state in many much poorer and as yet unindustrialized countries of Latin America. The combination has produced political demands so potent that the state is forced to accept responsibilities toward its citizens which, however admirable in themselves, divert into consumption resources needed for economic development. Again, Japanese governments could resist such demands until the Japanese economy could easily afford them.

(The postponement of change, however, usually implies eventual revolution, for those who cling to privilege and traditional authority rarely know when to give way. Whether Japan's rulers would eventually have shown a sufficiently acute sense of realities to avoid revolution we shall never know, for in Japan's case the cataclysm came from without—in the shape of a devastating defeat and a reformist Occupation.)

These are but particular aspects of the general situation of the late-developer. Economic growthmen of the Rostow school can demonstrate with a good deal of plausibility that industrialization is a process that takes more or less the same length of time anywhere; take-off to maturity requires sixty years whenever the society chooses to start. But in certain things there is only one time scale—a world time scale. Steel mills are not carried across frontiers on the feet of migrant birds, but certain things—ideas, ideals, consumer tastes, and the reverberations of revolutions and moonshots—do slip across almost as easily. So, for instance, Japan like Brazil had its temples of positivism in the nineties and impressionistic painters by the early nineteen-hundreds. In the first decade of this century, Japanese as well as Chilean mines were the scene of violently suppressed strikes, and Japan, too, had the beginnings of a more permanently organized labor movement by the end of the First World War.[18] Like many Latin American countries she had social realist novelists writing "proletarian novels" in the thirties;[19] and so on. It was just that isolation and the strength of tradition served until 1945 to keep the effects of these worldwide currents to a minimum.

Nor was this Japan's only advantage in the matter of timing. The situation of a late-developer can be significantly different in this respect from that of an even later developer, for ideological pressures tend to be cumulative, particularly in a postwar world with airplanes and transistor radios to provide the channels, and the United Nations to provide the pressures, for the global diffusion of political principles. Japan's advantage was that her industrialization began *early* enough and proceeded rapidly enough so that, by 1945, Japan *was* prepared for a version of liberal democracy and *could* begin to afford extensive welfare services.

The same point can be made in demographic terms. Drugs, like ideas, can cross frontiers fairly easily. The dramatic fall in the death rate came simultaneously in both Japan and Latin America in the late forties. But in Japan the industrial and educational revolution and the revolution in mobility aspirations had by then reached the point at which a simple legislative act permitting abortion could reduce the birth rate with dramatic suddenness, and so cut population growth back to manageable proportions.[20] Japan may well be the last country that started its take-off early enough to solve its population problem in this, the classical way, through the medium of unmanipulated individual preferences.

Another aspect of the demographic problem is that Japan was relatively free of "premature urbanization"—due to the push of rural poverty rather than the pull of urban opportunity—the social and political consequences of which in the shanty suburbs of Latin America are described in Frank Bonilla's paper, and the sources of which are described in Charles Wagley's. For this, however, something more than the manageable rate of population growth and the fact that Japan launched into machine industry in the days before the automatic factory is responsible. Also relevant is the importance to agriculture of the peasant family holding; the in-

stitution of the landholding peasant family was strong enough (as
it usually is, though in the Japanese case there was the extra element of ideological reinforcement) to give rural areas a far more
elastic capacity to absorb population than in a plantation economy. If an urban job was not easily to be found, the younger son
could more easily stay at home. If he found a job and was dismissed
at a time of recession, he could return home and by making himself marginally useful on the farm earn the right to sponge off his
inheriting elder brother. If unemployment one must have, there
is a good deal to be said for taking it in the concealed form of un-
deremployment in agriculture—as the Chinese, too, seem recently
to have concluded, to judge by their policy of returning population
from the cities. (And this, incidentally, is a consideration of general relevance to land-tenure policy. Reforms which seek to create owner-farmed peasant holdings used to be criticized on the
grounds, among others, that they inhibit the release of a fully committed urban labor force. Today a more common problem is to
slow the premature emergence of a committed but unemployed
urban labor force.)

To return from this digression on timing and agriculture to
the role of tradition, the contrast between Latin America and
Japan in this regard would seem clear enough. When a conscious
nationalistic urge for modernization began in the nineteenth century there was little in the Hispanic American tradition that could
serve at once (a) to so emphasize the specific differentiae of, say,
Chilean or Brazilian society as to satisfy the traditionalists, and
(b) to somehow facilitate change. The *indigenista* movement, it
seems, nowhere succeeded in making a substantial impact except
perhaps in Mexico, where the ideal of the ancient corporate Indian community combined with more modern forms of collectivism to produce the *ejido*. Cuauhtemoc may have proved an integrating symbol for the Mexicans, but a much weaker one than the
ancient Emperors of Japan, whose living descendant still resided
in Tokyo. There was no continuity with the Aztec tradition sufficient for anything comparable to, say, the Japanese family system
to be carried over into modern times. Although the solidarity of
the upper-class family, as described by Strassmann, does seem to
have been a distinctive Latin American characteristic, this was still

a class and not a national phenomenon and was never utilized ideologically as a symbol of the national essence.

There is another aspect of this search for traditions. When seeking to define a national self-image in a nationalistic frame of mind, one is most likely to seize on those features which supposedly differentiate one from one's major international antagonist. For Japan this point of counter-reference, the thou than which one has to feel more holy, has been the West generally and in the twentieth century America more particularly. For Latin America, since the beginning of this century at least, it has been almost exclusively America. But in differentiating themselves from Americans, the Japanese could point to the beauties of their tight family system; their patriotic loyalty to the Emperor contrasting with American selfish individualism; the pacific subtleties of Buddhism contrasting with the turbulent stridency of Christianity; and so on. But it was not so easy for a Latin American to establish the Latin American differentiae in terms of family, political, or legal institutions. He had to fall back on "spirit" and attitudes; and since the most visible American was the businessman, he tended—*vide arielismo* as Ellison describes it—to make his dimension of difference the materialist-spiritual one. Thus, by scorning American devotion to technology and profit, he made something of a virtue out of the stark fact of economic backwardness. For their part the Japanese had enough arguments with which to fortify their uncertain sense of their superior Japaneseness without resorting to this one, with its inhibiting effect on indigenous economic growth.

In *arielismo,* as in the serene and assured scorn of the modern world that sometimes characterizes England's older universities, there is an element that can only be explained by the continued existence of a traditional, landed upper class. And in this there is a powerful and important difference between Japan and almost any country in Latin America. In Japan the attenuation of the ties that had bound the feudal aristocracy and gentry to their lands began at the end of the sixteenth century and was completed in 1870.[21] During the late feudal period the samurai gentry left their small sub-fiefs to live in the castle towns of their feudal lords. Each of these larger fiefs was controlled from the castle town by an administration, staffed by the samurai gentry, which as time went on became increasingly bureaucratized. There were no longer any manors, any land-based knights. The exploitation of these large fiefs took the form of a standardized, impersonal, produce tax levied on the peasant producers, the proceeds from which were doled out to the samurai as hereditary rice stipends.

When the new central government took over in 1868 this system was fairly easily dismantled over the course of a few years. The fiefs were turned into prefectures; the feudal lords, compensated with titles and government bonds, were forced to break their ties with their former territories. The samurai gentry were also compensated for their lost hereditary revenues, though on a lesser scale; some were absorbed in the new centralized bureaucracy, some went into the new national army, others became teachers, lawyers, policemen, and businessmen.[22]

The old aristocratic fief-holders, the three hundred noble families who formed the new nineteenth-century peerage, had little effective power in modern Japan. One reason was that they had already, in the latter years of the feudal period, been effectively separated from the exercise of power by the development of fief bureaucracies—they had been bred to reign but not to rule. Another was that they had lost the power and the prestige direct ownership of land can give. This did not mean that there were no landlords in rural Japan. There were; and a few of them were rich. But the majority of them were members of the peasant class who had accumulated extra land through the improvidence or the misfortunes of their fellow peasants. They did manage to predominate in the early political parties and they retained some power as a veto group until the postwar land reform.[23] But they never exercised effective political leadership because they could not rival the prestige or the elitist traditions of the bureaucracy, recruited as it was predominantly from the samurai—their former feudal superiors.

And so any analysis of modern Japanese history in terms of the "emergence of the middle sectors" becomes complicated. If at the beginning of the industrialization process the samurai were Japan's ruling "upper" class, those among them who held effective power became upper-ranking bureaucrats, professional men of typically "middle sector" type who derived their income from salaries, not family wealth, and claimed their position on the basis not of lineage, but (especially after the beginning of civil service entrance examinations in 1887) of demonstrated ability. Later, other typically "middle" groups emerged to share their power. The unified bureaucracy soon generated a separate, contending military wing.[24] The Constitution of 1889 and the partial separation of legislative and executive functions gave birth to a new group of professional politicians (which, however, ex-bureaucrats soon dominated as they still do today).[25] The landlords have been mentioned. As industrialization proceeded, a new business class acquired influence through its financing of the political parties and more direct connections with the bureaucracy.

The work of journalists and intellectuals in molding an increasingly articulate public opinion imposed further constraints, and so, less directly, did the university teachers who controlled the training of the would-be bureaucrat. All these groups, with the exception of the landlords, were at first predominantly of samurai origin, and although they absorbed large numbers of commoners, continued to retain something of a common samurai ethos. They were interrelated by kinship and marriage ties, by school and university friendships. But if they may be spoken of as a single class, there was no doubt that until the last decade, at least, the bureaucracy constituted its core, absorbed its most talented members, and carried the highest prestige.

Whether they be called the upper class, or, because of the history of their development in the classical Western model, "middle sectors," it seems clear that today a similar combination of occupational groups dominates many Latin American countries. The important difference between Japan and these countries is the difference between, on the one hand, a society in which a new administrative class replaces the old landed upper class before industrialization begins; and on the other, a society in which the new professional groups, created as a *result* of economic and social change, gradually share power with an existing landed upper class and in the process merge with it (insofar, indeed, as they are not originally sprung from it) and take over many of its values. Even in Mexico, the post-revolutionary administrators took over much of the administrative structure and many values of the former regime, and only in the recent revolutions in Bolivia and Cuba have really sharp breaks occurred.

In contrast the new samurai bureaucracy that took power in 1868 was building from the ground up, and by eliminating the landed upper class from the scene Japan gained great advantages in industrializing. The salaried bureaucracy was not bound by landed ties to competing economic interests that might have made it lukewarm toward industry. Its very nature as a bureaucracy inclined it toward rationalizing legalistic procedures and the creation of predictable formal structures, rather than toward reliance on the more arbitrary wisdom and judgment of those who exercise authority by hereditary right. And since members of the bureaucracy were unquestionably top people, they were not tempted to improve their social standing by buying land or by imitating the manners of a landed aristocracy, with its typical scorn of menial occupations and pursuit of conspicuous leisure as well as conspicuous consumption. The Japanese did not suffer, therefore, from an analogue of *la pareza criolla;* they could, on the contrary, draw selectively on elements of the Confucian tradition to create that ethic of serious-minded diligence for which they are famed.[26] *Mañana,* for the Japanese, was the day against which one prudently prepares, not the day for which, hopefully, fate will bountifully provide.

I referred earlier to the fashion for studying Japan as a model of successful industrial transformation. Models should provide "lessons," and one who has succumbed to that fashion is perhaps obliged to hazard a few conclusions as to whether indeed Japan does offer any for modern Latin America. The last point, i.e., the advantage of discontinuity and revolutionary change *before* industrialization begins, particularly in the composition of the governing class, can hardly be generalized into a prescription for revolution in countries where these processes are already under way and much of the apparatus of the modern state is already built. In any case, the history of Cuba in the sixties is likely to provide far more relevant indications of the advantages and disadvantages of revolutionary change than the history of Japan in the nineteenth century. Similarly, the use of traditional channels and modes of authority in Japan's development again shows only that they can be used to promote industrial and even political change if the commanding heights of authority are firmly seized by innovating leaders *before* they are eroded away by economic and social change and the influence of egalitarian ideologies. It is too late to try to capture such traditional channels of authority when that process of erosion is already well advanced. Again, many of the factors indicated as differentiating Japan from Latin America—the Confucian tradition of education, the sense of cultural separateness and the coincidence of cultural and political boundaries, the timing of industrialization with respect to world-wide ideological and demographic trends—are advantages inherent in Japan's situation that can hardly be reproduced by an act of political will.

The only plausibly generalizable quantity in the equation is the strong identification with the nation and awareness of national purpose which in Japan undoubtedly helped create the cohesion needed to induce change and subordinate short-term sectional to long-run majority interests. Although Latin American countries are so much less favored by circumstances for the natural creation of such sentiments, perhaps they can be induced (there are, after all, far more effective means of communication now available) and utilized for development. But to recall earlier remarks about cost, it must be remembered that the national purposes of which the Japanese were aware and for which they unitedly strove were for most of Japan's modern history predominantly military in character. It remains to be demonstrated that a sense of national purpose can prove as effective and as compelling when defined in terms of economic growth rates and social welfare. Cuba may one day provide a crucial test of this. If eventually tempers cool and accommodations with her neighbors can be reached, we shall be able to see whether the emotional strength behind the slogan "Cuba Sí!" can remain undiminished when it ceases to be conditioned by its obverse, "Yanqui No!"

Notes

1. The Peasant

1. Examples of "urban" criteria are: Mexico—populated centers of more than 2,500 inhabitants; Guatemala—places with 2,000 or more inhabitants, and places with 1,500 or more inhabitants if running water service is provided in the houses; Brazil—administrative centers of *municipios* and centers of population of districts, including suburban zones.

2. Eric R. Wolf, "Aspects of Group Relations in a Complex Society: Mexico," *American Anthropologist*, LVIII (1956), 1065.

3. Robert Redfield, *The Folk Culture of Yucatan* (Chicago, 1941).

4. Elsewhere, e.g., Charles Wagley and Marvin Harris, "A Typology of Latin American Sub-cultures," *American Anthropologist*, LVII (1955), 428–51, the terms "Modern Indian" and "peasant" were used for these same subtypes or, as we called them, "subcultures." Eric Wolf, in his "Types of Latin American Peasantry," *American Anthropologist*, LVII (1955), 452–71, has termed them "corporate" and "open" peasant types, terms derived from the structure of the communities in which each type characteristically lives. I agree with Wolf that both types are "peasants," and thus I have chosen to use the terms "Indian peasant" and "mestizo peasant" in the present paper. They differ from one another both in culture content and in terms of their respective positions within the national social structure. Richard N. Adams, in "Cultural Components of Central America," *American Anthropologist*, LVIII (1956), 881–907, has provided a much more refined set of subtypes for Central America.

5. Wolf, "Types of Latin American Peasantry," p. 461.

6. One might also include as mestizo those rural groups that collect palm nuts, gather wild rubber, raise livestock, and fish, when these activities are performed outside the orbit of large estates and are combined with subsistence agriculture.

7. Conrad Arensberg, "The Community as an Object and as a Sample," *American Anthropologist*, LXIII (1961), 253.

8. Alfred L. Kroeber, *Anthropology* (New York, 1948). See also Robert Redfield, *The Primitive World and Its Transformations* (Ithaca, 1953), p. 31; George Foster, "What is Folk Culture?" *American Anthropologist*, LV (1953), 153ff; Wolf, "Types of Latin American Peasantry," p. 452.

9. Harry W. Hutchinson, *Village and Plantation Life in Northeastern Brazil* (Seattle, 1957).

10. John P. Gillin, *The Culture of Security in San Carlos: A Study of a Guatemalan Community of Indians and Ladinos* (New Orleans, 1951). See also Melvin M. Tumin, *Caste in a Peasant Society* (Princeton, 1952).

11. The author carried out intensive field research in both communities many years ago. Field research in Santiago Chimaltenango was done in 1937 (see Wagley, *Economics of a Guatemalan Village*, Memoir of the American Anthropology

Association, Washington, D.C., 1941, No. 58, and *The Social and Religious Life of a Guatemalan Village*, Memoir of the American Anthropology Association, Washington, D.C., 1949, No. 71). The research in Itá was spread over several periods from 1942 to 1948, but the longest period was in 1948 (see Wagley, *Amazon Town: A Study of Man in the Tropics*, New York, 1953). A short revisit to Santiago Chimaltenango was made in 1956, and one to Itá in 1962. It must not be thought that either of these revisits was in any way a restudy, but they did allow a quick eyewitness view of some obvious changes and trends in the communities in question.

12. Nathan L. Whetten, *Guatemala, the Land and the People* (New Haven, 1961), pp. 76ff.

13. The 1950 census puts it at about 1,800 people.

14. Whetten, *Guatemala*, p. 77.

15. For a time during the Ubico regime, Santiago Chimaltenango was attached to San Pedro Necta. The restoration of separate status was a major aim of community policy, and was achieved in 1946 during Arévalo's presidency. See Juan de Dios Rosales in Wagley, *Social and Religious Life*, pp. 133–34.

16. Manning Nash, "Cantel 1944–1954," in Richard N. Adams, ed., *Political Changes in Guatemalan Indian Communities* (New Orleans, 1957), p. 102.

17. Whetten, *Guatemala*, pp. 321–22.

18. Adams, *Political Changes*, pp. 1–54.

19. Manning Nash, "Cantel," p. 30.

20. Robert H. Ewald, "San Antonio Sacatepéquez 1932–1953," in Adams, *Political Changes*, pp. 20–21.

21. June Nash, in "Protestantism in an Indian Village in the Western Highlands of Guatemala," in *Alpha Kappa Delta* (Winter 1960), pp. 49–53, discusses the effect of Protestantism on the folk Catholic *cofradía* system in the Guatemalan community of Cantel and the fact that "the Protestant sects drew their younger and more alert members into a network of social relations which was national in scope" (p. 50). See also Harry S. McArthur, "La estructura política-religiosa de Aguacatán," in *Guatemala indígena*, I, No. 2 (1961), 63.

22. Jorge Arias B., "Aspectos demográficos de la población indígena de Guatemala," *Guatemala indígena*, I, No. 2 (1961), 16.

23. Richard W. Patch, "Bolivia: U.S. Assistance in a Revolutionary Setting," in Council on Foreign Relations, *Social Change in Latin America Today* (New York, 1960), pp. 108–76.

24. Ruben E. Reina, *Chinautla, A Guatemalan Indian Community* (New Orleans, 1960), p. 85.

25. William W. Stein, "Outside Contact and Cultural Stability in a Peruvian Highland Community," in American Ethnological Society, *Cultural Stability and Cultural Change* (Seattle, 1957), p. 19; see also his *Hualcán, Life in the Highlands of Peru* (Ithaca, 1961), pp. 18–21.

26. Reina, *Chinautla*, p. 85. It should not be thought that I am arguing against agrarian and land-tenure reform. It is perhaps the single most-needed change in Latin American society. Unless it is thorough and sweeping, however, it will not solve fundamental problems and might have some strange side effects.

27. Wolf, "Review of *Chinautla: A Guatemalan Indian Community* by Ruben Reina," *American Anthropologist*, LXIV, No. 1, Part 1 (1962), 198. See also Reina, *Chinautla*, p. 102.

28. Itá is a fictitious name for a real town. (See Wagley, *Amazon Town*.)

29. T. Lynn Smith, *Brazil, People and Institutions* (Baton Rouge, 1954), pp. 594ff.

30. At the time of my visit to Itá, the cruzeiro had fallen from 300 to 600 to the dollar, and the nation was wavering between presidential and parliamentary systems, an issue settled in January 1963 by a plebiscite in favor of a presidential system. In the state of Rio de Janeiro, there had just been riots resulting from food shortages. Peasant unrest was reported constantly from the arid northeastern region of the country.

31. Thomas Carroll, "The Land Reform Issue in Latin America," in Albert O. Hirschman, ed., *Latin American Issues* (New York, 1961), p. 61.

32. According to the Brazilian census, 34.4 per cent of all agricultural establishments were composed of tracts of less than ten hectares and altogether accounted for but 1.3 per cent of the land in cultivation. Another 51 per cent of all agricultural establishments was composed of tracts of between ten and 100 hectares accounting for 15.3 per cent of the total area. The remaining 14.6 per cent of agricultural holdings accounted for 83.4 per cent of the area.

33. Patch, "Bolivia," pp. 119ff.

34. During the discussion of the paper on "Rural Labor" by Richard Adams, Henry Dobyns reported that of 15 cases of violence in rural Peru, one case involved an inter-indigenous land feud and most of the others police intervention to protect the land ownership system (i.e., haciendas).

35. Wolf, describing Mexican Indian communities, has explained this conservatism in economic and functional terms. He wrote, "Lacking adequate resources in land, water, technical knowledge, and contacts in the market, the majority also lack the instruments which can transform use values into marketable commodities. At the same time, their inability to speak Spanish and their failure to understand the cues for the new patterns of nation-oriented behavior isolate them from the channels of communication between community and nation. Under these circumstances they must cling to the traditional 'rejection pattern' of their ancestors, because their narrow economic base sets limits to the introduction of new cultural alternatives. These are all too often nonfunctional for them. The production of sufficient maize for subsistence purposes remains their major goal in life. In their case the granting of *ejidos* tended to lend support to their accustomed way of life and reinforced their attachment to their traditional heritage." ("Aspects of Group Relations," p. 1073.)

36. The concept of the "cultural broker" and the importance of the relationship of peasant communities to the larger society were pointed out during the discussion of an earlier draft of this paper by Manning Nash at the Scottsdale meetings. Neither Nash nor the other participants are, of course, responsible for my own treatment of the "cultural broker" in these pages, which is meant to suggest important lines of future research.

37. Wolf, "Aspects of Group Relations," p. 1072.

38. *Ibid.*, p. 1075.

39. Adams, *Political Changes.* Juan Pérez Jolote, the Tzotzil-speaking Indian from Chamula in Chiapas, Mexico, whose story is told so vividly by Ricardo Pozas, is an example of an Indian who seems to have rejected his outside experience and to have reintegrated his life into the traditional community. (See Pozas, *Juan, the Chamula: An Ethnological Re-creation of the Life of a Mexican Indian,* trans. by Lysander Kemp, Berkeley, 1962.) José Rojas, a Quechua-speaking peasant from the community of Ucureña in Cochabamba department of Bolivia, is an example of a man who became a native leader upon his return. After living in Argentina, Rojas returned to Ucureña, where "he worked as a laborer while he assisted in organizing the *campesinos*." He ultimately became a national figure as a campesino leader. (See Patch, "Bolivia," pp. 119–20.)

2. Rural Labor

1. Charles Wagley and Marvin Harris, "A Typology of Latin American Sub-cultures," *American Anthropologist*, LVII (1955), 428–51; cf. Eric R. Wolf, "San José: Sub-cultures of a 'Traditional' Coffee Municipality," in Julian Steward *et al.*, *The People of Puerto Rico* (Urbana, 1956), pp. 171–264, and Wolf and Sidney W. Mintz, "Haciendas and Plantations in Middle America and the Antilles," *Social and Economic Studies*, VI (1957), 380–412.

2. See the contributions of Charles Wagley and Frank Bonilla in this volume.

3. George W. Hill, José A. Silva M., and Ruth Oliver de Hill, *La Vida rural en Venezuela* (Caracas, 1960), p. 14.

4. Wolf, "Specific Aspects of the Plantation System in the New World," in *Plantation Systems of the New World* (Washington, D.C., 1959), Pan American Union Social Science Monographs No. VII, pp. 136–46.

5. Allan R. Holmberg and Henry F. Dobyns, "The Process of Accelerating Community Change," *Human Organization*, XXI (1962), 107–9. See also Dobyns, Carlos Monge M., and Mario C. Vásquez, "Summary of Technical Organization Process and Reactions to It," *Human Organization*, XXI (1962), 109–15; and International Labor Organization (ILO), *Indigenous Peoples* (Geneva, 1953).

6. Manning Nash, *Machine Age Maya*, Memoir of the American Anthropological Association, Washington, D.C., 1958, No. 87, p. 80.

7. Wilburg Jiménez Castro, *Migraciones internas de Costa Rica* (Washington, D.C., 1956), pp. 89–90.

8. Louis J. Ducoff, *Human Resources of Central America, Panama, and Mexico, 1950–1980, in Relation to Some Aspects of Economic Development* (New York, 1960), p. 80.

9. Richard N. Adams, *A Community in the Andes, Problems and Progress in Muquiyauyo* (Seattle, 1959), p. 97.

10. George W. Hill, José A. Silva M., and Ruth Oliver de Hill, *Vida rural*, pp. 20–21.

11. George W. Hill, *Central Tacarigua* (Caracas, 1960); cf. George W. Hill, *El Estado Sucre: Sus Recursos humanos* (Caracas, 1961).

12. Wolf, "San José," pp. 202ff.

13. Ruben E. Reina, *Chinautla, A Guatemalan Indian Community* (New Orleans, 1960), pp. 55–130.

14. Richard N. Adams, *Cultural Surveys of Panama-Nicaragua-Guatemala-El Salvador-Honduras* (Washington, D.C., 1957), p. 305.

15. George McBride, *Chile: Land and Society* (New York, 1936).

16. Elena Padilla Seda, "Nocorá: The Subcultures of Workers on a Government Owned Sugar Plantation," in Steward *et al.*, *People of Puerto Rico*, p. 290.

17. Melvin M. Tumin, with Arnold S. Feldman, *Social Class and Social Change in Puerto Rico* (Princeton, 1961), pp. 448–49.

18. ILO, *Indigenous Peoples*, pp. 219–20.

19. Wolf, "Types of Latin American Peasantry," *American Anthropologist*, LVII (1955), 452–71. Cf. Wolf and Mintz, "Haciendas and Plantations"; Louis C. Faron, "The Formation of Two Indigenous Communities in Coastal Peru," *American Anthropologist*, LXII (1960), 437–53.

20. Duane Metzger, personal communication.

21. Mintz, "Cañamelar: The Subculture of a Rural Sugar Plantation Proletariat," in Steward *et al.*, *People of Puerto Rico*, pp. 314–417; and Elena Padilla Seda, "Nocorá," p. 281.

22. Henry F. Dobyns, personal communication.

23. Thomas McCorkle, "Community Persistence and Cultural Change in Margarita Island, Venezuela" (ms. in author's possession); Adams, *Community in the Andes*; and William Mangin, "The Role of Regional Associations in the Adaptation of Rural Populations in Peru," *Sociologus* (N.S.), IX (1959), 23–36.

24. In two Caracas samples, 7.14 per cent and 5.56 per cent gave this as the reason for the movement; in a Lima sample, 8.6 per cent did. See Organization of American States, *Exodo rural en Venezuela* (Washington, D.C., n.d.); and José Matos Mar, "Migration and Urbanization," in Philip M. Hauser, ed., *Urbanization in Latin America* (New York, 1961), p. 182.

25. Elena Padilla Seda, "Nocorá," p. 290.

26. Wilburg Jiménez Castro, *Migraciones internas*, p. 89.

27. George W. Hill, *Central Tacarigua*, p. 85b.

28. *Ibid.*, p. 74a.

29. Reina, *Chinautla*, pp. 74–75.

30. Thomas Norris, "Economic Systems: Large and Small Land Holdings," in Charles P. Loomis *et al.*, *Turrialba: Social Systems and the Introduction of Social Change* (Glencoe, 1953), p. 102.

31. Dobyns, in a comment on an earlier draft of this paper.

32. Steward *et al.*, *People of Puerto Rico*.

33. ILO, *Indigenous Peoples*, p. 388.

34. For Vicos, see Holmberg and Dobyns, "Process"; for Bolivia, Richard W. Patch, "Bolivia: U.S. Assistance in a Revolutionary Setting," in Council on Foreign Relations, *Social Change in Latin America Today* (New York, 1960), pp. 108–76; for rural labor unions, Héctor Martínez, *La Hacienda Capana*, Serie Monográfica No. 2, Plan Nacional de Integración de la Población Indígena (Lima, 1962), and Stokes Newbold, "Receptivity to Communist-Fomented Agitation in Rural Guatemala," *Economic Development and Cultural Change*, V (1957), 338–61; and for Mexico, Nathan L. Whetten, *Rural Mexico* (Chicago, 1948), pp. 182ff.

35. Adams, *Cultural Surveys*, pp. 300–301, 543–44.

36. For Puerto Rico, see Robert A. Manners, "Tabara: Subcultures of a Tobacco and Mixed Crop Municipality," in Steward *et al.*, *People of Puerto Rico*, pp. 93–170; for Colombia, Roberto Pineda Giraldo, *Estudio de la zona tabacalera santandereana*, Departamento Técnico de la Seguridad Social Campesina, No. 2 (Bogotá, 1955), pp. 40–43; and for Brazil, Manuel Dieguez Junior, "Land Tenure and Use in the Brazilian Plantation System," in *Plantation Systems of the New World*, pp. 104–22.

37. Carl Taylor, *Rural Life in Argentina* (Baton Rouge, 1948).

38. Arnold Strickon, "Class and Kinship in Argentina," *Ethnology*, I (1962), 500–515.

39. Mintz, "Cañamelar"; cf. his *Worker in the Cane: A Puerto Rican Life History* (New Haven, 1960), and Wolf, "Specific Aspects."

40. See Eugene A. Hammel, *Wealth, Authority and Prestige in the Inca Valley, Peru* (Albuquerque, 1962), University of New Mexico Publications in Anthropology No. 10.

41. Francis LeBeau, "Agricultura de Guatemala," in J. L. Arriola, ed., *Integración social en Guatemala* (Guatemala City, 1956), pp. 296–301.

42. Newbold, "Receptivity."

43. Charles P. Loomis, Thomas L. Norris, and Charles H. Proctor, "Social Status and Communication," in Loomis *et al.*, *Turrialba*, pp. 39–72; cf. Hammel, *Wealth*.

44. LeBeau, "Agricultura."

45. Strickon, "The Euro-American Ranching Complex as a Cultural-Ecological Type" (unpublished ms.).

46. Roy Clifford pointed this out for Turrialba, in Loomis *et al.*, *Turrialba*, pp. 231–57.

47. Elena Padilla Seda, "Nocorá," p. 312.

48. International Bank for Reconstruction and Development, *The Economic Development of Guatemala* (Washington, D.C., 1951), and *The Economic Development of Mexico* (Baltimore, 1953).

49. Héctor Martínez, *Hacienda Capana*, p. 7.

50. Dobyns records in detail 15 cases for Peru for 1960 in a manuscript in his possession: "The largest number of incidents . . . involved national police protection of the interests of hacienda managements against Indian serfs or peasants."

51. Mons German, Fals Borda, and Eduardo Umaña Luna, *La Violencia en Colombia* (Bogotá, 1962).

52. Charles Wagley, *Amazon Town* (New York, 1953); cf. Robert F. Murphy, "Credit vs. Cash: A Case Study," *Human Organization*, XIV (1955), 26–28.

53. Robert J. Alexander, *Today's Latin America* (New York, 1962), p. 103.

54. For Cantel, see Manning Nash, "The Recruitment of Wage Labor and the Development of New Skills," in Bert Hoselitz, ed., *Agrarian Societies in Transition*, special issue of *The Annals of the American Academy of Political and Social Science*, CCCV (1956); for Nocorá, Elena Padilla Seda, "Nocorá," pp. 277ff; Duane Metzger observed the same situation in Mexico.

55. Patch, "Bolivia."

56. Metzger, in a personal communication.

57. Elena Padilla Seda, "Nocorá," p. 313.

58. Mintz, "Cañamelar," pp. 394ff.

59. Indeed the disillusionment that concludes the story of Mintz's *Worker in the Cane* is more than the merely personal frustration of a man who has not satisfied his immediate needs in politics and unions; more important is the realization that the shift from the older, hated, personalistic hacienda has not provided the independence of action he anticipated. Rather, he has simply gained another master, the government—a master quite unreachable because of the many organizations between it and the individual worker.

60. It should be noted here that some observers characterize the paternalistic relation as personalistic. The distinction, however, is an important one. The term "familialistic" that has been used for some labor relations will not be used in this context, since many qualities it involves are discussed later, in the section on social structure and attitudes.

61. Charles Erasmus, "Culture Structure and Process: The Occurrence and Disappearance of Reciprocal Farm Labor," *Southwestern Journal of Anthropology*, XII (1956), 444–70.

62. Elman and Helen R. Service, *Tobati, Paraguayan Town* (Chicago, 1954), pp. 126–30.

63. Gerardo and Alicia Reichel-Dolmatoff, *The People of Aritama: The Culture and Personality of a Colombian Mestizo Village* (Chicago, 1961), pp. 259–71.

64. William F. Whyte and Allan R. Holmberg, "Human Problems of a U.S. Enterprise in Latin America," *Human Organization*, XV, No. 3 (1956), 1–40.

65. Manners, "Tabara," p. 115.

66. Adams, *Community in the Andes*.

67. Holmberg and Dobyns, "Process"; cf. Dobyns, Carlos Monge M., and Mario C. Vásquez, "Summary"; and LeBeau, "Agricultura."

68. Elena Padilla Seda, "Nocorá," pp. 296ff.

69. Manners, "Tabara," pp. 114–15.

70. Elizabeth E. Hoyt, "The Indian Laborer on Guatemalan Coffee Fincas," *Inter-American Economic Affairs*, IX (1955), 33–46.

71. Newbold, "Receptivity," p. 349.

72. Mintz, "Cañamelar" and *Worker in the Cane*; Elena Padilla Seda, "Nocorá"; Wolf, "Specific Aspects"; George W. Hill, *Central Tacarigua*; Héctor Martínez, "Hacienda Capana"; Loomis *et al.*, *Turrialba*; Nash, *Machine Age Maya*; and Strickon, "Class and Kinship in Argentina."

73. Wolf, "Specific Aspects."

74. Strickon, "Class and Kinship in Argentina."

75. Wolf, "San José," pp. 208ff.

76. Adams, *Cultural Surveys*, p. 331.

77. See especially Reina, "Two Patterns of Friendship in a Guatemalan Community," *American Anthropologist*, LXI (1959), 44–50.

78. Oscar Lewis, "Urbanization Without Breakdown," *Scientific Monthly*, LXXV (1952), 31–41; Mangin, "Role of Regional Associations"; cf. Strickon, "Class and Kinship in Argentina."

79. Bertram Hutchinson, *Mobilidade e trabalho* (Rio de Janeiro, 1960). See also the contribution of Frank Bonilla in this volume.

80. See the contributions of Loomis, Julio O. Morales, Ray A. Clifford, and Olen E. Leonard, in Loomis *et al.*, *Turrialba*.

81. For Puerto Rico, see Mintz, "Cañamelar," p. 412, and Wolf, "San José," p. 230; for Mexico, George Foster, *Empire's Children: The People of Tzintzuntzan* (Washington, D.C., 1948), pp. 128–29; for Colombia, Gerardo and Alicia Reichel-Dolmatoff, *People of Aritama*, pp. 259–66; for Peru, Humberto Ghersi Barrera, "El Indígena y el mestizo en la comunidad de Marcará," *Revista de Museo Nacional*, XXVIII (1959), 118–88 and *ibid.*, XXIX (1960), 48–128; for Paraguay, Elman and Helen R. Service, *Tobati*, pp. 126–27; and for Brazil, Emilio Willems, *Buzios Island* (New York, 1952). Monograph of the American Ethnological Society No. XX.

82. Wolf, "Specific Aspects" and "Types of Latin American Peasantry." In the latter, Wolf misses the point in attributing the cult of poverty to corporate, as opposed to open, societies.

83. Adams, *Community in the Andes*; Paul L. Doughty, "Peruvian Highlands in a Changing World: Social Integration and Culture Change in an Andean District," unpublished doctoral dissertation (Cornell University, 1963).

84. Nash, *Machine Age Maya*, p. 28.

3. The Writer

1. Edward A. Shils, "The Intellectuals and the Powers," *Comparative Studies in Society and History*, I (Oct. 1958), 5.

2. In regretting a want of style in the Uruguayan philosopher Carlos Vaz Ferreira, Alberto Zum Felde wrote that it had limited the diffusion of his writing and that such a deficiency would not matter anywhere else, perhaps, but in Latin America, "where culture continues to be predominantly literary." He adds, "and where, in general, a felicitous phrase achieves greater success than a true idea; where a brilliant metaphor or an oratorical paragraph is more convincing than the most exact or subtle argument." *Indice crítico de la literatura hispanoamericana: los ensayistas* (Mexico City, 1954), pp. 345–46.

3. Fernando de Azevedo, *A Cultura brasileira* (São Paulo, 1944), p. 173.

4. K. H. Silvert, *The Conflict Society: Reaction and Revolution in Latin America* (New Orleans, 1961), p. 142.

5. Rodolfo Vinacua, "Borges on Literature," *Américas*, XIII (Dec. 1961), 3.

6. Zum Felde, *Indice crítico*, p. 21.

7. Martínez, *Problemas literarios* (Mexico City, 1955), p. 142.

8. *Boletín cultural*, Ministry of Foreign Affairs (Havana, Nov. 1961), special number, p. 5.

9. *Ibid.*, pp. 24–25.

10. Azevedo, "A Escola e a literatura," in *A Literatura no Brasil* (Rio de Janeiro, 1956), Vol. 1, tomo 1, 150.

11. *Boletín cultural*, pp. 19–27.

12. *Ibid.*, p. 23.

13. Silvert, *The Conflict Society*, p. 143, commenting on Mannheim's observation.

14. Luis Merino Reyes, "The Writers of Chile," *Américas*, XIV (Oct. 1962), 40.

15. Nelson Werneck Sodré, *Historia da literatura brasileira: seus fundamentos económicos* (Rio de Janeiro, 1960), p. 396.

16. Consuelo dos Reis e Mello, "Resposta sôbre literatura," *Leitura*, XIX, No. 57 (March 1962), 24; and her "Remuneração de escritor," *ibid.*, XIX, No. 50 (Aug. 1961), 12–14. See also Fábio Lucas, "Livros na mesa," *Correio da Manhã* (Rio de Janeiro), May 19, 1962; Antônio d'Elia, "A Profissão de escritor," *Boletim bibliográfico brasileiro*, IX, No. 4 (May 1961), 96.

17. Albert D. Van Nostrand, mimeographed reports prepared for the USIS in São Paulo: "Book Distribution in the Argentine Market," Feb. 1962; "Book Distribution in Chile," March 1962; "Lima and Bogotá; Common Factors in Two Separate Book Markets," "The Book Trade in Brazil," and "The Brazilian University as a Book Market," all Oct. 1962.

18. Anon., "Por que lemos tão pouco?" *Para todos*, Ano I, No. 7 (Aug. 1956), 9.

19. See Madeiros Lima, "José Lins do Rego não foi menino prodígio," *Jornal de letras*, VI (Feb. 1954), 9.

20. For the extensive government-supported Brazilian cultural institutions, see Ministry of Foreign Relations, *Brazil: 1960* (Rio de Janeiro, n.d.), pp. 244–93. See also Margarita Michelena, "Tendencias culturales en México y Centroamérica," *Américas*, XIV (June 1962), 21–24; "Tendencias culturales en la Gran Colombia," *ibid.*, XIV (May 1962), 32–36.

21. Charles Wagley, "The Brazilian Revolution: Social Changes since 1930," in Council on Foreign Relations, ed., *Social Change in Latin America Today* (New York, 1960), pp. 201–6.

22. Martínez, *Problemas literarios*, pp. 216–17.

23. Martin E. Erickson, "Trends in Central American Literature," in *Intellectual Trends in Latin America* (Austin, 1945), p. 112.

24. Peregrino Junior, "Alocução," *Curso de jornalismo* (Rio de Janeiro, 1958), p. 9.

25. John P. Gillin, "Some Signposts for Policy," in *Social Change in Latin America Today*, p. 42.

26. Francisco Miró Quesada, "The University and Society," *Américas*, XII (Dec. 1960), 3.

27. Gillin, "Signposts for Policy," p. 42.

28. Zum Felde, *Indice crítico*, p. 214.

29. For both sides of this question, see Rosário Fusco, *Política e letras* (Rio de Janeiro, 1940), and Osório Borba, *A Comédia literária* (Rio de Janeiro-Bahia, 1959).

30. Miró Quesada, "University and Society," p. 3.

31. Arturo Torres-Rioseco, *Ensayos sobre literatura latinoamericana* (Berkeley, 1958), p. 115.

32. Professor Ricardo Gullón has developed a fruitful idea from the writings of Juan Ramón Jiménez. See his "Juan Ramón Jiménez y el modernismo," in *Direcciones del modernismo* (Madrid, 1963), p. 59.

33. See also Ricardo Gullón, "Indigenismo y modernismo," *Revista de la Universidad de México*, XVII, No. 3 (Nov. 1962), 18–20.

34. Gillin, "Signposts for Policy," p. 41.

35. Title IX, Art. 203, Brazilian Constitution of 1946.

36. Frank Tannenbaum, "Toward an Appreciation of Latin America," in *The United States and Latin America* (New York, 1959), p. 52.

37. *Ibid.*, p. 56.

38. Ayala, *El Escritor en la sociedad de masas* (Mexico City, 1956), p. 80.

39. See Seymour Martin Lipset, "The Real Status of American Intellectuals," in G. B. de Huszar, ed., *The Intellectuals* (Glencoe, 1960), pp. 510–16; he has shown that U.S. intellectuals are actually held in higher esteem than they themselves think they are.

40. Cited by Emilio Carilla, *El Romanticismo en Hispanoamérica* (Madrid, 1958), p. 19.

41. One should certainly add the name of the Emperor Dom Pedro II of Brazil, 1840–89. Pedro Henríquez Ureña, *Las Corrientes literarias en la América Hispánica* (Mexico City, 1954), p. 239.

42. *Ibid.*, p. 166.

43. *Ibid.*, p. 172.

44. *Ibid.*, pp. 191–92.

45. Agustín Yáñez has stated: "With frequent negative results and always at a risk to aesthetic value, even literature that aspires to the artistic—poetry, the novel, theatre—is generally linked in Iberoamerica with society's vital problems, which it diagnoses and for which it tries to prescribe therapy when it is a question of maladies. . . . Ours is an edifying literature, except in a few cases which are precisely those which have few or none of the characteristics of Iberoamerican works." "El contenido social de la literatura iberoamericana," *Jornadas*, No. 14 (Mexico City, n.d.), p. 17.

46. Angel F. Rojas, *La Novela ecuatoriana* (Mexico City, 1948), p. 218.

47. Fernando Alegría, *Breve historia de la novela hispanoamericana* (Mexico City, 1959), p. 210.

48. The two last-named works have recently become available in English translation: Carlos Fuentes, *Where the Air is Clear* (New York, 1960), and Jorge Amado, *Gabriela, Clove and Cinnamon* (New York, 1962).

49. "Imagen del Perú de hoy," *Cuadernos americanos*, CXX, No. 1 (Jan.–Feb. 1962), 114.

50. *Temas hispanoamericanos* (Mexico City, 1959), p. 80.

51. The Party was suppressed in May 1947.

52. Cited by Disraeli (*pseud.*), "Política e letras," *Letras e artes*, Nov. 9, 1947, p. 5.

53. "1960, Ano crucial," in *Anuário da literatura brasileira, 1961* (Rio de Janeiro, n.d.), p. 7.

54. This curious work announces the advent of a new epoch style in Brazil, that of "socialist realism," to which the author claims to have given "definitive philosophical form" in 1950 in one of his own essays. *Interpretação da literatura brasileira* (Rio de Janeiro, 1957), p. 39.

55. See the lists of adherents in the section "Homenaje a la Revolución cu-

bana," *Nueva revista cubana*, Año II, No. 1 (Jan.–March 1960), 11–22, with statements by Waldo Frank, Ezequiel Martínez Estrada, Miguel Angel Asturias, Benjamín Carrión, and others. See also *ibid.*, "Documentos," pp. 207ff.

56. *Ibid.*, pp. 11–12.

57. John J. Johnson, "Whither the Middle Sectors?" *The Virginia Quarterly Review*, XXXVII (Autumn 1960), 509.

58. *Ibid.*, p. 521.

59. It should be noted that in 1962 Jorge Amado withdrew from the Communist Party.

60. Robert J. Alexander, *Communism in Latin America* (New Brunswick, N.J., 1957), p. 72.

61. George Steiner, "The Writer and Communism," *Problems of Communism*, X, No. 3 (May–June 1961), 45.

62. "Teoría y plan de la Segunda Independencia," *Cuadernos americanos*, CXIV, No. 1 (Jan.–Feb. 1961), 66.

63. Anon., "Universidade do ponto de vista político-social," *O Metropolitano* (official weekly newspaper of the UNE, circulated with the *Diário de Notícias* of Rio de Janeiro on Saturdays), April 7, 1962, p. 4.

64. Benjamín Carrión, "Teoría y plan," pp. 63–65.

65. Octavio Paz, *Labyrinth of Solitude* (New York, 1962), pp. 186–87; Alfredo Pareja Díez-Canseco, "América Latina en el mundo de hoy," *Cuadernos americanos*, CXVII, No. 4 (July–Aug. 1961), 22.

66. Paz, *Labyrinth*, p. 184.

67. Adonias Filho, "Tendencias culturales en el Brazil," *Américas*, XIV (July 1962), 37. The works he cites are: Eduardo Portella, *Africa, colonos e cúmplices* (Rio de Janeiro, 1961), José Honório Rodrigues, *Africa e Brasil, outro horizonte* (Rio de Janeiro, 1961), and Adolfo Justo Bezerra de Menezes, *Asia, Africa e a política independente do Brasil* (Rio de Janeiro, 1961).

68. Zum Felde, *Indice crítico*, p. 17.

69. *Ibid.*, pp. 290–312.

70. *Ibid.*, p. 9.

71. *Ibid.*, p. 484.

72. See Roland Corbusier, *Responsabilidade dos elites* (São Paulo, 1956), pp. 41–43, and passim.

73. José Carlos Barbosa Moreira, "O Problema da cultura nacional," *Jornal do Brasil* (Rio de Janeiro), May 18, 1962, Sec. B, p. 3. Under the same title, see the continuations in *ibid.*, May 25, 1962, and May 31, 1962. On alienation among U.S. intellectuals, see Sidney Hook, "From Alienation to Critical Integrity: the Vocation of the American Intellectuals," in *The Intellectuals*, pp. 528ff.

74. Carrión, "Teoría y plan," pp. 62–63.

75. *La Crítica literaria contemporánea* (Buenos Aires, 1957), pp. 123–24.

76. William S. Stokes, "The Drag of the Pensadores," in James W. Wiggins and Helmut Schoeck, eds., *Foreign Aid Reexamined* (Washington, D.C., 1958), p. 66.

77. Portella, "A Literatura do desenvolvimento," *Anuário da literatura brasileira: 1960* (Rio de Janeiro, n.d.), p. 5.

78. Shils, "The Intellectuals," p. 11.

4. The Artist

1. In 1964 Professor Aurelio de la Vega of San Fernando Valley State College completed "A Study of the Sociological Aspects of Latin American Serious Music"; but no coordinated study of all the arts has been undertaken.

2. Literature is excluded by mandate, since it has been covered in the preceding chapter. The motion picture and the dance should be included among the major fine arts, but are omitted here because of their incipient situation in Latin America.

3. Noel P. Gist and L. A. Halbert, *Urban Society* (New York, 1957), p. 24.

4. John J. Johnson, *Political Change in Latin America* (Stanford, 1958), p. 24.

5. *Ibid.*, p. 5.

6. A consideration of folklore in any of its forms (including folk music and dances, and native crafts) would involve an entirely different approach to the subject, since folklore is a retention from the past and functions primarily in a rural rather than an urban environment. It is therefore not pertinent to a discussion of cultural dynamics in a modern society.

7. *Encyclopedia of the Social Sciences*, II, 175.

8. Virgil Thomson, *The State of Music* (New York, 1962), p. 15.

9. *Ibid.*, p. 132.

10. *Ibid.*, pp. 132–36, and passim.

11. Dilman W. Gotshalk, *Art and the Social Order* (Chicago, 1947), p. 221.

12. Quoted by Laurence E. Schmeckebier, *Modern Mexican Art* (Minneapolis, 1939), p. 31.

13. Marta Traba, *Art in Latin America Today: Colombia* (Washington, D.C., 1959), p. 4.

14. *Ibid.* It should be remembered that the influence of the Mexican muralists was widespread in Latin America.

15. The term "Revolutionary art" has been used by many writers to designate the art associated with the Mexican Revolution; in this strictly limited sense there is no objection to the term. But unless this limitation is made clear, there is danger of confusion with the term "revolutionary art," meaning art that has revolutionized accepted aesthetic concepts. The Mexican Revolution stood apart from the revolution in modern art, although both began about the same time—around 1910.

16. Bernard S. Myers, *Mexican Painting in Our Time* (New York, 1956), p 167.

17. *Ibid.*, p. 174.

18. *Ibid.*, p. 213.

19. José V. Acha, *Art in Latin America Today: Peru* (Washington, D.C., 1961), p. 7.

20. The case for artistic values was most strongly stated by Tamayo: "It seems to me that to pretend that its [i.e., painting's] value is derived from other elements, particularly from ideological content which is not otherwise related to plastic content, cannot but be considered a fallacy which can temporarily deceive the unwary, but which Time, ruthless enemy of everything specious, will undertake to refute." Quoted by Myers, *Mexican Painting*, p. 129, from "Unas palabras de Rufino Tamayo," *Espacios* (Spring 1949).

21. Quoted from an unsigned article in *Américas* (1962).

22. See the article by José Roberto Teixeira Leite, "Cândido Portanari," *Módulo*, No. 27 (March 1962), pp. 23–26.

23. Luiz Almeida da Cunha, *Art in Latin America Today: Brazil* (Washington, D.C., 1960), p. 2.

24. *Ibid.*, p. 4.

25. David D. Zingg, "The Wind of Change: South America's Lively New Generation of Artists," in special issue of *Show: The Magazine of the Arts* (Vol. II, Nov. 1962), p. 56.

26. *Ibid.*, p. 58.

27. *Ibid.*, p. 96. Interview with Robert M. Wool.

28. *Ibid.*

29. The two exceptions among Mexican painters were Rufino Tamayo and Carlos Mérida. Writing of the latter, Myers said, "He has led a constant series of experimental developments that have perpetuated among Mexicans the idea of painting as painting." *Mexican Painting*, p. 127.

30. Fernando de Szyszlo, "Contemporary Latin American Painting," *College Art Journal*, XIX, No. 2 (1959–60), 134–45.

31. All the quotations from Orozco are taken from the English translation of his autobiography: *José Clemente Orozco: An Autobiography*, trans. by Robert C. Stephenson (Austin, 1962).

32. Cf. Myers, *Mexican Painting*, p. 42: "Orozco emerges as the towering figure of the Mexican school. . . . Neither self-conscious polemics nor programmatic political attitudes have ever affected his point of view."

33. Cf. the interesting, but to me not completely convincing, article by Virginia Derr, "The Rise of a Middle Class Tradition in Mexican Art," in *Journal of Inter-American Studies*, III (July 1961), 385–409.

34. Robert Motherwell, in *Perspectives* (Autumn 1954), p. 109.

35. According to John Cage, "Once when Virgil Thomson was giving a talk at Town Hall in New York City, he spoke of the necessity of originality. The audience immediately hissed." (Cage, *Silence*, Middletown, Conn., 1962, p. 75.) Originality is always hissed because it disturbs the status quo or because it gives people a sense of inferiority.

36. Almeida da Cunha, *Art in Latin America: Brazil*, p. 4.

37. Myers, *Mexican Painting*, p. 257.

38. Tamayo has stated that there is "no place in art for political or ideological manifestations. Painting is painting . . . and there is no need of mixing it with any other thing. That has been the error of Mexican painting," in *Diario de las Américas* (Miami, Fla.), April 5, 1960, quoted by Derr, "Rise of Middle Class Tradition," p. 407.

39. *Ibid.*, p. 393.

40. José Luis Cuevas, "Recollections of Childhood," in *Evergreen Review*, VII, No. 29 (March–April 1963), 49.

41. Quoted by Stanton L. Catlin, "New Vistas in Latin American Art," *Art in America*, XLVII (Fall 1959), 30.

42. Seldon Rodman, "Rumblings from the South," *Show*, special issue, p. 30.

43. *Ibid.*

44. *Ibid.*

45. *Ibid.*, p. 58.

46. Cf. Roberto García Morillo, *Carlos Chávez: Vida y obra* (Mexico City, 1960), pp. 83–84.

47. For a self-analysis of Chávez's position, see the chapter on "A Latin American Composer" in his book, *Musical Thought* (Cambridge, Mass., 1961). Also pertinent is Chap. 2, "Art as Communication."

48. Quoted from Alberto Ginastera, in Robert M. Wool, "The Future Is Not Soon Enough," *Show*, special issue, p. 97.

49. Typical of this trend is a brochure published in Santiago de Cuba in 1960 by Juan Marinello, *Conversación con nuestros pintores abstractos*, which is described by Professor Donald Robertson as "a polemic against abstract artists and abstract art, and an exhortation to Cuban artists to turn from it to social realism." See *Handbook of Latin American Studies*, Vol. 24, Item No. 1722. On the other hand, the review *Arquitectura* of Havana, in its issue of March 1960, re-

prints a "Lesson on Architecture" by Le Corbusier advocating the utmost creative freedom for the architect, which would seem to indicate that the attitude toward modern architecture may be more permissive than that toward modern painting.

50. See Gilbert Chase, "Problemática de la música americana actual," in *Cuadernos* (Paris), No. 30 (May–June 1958), 37–41.

51. See the article by Luis Lastra Almeida, "Artists Among Skyscrapers," in *Américas*, XV, No. 1 (January 1963), 26–31.

52. Quoted by Robert Van Steen, "The Look of the Future: Oscar Niemeyer and Brasilia," in *Show*, special issue, p. 73.

53. Quoted in Le Corbusier, *Creation Is a Patient Search: A Self-Portrait* (New York, 1960), p. 49.

54. *Ibid.*, p. 124.

55. Quoted by David Crease, "Progress in Brasilia," *The Architectural Review*, CXXXI, No. 782 (April 1962), 257–62. Cf. Oscar Niemeyer, *Minha experiencia em Brasilia* (Rio de Janeiro, 1960).

56. Stamo Papadake, *Oscar Niemeyer* (New York, 1960), p. 31.

57. Robert Van Steen, *Show*, special issue, p. 70.

58. Crease, "Progress in Brasilia," p. 261.

59. Helvidia Saal, "Sala de Conciertos y Teatro Espacial," in *Lyra* (Buenos Aires), XVI (1958), Nos. 171–73, with illustrations and diagrams.

60. Typical of such groups is Spartacus of Buenos Aires, which emphasizes the social aspect of art. Cf. Ricardo Carpani, *Arte y revolución en América Latina* (Buenos Aires, 1960).

61. Quoted by Robert Van Steen in *Show*, special issue, p. 70.

5. The Military

1. There are exceptions to this generalization. The state militias of Brazil, for example, are significant political forces.

2. Trans. by Anita Brenner (New York, 1961), p. 234.

3. Richard W. Patch, "Bolivia: U.S. Assistance in a Revolutionary Setting," in Council on Foreign Relations, *Social Change in Latin America Today* (New York, 1960), pp. 115, 141.

4. As quoted in Robert J. Alexander, *The Bolivian National Revolution* (New Brunswick, N.J., 1958), p. 152.

5. "The Aspirations for Economic Development," in Robert N. Burr, ed., *Latin America's Nationalistic Revolutions*, special issue of *The Annals of the American Academy of Political and Social Science*, CCCXXXIV (March 1961), 17.

6. Lieuwen divides the Latin American countries into three types according to the degree to which the armed forces participate in the political process. Group I is constituted by those in which they dominate politics, Group II by those in which the armed forces are in transition from political to non-political bodies, and Group III by those in which they are non-political. See his *Arms and Politics in Latin America* (New York, 1961), chap. 6.

7. John J. Johnson, *The Military and Society in Latin America* (Stanford, 1964), pp. 106–13.

8. As quoted in Alexander, *The Bolivian National Revolution*, p. 151.

9. *The Conflict Society: Reaction and Revolution in Latin America* (New Orleans, 1961), p. 86, n. 13.

10. Comments on an earlier draft of this paper.

11. Javier Romero, *Aspectos psicobiométricos y sociales de una muestra de la juventud mexicana* [Dirección de Investigaciones Antropológicas, 1] (Mexico City, 1956), pp. 13–15, 45–51.

12. Víctor Alba, *El Militarismo* (Mexico City, 1959), pp. 56–72.

13. This expression refers to officers from the Andean region of Venezuela and primarily the Andean province of Tachira.

14. Juan Bautista Alberdi, *Bases y puntos de partida para la organización política de la República Argentina* (Buenos Aires, 1943), p. 45, as quoted in R. A. Gomez, *Government and Politics of Latin America* (New York, 1963), p. 56.

15. Alfred Vagts, *A History of Militarism* (New York, 1959), pp. 29–32.

16. As quoted in Charles W. Simmons, "The Rise of the Brazilian Military Class: 1870–1890," *Mid-America*, XXXIX (October 1957), 237.

17. As quoted in Robert J. Alexander, *The Perón Era* (New York, 1951), p. 116.

18. Speech, March 14, 15, 1960, as quoted in Arthur P. Whitaker, "The Argentine Paradox," in Burr, ed., *Latin America's Nationalistic Revolutions*, p. 106.

19. As quoted in John J. Johnson, "The Latin-American Military as a Politically Competing Group in Transitional Society," in John J. Johnson, ed., *The Role of the Military in Underdeveloped Countries* (Princeton, 1962), p. 124.

20. *Ibid.*, p. 119.

21. Quoted in Dankwart A. Rustow, "The Army and the Founding of the Turkish Republic," *World Politics*, XI (July 1959), 520.

22. In Roberto MacLean y Estenós, *Historia de una revolución* (Buenos Aires, 1953), pp. 158–59.

23. Alan K. Manchester, "Brazil in Transition," *South Atlantic Quarterly*, LIV (April 1955), 175.

24. These words were used to describe contemporary Indonesian society. See "The Role of the Military in Indonesia," in Johnson, ed., *The Role of the Military*, p. 220. They aptly describe, without paraphrase, Latin America.

25. Zevedei Barbu, *Democracy and Dictatorship* (New York, 1956), p. 34, as quoted in Vernon L. Fluharty, *Dance of the Millions: Military Rule and the Social Revolution in Colombia* (Pittsburgh, 1957), p. 169.

26. Samuel P. Huntington, *The Soldier and the State* (Cambridge, Mass., 1957), p. 98.

27. Vagts, *A History of Militarism*, p. 144.

28. See the remarks of Samuel E. Finer on the relationship between military professionalism and political activity in *The Man on Horseback: The Role of the Military in Politics* (London, 1962), pp. 23–30.

29. Gruening, Remarks in the United States Senate, *Congressional Record, Senate*, Aug. 2, 1962, p. 14412.

30. On this point see the speech of Argentine General Luis Rodolfo González published in September 1956 and translated in Silvert, *Conflict Society*, pp. 81–112.

6. The Industrialist

1. Among the many who have helped me, Lic. Victor Urquidi and Dr. Miguel Wionczek were most generous with their time and stimulating with ideas. Their comments, as well as suggestions by Professors David Chaplin, Thomas Mayer, and Daniel Goldrich, have reduced the number of errors.

2. Hollis B. Chenery, "Patterns of Industrial Growth," *American Economic Review*, I (Sept. 1960), 646.

3. R. E. Baldwin, "Patterns of Development in Newly Settled Regions," *Manchester School of Economic and Social Studies*, XXIV (May 1956), 161–79.

4. Chenery, "Patterns," p. 636. Twenty-eight years appears to be the lag for Costa Rica and Lebanon, countries in which size is obviously significant.

5. *Ibid.*, p. 637. Other Latin American countries were not included.

6. Stanley J. Stein, "The Brazilian Cotton Textile Industry, 1850–1950," in Simon Kuznets, Wilbert E. Moore, and Joseph J. Spengler, eds., *Economic Growth: Brazil, India, Japan* (Durham, N.C., 1955), pp. 432–40.

7. A few studies using other categories have been attempted. McClelland reports that 12 per cent of a sample of 60 United States "business managers" had lower-class backgrounds, indicating mobility. David C. McClelland, *The Achieving Society* (Princeton, 1961), p. 277. An interesting account of the origins of several Peruvian textile firms occurs in David Chaplin, "The Recruitment of the Peruvian Industrial Labor Force," unpublished doctoral dissertation (Princeton University), 1962, pp. 117–23, 198–367 passim.

In May 1963 papers on "El Empresario Industrial en América Latina" were presented at the meetings of the Economic Commission for Latin America at Mar del Plata, Argentina, E/CN.12/642/Add.1–4. Country reports included were those of Eduardo A. Zalduendo on Argentina, Fernando H. Cardoso on Brazil, Guillermo Briones on Chile, and Aarón Lipman on Colombia. The reports on Argentina, Chile, and Colombia present the entrepreneurs as risk-shunning and most upset by labor trouble but as nevertheless "modern" in approach toward problems of the firm and society. Based almost entirely on replies to questionnaires, these findings are admittedly preliminary. The more comprehensive paper by Professor Cardoso rightly stresses that "correspondence between words and deeds is rare" (p. 59), and that modern behavior is neither widespread nor always rational in the prevailing unstable political and economic setting. He found that industrialists who most emphasize the modern values of hard work and thrift may in fact be old-fashioned and even irrational in refusing to see the yield from lightening intense physical strain of workers and paying adequate wages for obtaining various skills (pp. 47–48).

8. Albert O. Hirschman, "Ideologies of Economic Development in Latin America," in Albert O. Hirschman, ed., *Latin American Issues: Essays and Comments* (New York, 1961), pp. 4–9.

9. Gilberto Freyre, *The New World in the Tropics: The Culture of Modern Brazil* (New York, 1959), pp. 161–62.

10. Simon G. Rottenberg, "Entrepreneurship and Economic Progress in Jamaica," *Inter-American Economic Affairs*, VII, No. 2 (Autumn 1953), 74–79.

11. Tomás Roberto Fillol, *Social Factors in Economic Development: The Argentine Case* (Cambridge, Mass., 1961), pp. 35–39.

12. Bernard J. Siegel, "Social Structure and Economic Change in Brazil," in Kuznets *et al.*, *Economic Growth*, p. 397.

13. For bibliographies of relevant Latin American works, refer to Mary Catherine Megee, *Monterrey, Mexico: Internal Patterns and External Relations* (Chicago, 1958), and James J. Parsons, *Antioqueño Colonization in Western Colombia* (Berkeley, 1949). See also McClelland, *The Achieving Society*, pp. 355–65.

14. Everett E. Hagen, *On the Theory of Social Change: How Economic Growth Begins* (Homewood, Ill., 1962), pp. 353–84.

15. Preston E. James, *Latin America*, rev. ed. (New York, 1950), pp. 153–54.

16. Albert O. Hirschman, *The Strategy of Economic Development* (New Haven, 1958), pp. 185–87.

17. Henry G. Aubrey, "Industrial Enterprise in Underdeveloped Countries,"

Conference on *Capital Formation and Economic Growth* (Princeton, 1953), pp. 415–18, and "Industrial Investment Decisions: A Comparative Analysis," *Journal of Economic History*, XV (Dec. 1955), 335–57. In examining the apparent faltering of British entrepreneurship compared with American in the late nineteenth century, H. J. Habakkuk similarly concludes that "many of the deficiencies can be explained in more narrowly economic terms with less recourse to sociological influences," *American and British Technology in the Nineteenth Century: The Search for Labour-Saving Inventions* (Cambridge, Eng., 1962), p. 194.

18. Sanford A. Mosk, *Industrial Revolution in Mexico* (Berkeley, 1950), pp. 21–31. Cf. various comments on this book in *Problemas agrícolas e industriales de México*, Vol. III, No. 2.

Frank R. Brandenburg included only six politicians in his list of thirty outstanding Mexican businessmen. Since there were eighty cabinet-level officials between 1934 and 1958, he considers the proportion low. Brandenburg, "A Contribution to the Theory of Entrepreneurship and Economic Development: The Case of Mexico," *Inter-American Economic Affairs*, XVI (Winter 1962), 3–23.

19. In Argentina, incorporation is a way to avoid inheritance taxes. As in Mexico and other countries, stocks are made out "to the bearer," and the government is not entitled to know who owns what. This limitation was abandoned by Aramburu in 1956, but restored by Frondizi in 1958. Robert J. Alexander, *Labor Relations in Argentina, Brazil, and Chile* (New York, 1962), pp. 148–49. Professor Cardoso, moreover, has shown how inflation discourages sales of stock to the public by groups seeking to maintain control and to minimize tax payments. See p. 31 of his paper cited in note 7 above.

20. Thomas C. Cochran, *The Puerto Rican Businessman: A Study in Cultural Change* (Philadelphia, 1959), p. 108.

21. Frederick H. Harbison and Eugene W. Burgess, "Modern Management in Western Europe," *American Journal of Sociology*, LX, No. 1 (July 1954), 15–23; and Harbison, "Entrepreneurial Organization as a Factor in Economic Development," *Quarterly Journal of Economics*, LXX (Aug. 1956), 364–79.

22. Fillol, *Social Factors*, pp. 19–23; Cochran, *Puerto Rican Businessman*, pp. 85–90.

23. Cf. Clark Kerr, John T. Dunlop, Frederick H. Harbison, and Charles A. Myers, *Industrialism and Industrial Man: The Problems of Labor and Management in Economic Growth* (Cambridge, Mass., 1960), p. 83. But delegation of authority may entail a dangerous loss of rapid flexibility in countries undergoing great political and economic flux. See Cardoso's report on Brazilian industrialists, p. 27.

24. Haya de la Torre, *El Antiimperialismo y el APRA* (Santiago, 1939).

25. Ernesto López Malo, *Ensayo sobre localización de la industria en México* (Mexico City, 1960), pp. 171–73.

26. Domingo Alberto Rangel, *La Industrialización de Venezuela* (Caracas, 1958), pp. 17–19, 51–65.

27. Productivity in many import-substituting industries was low. Population growth aggravated the problem of creating employment and urban social overhead. Neglect of agriculture led to rising food prices, and inevitably wages rose but without a corresponding increase in mass markets and mass production economies for manufactured goods. The growing numbers of urban workers were mobilized by political parties supporting social welfare measures as expected, but the countries could not afford these while sustaining mercantilist investment. Demanding tax reductions, subsidies, and protection from labor's demands, the industrialists tended to bolster their new power by siding with land-

owners. Inflationary credit expansion seemed necessary to salve everybody's discontent but failed to lubricate the economic machinery. On the contrary, it often aggravated the very income inequality and balance-of-payments problems that welfare-mercantilism was supposed to mitigate.

For a clear analysis of the "mercantilist–welfare state cleavage" see David Felix, "Industrialization and Stabilization Dilemmas in Latin America," *Journal of Economic History*, XIX (Dec. 1959), 584–99, and "An Alternative View of the 'Monetarist'-'Structuralist' Controversy," in Hirschman, ed., *Latin American Issues*, pp. 81–93.

Mexico, as Felix points out, was probably the only country, aside from the special case of Puerto Rico, that could promote both welfare and industrialization. Its agrarian revolution made a fairly adequate support of agriculture politically acceptable, and tourism helped prevent balance-of-payments difficulties. Nevertheless, inequality increased sharply in the course of industrialization, a result that was not unexpected. The worker was told he was no longer entitled to the support he had had when he was the "protagonist against foreign rapacity" (Avila Camacho in 1945, quoted by John J. Johnson, *Political Change in Latin America: The Emergence of the Middle Sectors*, Stanford, 1958, p. 144) and that "the conviction that the decisive thing is to produce more has defeated the generous, although vague, decision to achieve a fair distribution of wealth" (Antonio Carillo Flores, Minister of Finance, in 1948, quoted by Felix, "Industrialization and Stabilization," p. 587). See Ifigenia M. de Navarrete, *La Distribución del ingreso y el desarrollo económico de México* (Mexico City, 1960), for statistical support of growing income inequality.

28. Cochran, *Puerto Rican Businessman*, p. 131.

29. The view that preference for real estate over other investments can be attributed to its superior value as an inflation-hedge is probably erroneous. See Martin J. Bailey, "Construction and Inflation: A Critical Scrutiny," *Economic Development and Cultural Change*, X, No. 3 (April 1962), 264–74.

30. The *growth rate* of private investment in Mexico fell from 15.4 per cent annually during 1953–58 to 1 per cent during 1959–61, with an actual decline from 1960 to 1961 of .09 per cent. Address by Antonio Ortíz Mena, Secretary of the Treasury, reported in *Excelsior*, March 30, 1962, and reprinted in *El Mercado de Valores*, April 2, 1962. See also Nacional Financiera, S.A., *Informe anual, correspondiente a 1961* (Mexico City, 1962), p. 41.

Yet throughout the year the government had sought to soothe the anxieties of the industrialists. As early as January 24, 1961, President Adolfo López Mateos took the unprecedented step of personally attending and addressing a session of the general assembly of the Cámara Nacional de la Industria de Transformación. *Excelsior*, Jan. 25, 1961.

31. This view is heavily stressed by Aubrey, "Industrial Enterprise," pp. 339–43.

32. Hernán Echavarría Olózaga, *El Sentido común en la economía colombiana* (Bogotá, 1958), p. 301, quoted by Hirschman, "Ideologies," p. 26. A number of Mexican industrialists told me in 1960 and 1961 that fear of retaliation and the need for official favor alone kept them buying wood pulp, copper, and other materials from government enterprises and from competing openly with such enterprises.

33. This pattern has been identified by Hirschman as the "ego-focussed image of change," in *Strategy of Economic Development* and Hirschman, ed., *Latin American Issues*, pp. 14–20, and by Harvey Leibenstein as "zero-sum enterpreneurship," in *Economic Backwardness and Economic Growth: Studies in the*

Theory of Economic Development (New York, 1957), pp. 112–19. Victor Urquidi has written to me that a similar reluctance to communicate may also exist within government with consequent uncertainty in public sector policies and activity.

34. Cochran, *Puerto Rican Businessman*, p. 73.

35. Cf. Harbison, "Entrepreneurial Organization," p. 367; Urquidi, *Viabilidad económica de América Latina* (Mexico, 1962), pp. 84–85.

36. Kerr *et al., Industrialism and Industrial Man*, p. 55. James C. Abegglen, however, reports claims of Catholic revival as responsible for social responsibility and therefore entrepreneurship among the industrial elite of Monterrey (field report cited by McClelland, *The Achieving Society*, p. 412). For a neo-Marxist view, see Ricardo Lagos Escobar, *La Concentración del poder económico —su teoría: realidad chilena* (Santiago de Chile, 1961).

37. Alexander, *Labor Relations*, pp. 104ff.

38. This point is made with force and clarity by Cardoso, pp. 63–69. By contrast, landowners are also proprietors of enterprises, but these involve far less personal attention, much less entrepreneurship. Neglect is not only possible, but a tradition. The chief uncertainties come not from purchasing, production, and sales, but from weather and government. Survival depends less on correct day-to-day decisions than on avoiding taxes, price control, competition from imports, and expropriation. Hence landlords, in contrast with industrialists, are likely to be managerially passive and politically active.

39. Note for example the experience of Governor Tugwell in Puerto Rico: "All the public-service enterprises were faced with the choice of strikes or labor management by union officials. . . . It was to the workers' interest, of course, to make these enterprises succeed; they, and other citizens, were their owners. But there was no recognition of this. These governmental enterprises were forced to increase their costs much faster than comparable private employers; and steady advantage was taken of the fact that the Government, for political reasons, could ill afford labor disputes." Rexford Guy Tugwell, *The Stricken Land: The Story of Puerto Rico* (Garden City, 1947), p. 570. The Puerto Rican government sold its manufacturing enterprises.

40. This position was actually taken by the commercial and industrial community of Mexico and was sufficiently strong to delay substantial land reform until the presidency of Lázaro Cárdenas. Johnson, *Political Change*, pp. 138–39.

41. *New York Times*, Aug. 19, 1962.

42. Segundo Congreso Nacional de la Industria de Transformación, *Memoria y documentos* (Mexico City, 1953), pp. 121–27, 148–54, 193–98, 228–34, 249–50, 297–98, 345, 370–72.

43. Gustavo R. Velasco, "O Importamos capitales O exportamos hombres," IV Congreso de Industriales, *Boletín Confederación*, No. 202, p. 13, quoted by López Malo, *Localización*, p. 203.

44. *Excelsior*, March 30, 1962. For an extended analysis of the ideology of Mexican business leaders, see Raymond Vernon, *The Dilemma of Mexico's Development: The Roles of the Private and Public Sectors* (Cambridge, Mass., 1963), pp. 155–75.

45. Decreto No. 19.739, March 7, 1931, cited by Stanley J. Stein, "Brazilian Cotton," pp. 442–43.

46. David Felix, "Structural Imbalances, Social Conflict, and Inflation: An Appraisal of Chile's Recent Anti-Inflationary Effort," *Economic Development and Cultural Change*, VIII, No. 2 (Jan. 1960), 123.

47. Alexander, *Labor Relations*, pp. 104–12, 327–36. The paternalistic orientation of Brazilian workers did not give way to class-conscious militancy, as in

Chile, but was diverted by Getulio Vargas, who "twisted the old patriarchal traditions to make himself patriarch of all Brazil" (p. 44).

48. International Bank for Reconstruction and Development, *Report on Cuba: Findings and Recommendations of an Economic and Technical Mission* (Baltimore, 1951), pp. 136–48. Twelve years later an official Cuban study was quoted as finding that the mass of workers "appears in great part to have confused the purposes of the revolution and interpreted it as meaning they can work less." Communist indoctrination was recommended to combat absenteeism, irresponsibility, negligence, and lack of interest in work. (*New York Times,* Aug. 3, 1962.) A few weeks later Labor Minister Augusto Martínez issued a decree instituting such penalties as one day's pay for six late arrivals or early departures. (*New York Times,* Aug. 30, 1962.)

49. Cf. Johnson, *Political Change,* pp. 148–49.

50. Robert E. Scott, *The Mexican Government in Transition* (Urbana, 1959), p. 163.

51. Edwin Lieuwen, *Venezuela* (London, 1961), pp. 64–88, 105–9.

52. Johnson, *Political Change,* pp. 56–57.

53. Through a resolution introduced by Congressman D. R. McGehee, the inflated charge reached the US Congress that "Governor Tugwell has enjoyed nominal as well as actual control over the insular legislature through his powers to appoint individuals to public office and has used that power for the establishment of a socialized form of government to the extent that private business enterprises have been coerced and intimidated while the insular government continued its concerted drive to bring all economic life under bureaucratic and socialized controls." H. Res. 496, April 1, 1944, quoted by Tugwell, *Stricken Land,* p. 640.

54. Scott, *Mexican Government,* pp. 182–86, 278–93. Frank R. Brandenburg, *Mexico: An Experiment in One-Party Democracy* (Ann Arbor, 1956), pp. 297–300, and "Organized Business in Mexico," *Inter-American Economic Affairs,* XII, No. 3 (Winter 1958), 26–50.

55. Francisco Cerda, "Patines y Cadillacs," *El Porvenir,* Monterrey, Dec. 19, 1960.

7. The Urban Worker

1. UNESCO, "Proyecto principal de educación," *Boletín trimestral,* No. 13 (Jan.– March 1962), pp. 16–18.

2. *Ibid.,* p. 22. Only Panama among the still primarily rural nations outstrips a primarily urban country (Chile) in per capita income.

3. Jorge Ahumada, *El Desarrollo económico y los problemas del cambio social en América Latina* (Mexico City, 1960).

4. Pompeu Accioly Borges, "Graus de desenvolvimento na América Latina," *Desenvolvimento e conjuntura* (Rio de Janeiro, Feb. 1961).

5. *Statistical Abstract for Latin America,* University of California (Los Angeles, 1961).

6. See, for example, the preface by Don Martindale and Gertrud Neuwirth to their translation of Max Weber's *The City* (Glencoe, 1958).

7. A UNESCO-sponsored study of social stratification and mobility in Buenos Aires, Santiago de Chile, Rio de Janeiro, and Montevideo is now nearing completion and may prove a major advance in this area. A notable effort at conceptualization of the basic problem of urbanization supported by some empirical research is reported in Philip M. Hauser, *Urbanization in Latin America*

(New York, 1961). A theoretical review of the more abundant community studies in Latin America can be found in Richard N. Adams, "The Community in Latin America: A Changing Myth," *The Centennial Review* (Summer 1962), pp. 409–34.

8. See Frank Bonilla, "Rio's Favelas: The Rural Slum Within the City," in *American Universities Field Staff Report* (New York, 1961). Some data on urban occupational distributions are given in Economic Commission for Latin America, *Estudio sobre la mano de obra en América Latina* (La Paz, 1957).

9. UNESCO, "Proyecto," p. 45.

10. Bertram A. Hutchinson, *Mobilidade e trabalho* (Rio de Janeiro, 1960), p. 229.

11. K. H. Silvert and Frank Bonilla, *Education and the Social Meaning of Development: A Preliminary Statement* (New York, 1961), pp. 152–53.

12. United States Department of Labor, Bureau of Labor Statistics, *Labor in Brazil* (Washington, D.C., 1962), p. 15.

13. A direct comparison of prevailing wage rates with the prices of essential Post, Telegraph and Telephone International items is enough to demonstrate this in most cases. See, for example, *Purchasing Power 1961* (Bern, 1961).

14. A general treatment of the process for the middle sectors is given in John J. Johnson, *Political Change in Latin America: The Emergence of the Middle Sectors* (Stanford, 1958). There are many excellent analyses of individual countries by Latin Americans. A compact history of labor organization with an extensive bibliography is Moisés Poblete Troncoso and Ben G. Burnett, *The Rise of the Latin American Labor Movement* (New York, 1960).

15. See, for example, Julio César Jobet, *Ensayo crítico del desarrollo económico-social de Chile* (Santiago, 1955) and *Los Precursores del pensamiento social de Chile* (Santiago, 1955–56); and Hernán Ramírez Necochea, *Historia del movimiento obrero en Chile* (Santiago, 1956).

16. Refer to Víctor Alba, "Labor in Latin America," *Dissent* (Autumn 1962), pp. 387–401. See also his "El Movimiento obrero en la América Latina—presente y futuro," *Cuadernos americanos*, XII (May–June 1953), 33–51.

17. See Robert J. Alexander's *Labor Relations in Argentina, Brazil, and Chile* (New York, 1962). A comparative summary of selected provisions of labor laws is given in US Department of Labor, *Latin American Labor Legislation* (Washington, D.C., 1956). Refer also to Poblete Troncoso and Burnett, *Rise of the Latin American Labor Movement*, especially chap. 2.

18. This is one of the conclusions of a recent and penetrating examination of poverty in the United States: Michael Harrington, *The Other America: Poverty in the United States* (New York, 1962). See also Dwight Macdonald, "Our Invisible Poor," *The New Yorker*, Jan. 19, 1963, pp. 82–132.

19. In addition to the sources already cited, there is a growing series of studies on labor published over the last few years by the Bureau of Labor Statistics of the US Department of Labor. Among the countries covered thus far are Mexico, Argentina, Bolivia, Uruguay, Honduras, Brazil, Colombia, and Chile.

20. Some of the current difficulties of this kind of enterprise in Rio de Janeiro are discussed at length in the magazine *Visão*, Oct. 26, 1962.

21. *Statistical Abstract for Latin America.*

22. *The Hispanic American Report*, XVI (Nov. 1962), 861, gives some details of the meeting held for this purpose in September 1962 in Santiago de Chile.

23. Personal communication from the ORIT (Inter-American Regional Organization of Workers) economic and social affairs section. ORIT is the regional arm of the International Confederation of Free Trade Unions. A brief history of

international labor organization in Latin America is given in Robert J. Alexander's "Labor and Inter-American Relations," *Annals of the American Academy of Political and Social Science,* CCCXXXIV (March 1961), 41–53. Alexander's estimate of organized union strength for 1960 (about 6,640,000) is considerably more conservative than any of the above figures. (See his *Today's Latin America,* Garden City, N.Y., 1962, p. 95.)

24. ORIT-ICFTU, *The Cuban Trade Union Movement Under the Regime of Dr. Castro* (Mexico City, Oct. 1960). Anonymous pamphlet.

25. *New York Times,* Nov. 11, 1962, p. 42.

26. *Hispanic American Report,* XV (Oct. 1962), 702.

27. Solomon Barkin, *The Decline of the Labor Movement* (Santa Barbara, Calif., 1961).

28. See, for example, Philip Taft, "El rumbo pragmático del sindicalismo norteamericano," in *Mundo del trabajo libre, organo oficial de la Confederación Internacional de Organizaciones Sindicales Libres* (Aug.–Sept. 1962). Contrast this presentation with Leon Litwack, *The American Labor Movement* (Englewood Cliffs, N.J., 1962).

8. The University Student

1. For a fuller statement of the traditional-modern dichotomy being used here with special reference to the Latin American city, see Gino Germani's construction in Philip M. Hauser, ed., *Urbanization in Latin America* (New York, 1961), pp. 47–48. My amendments to these views appeared in UNESCO, *International Social Science Journal,* XV (1963), 560–70, under the title, "National Values, Development, and Leaders and Followers."

2. Oscar Vera, "La Situación educativa en América Latina," paper read at UNESCO meeting on the Social Aspects of Economic Development in Latin America, in Mexico City, Dec. 1960, pp. 2–3.

3. As quoted in Mexican news accounts of Oct. 28, 1959.

4. See Eduardo Hamuy, *El Problema educacional del pueblo de Chile* (Santiago, 1961), especially chap. 5, for Chilean experiences analogous to the Mexican problem.

5. Marshall Wolfe, "Las Clases medias en Centroamérica; Características que presentan en la actualidad y requisitos para su desarrollo," CEPAL, Comité de Cooperación Económica del Istmo Centroamericano, Oct. 18, 1960, p. 29 (mimeo).

6. Daniel Goldrich, *Radical Nationalism: The Political Orientations of Panamanian Law Students* (East Lansing, 1961), p. 30. Robert C. Williamson has completed a study of students in the National University of Colombia which also clearly supports these statements as well as many of those which follow. See his *El estudiante colombiano y sus actitudes* (Bogotá, 1962), especially pp. 16, 75–76.

7. Frank Bonilla, "The Student Federation of Chile: 50 Years of Political Action," *Journal of Inter-American Studies* (July 1960), p. 313.

8. Bonilla, "Students in Politics: Three Generations of Political Action in a Latin-American University," unpublished doctoral dissertation (Harvard University, 1959).

9. Eduardo Frei Montalva, "La Universidad, conciencia social de la Nación," *Prólogo* (Oct.–Nov. 1962), pp. 8–11 and passim. *Prólogo* is a Christian Democratic review published in Buenos Aires.

10. These figures are estimates based on the various charts in UNESCO, *La*

Situación educativa en América Latina (Paris, 1960), and on Bonilla, "Student Federation of Chile," for the Chile data missing in the UNESCO survey. Comparable reliable data for Bolivia, also missing in the UNESCO monograph, were unobtainable.

11. The drop-out rate is discussed on p. 214.

12. For example, Juan Mantovani, "Idea, forma y misión de las universidades en los países latinoamericanos," *Política* (Caracas), No. 21 (April–May 1962), p. 39, estimates the number of institutions of higher learning as 88 universities, 31 technical schools, and "another 114 higher schools of university category, not counting those of theology, fine arts, music, and physical culture."

13. See, for example, the editorial in *Panorama* (Washington, D.C., Dec. 1962), OAS Task Force for Programming and Development of Education, Science, and Culture in Latin America, Bulletin No. 9.

14. José Babini, *Historia de la ciencia argentina* (Mexico City, 1949), pp. 131–32. See also Arthur P. Whitaker, *The United States and Argentina* (Cambridge, Mass., 1954), p. 74, for an easily available summary statement in English of the echoes of the Reform within the general Argentine university system.

15. All figures in this section are taken from University of Buenos Aires, *Censo universitario* (Buenos Aires, 1959). The census was taken in 1958.

16. These figures are not unusual in Latin America. In Lucio Mendieto y Núñez and José Gómez Robleda, *Problemas de la Universidad* (Mexico City, 1948), chaps. 1 and 2, we find a desertion rate of 53 per cent for the University of Mexico. From 1931 to 1943 the University granted only 7,532 degrees. Total enrollment in 1931 was 9,722 and in 1943 was 22,230. As late as 1953 the total enrollment in all universities in Mexico was 27,200, and the University of Mexico continued to serve about 20,000 of these. The Asociación Nacional de Universidades e Institutos de Enseñanza Superior in *The Teaching of Engineering in Mexico* (Mexico City, 1962), pp. 21–23, now gives the total student population in higher education at 101,236 for 1961, of whom 44,319 were in the National University of Mexico. This figure does not include 23,561 students in the preparatory levels controlled by the University of Mexico.

17. More details on this poll and other University of Buenos Aires matters can be found in my *The Conflict Society* (New Orleans, 1961), chap. 8.

18. See John P. Harrison, "The Confrontation with the Political University," in Robert N. Burr, ed., *Latin America's Nationalistic Revolutions*, special issue of *The Annals of the American Academy of Political and Social Science* CCCXXXIV (March 1961), pp. 74–83, for a concise and easily available digest of current understandings of the Reform. The writings of Gabriel del Mazo are usually considered the most definitive Spanish sources on the Reform.

19. Tentative findings are reported in Silvert and Bonilla, *Education and the Social Meaning of Development: A Preliminary Statement* (New York, 1961), Part II.

20. *Ibid.*, p. 100.

21. Harrison, "Confrontation," pp. 77 and 80.

22. Risieri Frondizi, "La Universidad y sus misiones," *Comentario* (Oct.–Nov.–Dec. 1956), pp. 309 and passim.

23. Goldrich, *Radical Nationalism*, p. 19.

24. Figures are from my article, "Political Leadership and Institutional Weakness in Argentina," read at the 1961 American Political Science Association meetings, and published in Spanish under the title, "Liderazgo político y debilidad institucional en la Argentina," *Desarrollo económico* (Buenos Aires), I, No. 3 (Oct.–Dec. 1961).

25. Bonilla, "Student Federation of Chile," p. 330.

26. For all the material in this paragraph, see Silvert and Bonilla, "Education and Social Meaning," pp. 104, 114–15, 127–28, 237, 256, 276.

27. Roberto Moreira, *Educação e desenvolvimento no Brasil* (Rio de Janeiro, 1960), pp. 192–93.

28. Bonilla, "Student Federation of Chile," p. 315.

9. Latin America and Japan Compared

1. J. F. Embree, *Suye Mura: A Japanese Village* (Chicago, 1939).

2. See Thomas C. Smith, *The Agrarian Origins of Modern Japan* (Stanford, 1959), for the technical and social organization; and for an impression of the form this "public spirit" could take in exceptional men, see Tadaatsu Ishiguro, *Ninomiya Sontoku: His Life and Evening Talks* (Tokyo, 1955).

3. My own estimate is that between 40 and 50 per cent of boys and about 15 per cent of girls were getting some kind of schooling by 1870. See "The Legacy of Tokugawa Education" in a forthcoming volume (*Changing Japanese Attitudes Toward Modernization*) to be edited by Marius B. Jansen and published by Princeton University Press.

4. For an illustration of Confucian attitudes toward popular education, see Donald H. Shively, "Motoda Eifu, Confucian Lecturer to the Meiji Emperor," in David S. Nivison and Arthur F. Wright, eds., *Confucianism in Action* (Stanford, 1959).

5. For the early development of education in the modern period, see Dairoku Kikuchi, *Japanese Education* (London, 1909).

6. A good insight into the stresses involved for Japanese intellectuals may be gathered from John W. Bennett and Herbert Passin, *In Search of Identity* (Minneapolis, 1958).

7. The development of this nationalistic ideology is described in Delmer M. Brown, *Nationalism in Japan* (Berkeley, 1955), and its final form in Ruth Benedict, *The Chrysanthemum and the Sword* (Boston, 1946), and in Masao Maruyama, *Thought and Behaviour in Modern Japanese Politics* (London, 1963).

8. On the element of patriotism in Meiji businessmen, see G. Ranis, "The Community-Centered Entrepreneur in Japanese Development," *Explorations in Entrepreneurial History*, VIII, No. 2 (Dec. 1955), and my "Agricultural Improvement in Japan: 1870–1900," *Economic Development and Cultural Change*, IX, No. 1, Part 2 (Oct. 1960), 69–91.

9. James C. Abeg glen, *The Japanese Factory* (Glencoe, 1958), pp. 14–15.

10. For an evocative account of the innovating zeal of the early Meiji period see George B. Sansom, *The Western World and Japan* (New York, 1950), and Yukichi Fukuzawa, *The Autobiography of Fukuzawa Yukichi* (Tokyo, 1947).

11. This oscillation is well described in Brown's *Nationalism in Japan*.

12. For a good general discussion of the use of tradition in Japanese development, see the editors' introduction to Robert E. Ward and Dankwart A. Rustow, *Political Modernization in Japan and Turkey* (Princeton, 1964).

13. See Cabot Coville, "Shinto, Engine of Government," *Trans. Asiatic Society of Japan*, 3d series, I (1948), 1–23, and Daniel Holtom, *Modern Japan and Shinto Nationalism* (Chicago, 1943).

14. Compare the use of Imperial Rescripts as a last-resort measure to force budgets through the Diet, as described by Hugh Borton, *Japan's Modern Century* (New York, 1955).

15. See, for instance, the appendix "Bushido, the Invention of a New Reli-

gion" in the later editions of Basil H. Chamberlain, *Things Japanese* (London, 1939).

16. For the content of these ethics courses see Robert K. Hall, *Shūshin: The Ethics of a Defeated Nation* (New York, 1949).

17. This ideology and its legal embodiment are described in Baron Nobushige Hozumi, *Ancestor Worship and Japanese Law* (Tokyo, 1938).

18. See Andrew Roth, *Dilemma in Japan* (London, 1948), and George O. Totten, "Labor and Agrarian Disputes in Taisho Japan Following World War I," *Economic Development and Cultural Change*, IX, No. 1, Part 2 (Oct. 1960), 187–212.

19. Donald Keene, *Modern Japanese Literature* (New York, 1959).

20. Irene B. Taeuber, *The Population of Japan* (Princeton, 1958).

21. A good recent account of the structure of latter-day Japanese feudalism is contained in Edwin O. Reischauer and John K. Fairbank, *East Asia: The Great Tradition* (Boston, 1960).

22. On the character of this transition and the nature of the new bureaucracy see E. Herbert Norman, *Japan's Emergence as a Modern State* (New York, 1940); Thomas C. Smith, "Japan's Aristocratic Revolution," *Yale Review* (Spring 1961), pp. 370–83; William G. Beasley, "Councillors of Samurai Origin in the Early Meiji Government," *Bulletin of the School of Oriental and African Studies*, XX (1957), 89–103; Roger F. Hackett, "Nishi Amane: a Tokugawa-Meiji Bureaucrat," *Journal of Asian Studies*, XVIII (Feb. 1959), 213–25.

23. Robert A. Scalapino, *Democracy and the Party Movement in Pre-War Japan* (Berkeley, 1953).

24. For military control over policy see, e.g., Yale C. Maxon, *Control of Japanese Foreign Policy* (Berkeley, 1957).

25. See the work of Scalapino cited above, and Scalapino and Junnosuke Masumi, *Parties and Politics in Contemporary Japan* (Berkeley, 1962).

26. On the origins of this ethic see Robert Bellah, *Tokugawa Religion* (Glencoe, 1957).

Index